ON SCHISM

John Owen

Vintage Puritan Series
GLH Publishing
LOUISVILLE, KY

Sourced from *The Works of John Owen,* Vol. XIII.
Edited by William Goold. Johnstone & Hunter, London, 1852.

Republished by GLH Publishing, 2020.

ISBN:
  Paperback 978-1-64863-022-4
  Epub 978-1-64863-023-1

CONTENTS

OF SCHISM

Prefatory Note.	1
Chapter I.	4
Chapter II.	13
Chapter III.	38
Chapter IV.	44
Chapter V.	59
Chapter VI.	79
Chapter VII.	103
Chapter VIII.	113

A VINDICATION OF THE TREATISE ABOUT THE TRUE NATURE OF SCHISM, ETC.

Prefatory Note.	143
To The Reader.	146
Chapter I.	148
Chapter II.	161
Chapter III.	168
Chapter IV.	171
Chapter V.	183
Chapter VI.	190
Chapter VII.	193
Chapter VIII.	201
Chapter IX.	207
Chapter X.	215

AN ANSWER TO A LATE TREATISE ABOUT THE NATURE OF SCHISM.

Prefatory Note.	229
To The Reader.	231

A BRIEF VINDICATION OF THE NONCONFORMISTS FROM THE CHARGE OF SCHISM.

Prefatory note.	271
A Brief Vindication of the Nonconformists from the Charge of Schism.	275

OF SCHISM

The True Nature of it Discovered and Considered with
Reference to the Present Differences in Religion.

PREFATORY NOTE.

UNLIKE most of Owen's works, the following treatise on schism has neither dedication, nor preface, nor note to the reader, from which we might have inferred his reasons for undertaking the preparation of it. There is no reference to any authors of the day by whose writings he might have been stimulated to defend his position as an Independent. Perhaps the design of Owen was more effectually promoted by the care with which he abstains from all personal controversies. The charge of schism was frequently resorted to by the different ecclesiastical parties of that age; and so long as the term was shrouded in a certain vague mystery of import, it told on some minds with peculiar effect. Romanists were fond of it as a weapon of no mean power in their dispute with the Church of England, and several treatises might be named, written about this period, in which the latter is earnestly defended from the charge. The members of that church, on the other hand, used the same plea against the Presbyterians and Independents; while Presbyterians, fresh from the task of replying to the charge of schism preferred against themselves, delighted in urging it against their brethren of Congregational views.

As the nature of the sin itself was left undefined, and the term, as borrowed from Scripture, was employed with much laxity of application, the religions party to which Owen belonged stood especially obnoxious to the reproach of following a divisive and schismatic course. If not a new denomination, they had only of late risen to such strength as to exert an influence on the national movements; and their first appearance in public affairs had traversed the designs of the Presbyterians, by first thwarting and latterly superseding them in the enjoyment of political supremacy. The latter were thus tempted to resort to the accusation of schism against the Independents, while the acrimony with which the accusation was made could not fail to be enhanced by the circumstance that Independency, as new to its opponents, would be in some measure misunderstood. Its theory of particular churches, united under no bond of common jurisdiction, seemed to involve the essence of schism and a palpable breach of Christian unity; and its practice of "gathering churches out of churches" wore an aspect too aggressive to meet with silent connivance on the part of other Christian bodies. Our author, in defence of his party, refrains from all recrimination, and, instead of bandying with their opponents the charge of schismatic views and tendencies, in one of those bread, masterly, and comprehensive statements which shed such light upon a complex question as effectually redeems it from a world of error and confusion, examines the scriptural import of the term "schism," and proves that it denotes, not a rupture in ecclesiastical communion, but causes less divisions within the pale of a church. This argument was obviously not the less effective that it was of equal avail to the Anglican church against the Romanist, and to the Presbyterian against the former, while it was of peculiar service to the Independent against them all. The questions on which they differed came to be adjusted on their proper merits, and not under the perverting influence of the magic and mystery of an ambiguous word.

Thus far the discussion has been brought in the course of the first three chapters. The task, however, was but half done, if, whatever might be the scriptural usage of the term "schism," a breach of Christian unity were still a sin, and Independents, from their views of the nature of a church, were involved in it. That they were not justly open to this charge, he proves in reference to the different meanings of the word "church." If it be taken to denote *the body of the elect*. Independents, though separate from other religious bodies, and contending for a certain isolation among their churches, so far as jurisdiction was concerned, might still be saints of God, and in the church of the elect, chap. iv. If by the "church" is meant *the universal body of Christian professors*, the bond that connects them is not subjection to the authority of rulers or to the decrees of councils, but the maintenance of the common faith, so that deviation from it, not merely a separate fellowship, must constitute the evidence and measure of the guilt of schism, chap. v.; and our author links in connection with this argument a reply to the Romish charge of schism, which is met on the principle just stated, chap. vi. Finally, he makes reference to *particular churches*, and after showing in what their unity consists, — submission to the authority of Christ, and the exercise of Christian love among the brethren, — he claims it for his own denomination, and falls back on his original argument, as to the meaning of schism in Scripture, affirming it to be inapplicable "to the secession of any man or men from any *particular church*," or to the refusal of one church to hold communion with another, or, lastly, to the departure of any man quietly, and under the dictates of conscience, from the communion of *any church whatever*, chap. vii. In the last chapter he meets the charge of schism as urged by the church of England against all Christians who cannot acquiesce in an episcopal polity.

Much of all this discussion may now be superseded and out of date by the prevalence of sounder views and a spirit more benign and charitable among evangelical churches, since the time when a vague charge of schism helped a limping argument and heightened the zeal of partisanship; this treatise of Owen, however, is a model, for the Christian temper with which the reasoning is prosecuted, and a master-piece of controversial tact, even though we may demur to some of his most important conclusions. It should be added, that he guards himself against any disparagement of the obligation to unity, and deplores in strong terms the divisions that rend the church of Christ. — ED.

Chapter I.

Aggravations of the evil of schism, from the authority of the ancients — Their incompetency to determine in this case, instanced in the sayings of Austin and Jerome — The saying of Aristides — Judgment of the ancients subjected to disquisition — Some men's advantage in charging others with schism — The actors' part privileged — The Romanists' interest herein — The charge of schism not to be despised — The iniquity of accusers justifies not the accused — Several persons charged with schism on several accounts — The design of this discourse in reference to them — Justification of differences unpleasant — Attempts for peace and reconciliation considered — Several persuasions hereabout, and endeavours of men to that end — Their issues.

It is the manner of men of all persuasions who undertake to treat of schism, to make their entrance with invectives against the evils thereof, with aggravations of its heinousness. All men, whether intending the charge of others or their own acquitment, esteem themselves concerned so to do. Sentences out of the fathers, and determinations of schoolmen, making it the greatest sin imaginable, are usually produced to this purpose. A course this is which men's apprehensions have rendered useful, and the state of things in former days easy. Indeed, whole volumes of the ancients, written when they were actors in this cause, charging others with the guilt of it, and, consequently, with the vehemency of men contending for that wherein their own interest lay, might (if it were to our purpose) be transcribed to this end. But as they had the happiness to deal with men evidently guilty of many miscarriages, and, for the most part, absurd and foolish, so many of them having fallen upon such a notion of the catholic church and schism as hath given occasion to many woeful mistakes and much darkness in the following ages, I cannot so easily give up the nature of this evil to their determination and judgment. About the aggravations of its sinfulness I shall not contend.

The evidence which remains of an indulgence in the best of them τῇ ἀμετρίᾳ τῆς ἀνθολκῆς, in this business especially, deters from that procedure. From what other principle were these words of Augustine: "Obscurius dixerunt prophetæ de Christo quam de ecclesia: puto propterea quia videbant in spiritu contra ecclesiam homines facturos esse particulas; et de Christo non tantam litem habituros, de ecclesia magnas contentiones excitaturos?" Conc. 2 ad Ps. xxx. Neither the affirmation itself nor the reason assigned can have any better root. Is any thing more clearly and fully prophesied of than Christ? or was it possible that good men should forget with what contests the whole church of God, all the world over, had been exercised from its infancy about the person of Christ? Shall the tumultuating of a few in a corner of Africa blot out the remembrance of the late diffusion of Arianism over the world? But Jerome hath given a rule for the interpretation of what they delivered in their polemical engagements, telling us plainly, in his Apology for himself to Pammachius, that he had not so much regarded what was exactly to be spoken in the controversy he had in hand, as what was fit to lay load upon Jovinian. And if we may believe him, this was the manner of all men in those days. If they were engaged, they did not what the truth only, but what the defence of their cause also required! Though I believe him not as to all he mentions, yet, doubtless, we may say to many of them, as the apostle in another case, Ὅλως ἥττημα ἐν ὑμῖν ἐστιν. Though Aristides obtained the name of Just for his uprightness in the management of his own private affairs, yet being engaged in the administration of those of the commonwealth, he did many things professedly unjust, giving this reason, he did them πρὸς τὴν ὑπόθεσιν τῆς πατρίδος συχνῆς ἀδικίας δεομένης.

Besides, the age wherein we live having, by virtue of that precept of our Saviour, "Call no man master," in a good measure freed itself from the bondage of subjection to the dictates of men (and the innumerable evils, with endless entanglements, thence ensuing), because they lived so many hundreds of years before us, that course of procedure, though retaining its facility, hath lost its usefulness, and is confessedly impertinent. What the Scripture expressly saith of this sin, and what from that it saith may regularly and rationally be deduced (whereunto we stand and fall), shall be afterward declared; and what is spoken sensibly thereunto by any, of old or of late, shall be cheerfully also received. But it may not be expected that I should build upon their authority whose principles I shall be necessitated to examine; and I am therefore contented to lie low as to any expectation of success in my present undertaking, because I have the prejudice of many ages, the interest of most Christians, and the mutual consent of parties at variance (which commonly is taken for an unquestionable evidence of truth), to contend withal. But my endeavours being to go "non quà itur, sed quà eundum est," I am not solicitous about the event.

In dealing about this business among Christians, the advantage hath been extremely hitherto on their part who found it their interest to begin the charge; for whereas, perhaps, themselves were and are of all men most guilty of the crime, yet by their clamorous accusation, putting others upon the defence of themselves, they have in a manner clearly escaped from the trial of their own guilt, and cast the issue of the question purely on them whom they have accused. The actors' or complainants' part was so privileged by some laws and customs, that he who had desperately wounded another chose rather to enter against him the frivolous plea that he received not his whole sword into his body, than to stand to his best defence, on the complaint of the wounded man. An accusation managed with the craft of men guilty, and a confidence becoming men wronged and innocent, is not every one's work to slight and waive; and he is, in ordinary judgments, immediately acquitted who avers that his charge is but recrimination. What advantage the Romanists have had on this account, how they have expatiated in the aggravation of the sin of schism, whilst they have kept others on the defence, and would fain make the only thing in question to be whether they are guilty of it or no, is known to all; and, therefore, ever since they have been convinced of their disability to debate the things in difference between them and us unto any advantage from the Scripture, they have almost wholly insisted on this one business; wherein they would have it wisely thought that our concernment only comes to the trial, knowing that in these things their defence is weak who have nothing else. Nor do they need any other advantage; for if any party of men can estate themselves at large in all the privileges granted and promises made to the church in general, they need not be solicitous about dealing with them that oppose them, having at once rendered them no better than Jews and Mohammedans,[1] heathens or publicans, by appropriating the privileges mentioned unto themselves. And whereas the parties litigant, by all rules of law and equity, ought to stand under an equal regard until the severals of their differences have been heard and stated, one party is hereby utterly condemned before it is heard, and it is all one unto them whether they are in the right or wrong. But we may possibly, in the issue, state it upon another foot of account.

In the meantime, it cannot be denied but that their vigorous adhering to the advantage which they have made to themselves (a thing to be expected from men wise in their generation), hath exposed some of them whom they have wrongfully accused to a contrary evil, whilst, in a sense of their own innocency, they have insensibly slipped (as is the manner of men) into slight and contemptible thoughts of the thing itself whereof they are accused. Where the thing in question is but a name or *term of reproach*, invented amongst men, this is incomparably the best way of defence. But this contains a *crime*, and no man is to set light by it. To live in *schism* is to live in *sin*; which, unrepented of, will ruin a man's eternal condition. Every one charged with it must either desert his station, which gives foundation to this charge, or acquit himself of the crime in that station. This latter is that which, in reference to myself and others, I do propose, assenting in the gross to all the aggravations of this sin that, with any pretence from Scripture or reason, are heaped on it.

And I would beg of men fearing God that they would not think that the iniquity of their accusers doth in the least extenuate the crime whereof they are accused. Schism is schism still, though they may be unjustly charged with it; and he that will defend and satisfy himself by prejudices against them with whom he hath to do, though he may be no schismatic, yet, if he were so, it is certain he would justify himself in his state and condition. Seeing men, on false grounds and self-interest, may yet sometimes manage a good cause, which perhaps they have embraced upon better principles, a conscientious tenderness and fear of being mistaken will drive this business to another issue. "Blessed is he who feareth alway."

It is well known how things stand with us in this world. As we are *Protestants*, we are accused by the *Papists* to be schismat-

---

1 "Solis nosse Deos et Cœli numina vobis —— aut solis nescire datum."

ics; and all other pleas and disputes are neglected. This is that which at present (as is evident from their many late treatises on this subject, full of their wonted confidence, contempt, reviling, and scurrility) is chiefly insisted on by them.

Farther; among Protestants, as being *Reformatists,* or as they call us, *Calvinists,* we are condemned for schismatics by the *Lutherans,* and for sacramentarian sectaries, for no other crime in the world but because we submit not to all they teach, for in no instituted church relation would they ever admit us to stand with them; which is as considerable an instance of the power of prejudice as this age can give. We are condemned for separation by them who refuse to admit us into union! But what hath not an irrational attempt of enthroning opinions put men upon?

The differences nearer home about episcopal government, with the matter of fact in the rejecting of it, and somewhat of the external way of the worship of God formerly used amongst us, hath given occasion to a new charge of the guilt of the same crime on some; as it is not to be supposed that wise and able men, suffering to a great extremity, will oversee or omit any thing from whence they may hope to prevail themselves against those by whose means they think they suffer. It cannot be helped (the engagement being past), but this account must be carried on one step farther. Amongst them who in these late days have engaged, as they profess, unto *Reformation* (and not to believe that to have been their intention is fit only for them who are concerned that it should be thought to be otherwise, whose prejudice may furnish them with a contrary persuasion), not walking all in the same light as to some few particulars, whilst each party, as the manner is, gathered together what they thought conduced to the furtherance and improvement of the way wherein they differed one from another, some, unhappily, to the heightening of the differences, took up this charge of schism against their brethren; which yet, in a small process of time, being almost sunk of itself, will ask the less pains utterly to remove and take off. In the meantime, it is, amongst other things (which is to be confessed), an evidence that we are not yet arrived at that inward frame of spirit which was aimed at, Phil. iii. 15, 16, whatever we have attained as to the outward administration of ordinances.

This being the state of things, the concernment of some of us lying in all the particulars mentioned, of all Protestants in some, it may be worth while to consider whether there be not general principles, of irrefragable evidence, whereon both all and some may be acquitted from their several concernments in this charge, and the whole guilt of this crime put into the ephah, and carried to build it a house in the land of Shinar, to establish it upon its own base.

I confess I would rather, much rather, spend all my time and days in making up and healing the breaches and schisms that are amongst Christians than one hour in justifying our divisions, even therein wherein, on the one side, they are capable of a fair defence. But who is sufficient for such an attempt? The closing of differences amongst Christians is like opening the book in the Revelation, — there is none able or worthy to do it, in heaven or in earth, but the Lamb: when he will put forth the greatness of his power for it, it shall be accomplished, and not before. In the meantime, a reconciliation amongst all Protestants is our *duty*, and *practicable*, and had perhaps ere this been in some forwardness of accomplishment had men rightly understood wherein such a reconciliation, according to the mind of God, doth consist. When men have laboured as much in the improvement of the principle of forbearance as they have done to subdue other men to their opinions, religion will have another appearance in the world.

I have considered and endeavoured to search into the bottom of the two general ways fixed on respectively by sundry persons for the compassing of peace and union among Christians, but in one nation, with the issue and success of them in several places; — namely, that of *enforcing uniformity* by a secular power on the one side, as was the case in this nation not many years ago (and is yet liked by the most, being a suitable judgment for the most); and that of *toleration* on the other, which is our present condition. Concerning them both, I dare say that though men of a good zeal and small experience, or otherwise on any account full of their own apprehensions, may promise to themselves much of peace, union, and love, from the one or the other (as they may be severally favoured by men of different interests in this world, in respect of their conducingness to their ends), yet a little observation of events, if they are not able to consider the causes of things, with the light and posture of the minds of men in this generation, will unburden them of the trouble of their expectations. It is something else that must give peace unto Christians than what is a product of the prudential considerations of men.

This I shall only add as to the former of these, — of enforcing uniformity: As it hath lost its reputation of giving temporal tranquillity to states, kingdoms, and commonwealths (which with some is only valuable, whatever became of the souls of men, forced to the profession of that which they did not believe), [and is] the readiest means in the world to root out all religion from the hearts of men, — the letters of which plea are, in most nations in Europe, washed out with rivers of blood (and the residue wait their season for the same issue); so it continues in the possession of this advantage against the other, that it sees and openly complains of the evil and dangerous consequences of it, when against its own, where it prevails, it suffers no complaints to lie. As it is ludicrously said of physicians, the effects of their skill lie in the sun, but their mistakes are covered in the churchyard; so is it with this persuasion: what it doth well, whilst it prevails, is evident; the anxiety of conscience in some, hypocrisy, formality, no better than atheism, in others, wherewith it is attended, are buried out of sight.

But as I have some while since ceased to be moved by the clamours of men concerning "bloody *persecution*" on the one hand, and "cursed, intolerable *toleration*" on the other, by finding, all the world over, that events and executions follow not the conscientious embracing of the one or other of these decried principles and persuasions, but are suited to the providence of God, stating the civil interests of the nations: so I am persuaded that a general alteration of the state of the churches of Christ in this world must determine that controversy; which when the light of it appears, we shall easily see the vanity of those reasonings wherewith men are entangled, and [which] are perfectly suited to the present condition of religion. But hereof I have spoken elsewhere.

Farther; let any man consider the proposals and attempts that have been made for ecclesiastical peace in the world, both of old and in these latter days; let him consult the rescripts of princes, the edicts of nations, advices of politicians, that would have the world in quietness on any terms, consultations, conferences, debates, assemblies; councils of the clergy, who are commonly zealots in their several ways, and are by many thought to be willing rather to hurl the whole world into confusion than to abate any thing of the rigour of their opinions, — and he will quickly assume the liberty of affirming concerning them all, that as wise men might easily see flaws in all of them, and an unsuitableness to the end proposed; and as good men might see so much of carnal interest, self, and hypocrisy in them, as might discourage them from any great expectations; so, upon many other accounts, a better issue was not to be looked for from them than hath been actually obtained: which hath, for the most part, been this, that those that could dissemble most deeply have been thought to have the greatest advantage. In disputations, indeed, the truth, for the most part, hath been a gainer; but in attempts for reconciliation, those who have come with the least candour, most fraud, hypocrisy, secular baits for the subverting of others, have, in appearance, for a season seemed to obtain success. And in this spirit of craft and contention are things yet carried on in the world.

Yea, I suppose the parties at variance are so well acquainted at length with each other's principles, arguments, interests, prejudices, and real distance of their causes, that none of them expect any reconciliation, but merely by one party keeping its station and the other coming over wholly thereunto. And therefore a Romanist, in his preface to a late pamphlet about schism, to the two universities, tells us plainly, "That if we will have any peace, we must, without limitation, submit to and receive those κυρίας δόξας, those commanding oracles which God by his holy spouse propoundeth to our obedience:" the sense of which expressions we are full well acquainted with. And in pursuit of that principle, he tells us again, p. 238, "That suppose the church should in necessary points teach error, yet even in that case every child of the church must exteriorly carry himself quiet, and not make commotions" (that is, declare against her); "for that were to seek a cure worse than the disease." Now, if it seem reasonable to these gentlemen that we should renounce our sense and reason, with all that understanding which we have, or at least are fully convinced that we have, of the mind of God in the Scripture, and submit blindly to the commands and guidance of their church, that we may have peace and union with them, because of their huge interest and advantage, which lies in our so doing, we profess ourselves to be invincibly concluded under the power of a contrary persuasion, and consequently an impossibility of reconciliation.

As to attempts, then, for reconciliation between parties at variance about the things of God, and the removal of schism by that means, they are come to this issue among them by whom they have been usually managed, — namely, *politicians* and *divines*, — that the former, perceiving the tenaciousness in all things of the latter, their promptness and readiness to dispute, and to continue in so doing with confidence of success (a frame of spirit that indeed will never praise God, nor be useful to bring forth truth in the world), do judge them at length not to have that prudence which is requisite to advise in matters diffused into such variety of concernments as these are, or not able to break through their unspeakable prejudices and interests to the due improvement of that wisdom they seem to have; and the latter, observing the facile condescension of the former in all things that may have a consistency with that peace and secular advantage they aim at, do conclude that, notwithstanding all their pretences, they have indeed in such consultations little, or no regard to the truth. Whereupon, having a mutual diffidence in each other, they grow weary of all endeavours to be carried on jointly in this kind; — the one betaking themselves wholly to keep things in as good state in the world as they can, let what will become of religion; the other, to labour for success against their adversaries, let what will become of the world or the peace thereof. And this is like to be the state of things until another spirit be poured out on the professors of Christianity than that wherewith at present they seem mostly to be acted.

The only course, then, remaining to be fixed on, whilst our divisions continue, is to inquire wherein the guilt of them doth consist, and who is justly charged therewith; in especial, what is and who is guilty of the sin of schism. And this shall we do, if God permit.

It may, I confess, seem superfluous to add any thing more on this subject, which hath been so fully already handled by others. But, as I said, the present concernment of some fearing God lying beyond what they have undertaken, and their endeavours, for the most part, having tended rather to convince their adversaries of the insufficiency of their charge and accusation than rightly and dearly to state the thing or matter contended about, something may be farther added as to the satisfaction of the consciences of men unjustly accused of this crime; which is my aim, and which I shall now fall upon.

Chapter II.

The nature of schism to be determined from Scripture only — This principle by some opposed — Necessity of abiding in it — Parity of reason allowed — Of the name of schism — Its constant use in Scripture — In things civil and religious — The whole doctrine of schism in the epistles to the Corinthians — The case of that church proposed to consideration — Schism entirely in one church; not in the separation of any from a church; nor in subtraction of obedience from governors — Of the second schism in the church of Corinth — Of Clement's epistle. — The state of the church of Corinth in those days: Ἐκκλησία παροικοῦσα Κόρινθον, — Πάροικος, who; παροικία, what — Πάροχος, "parœcia" — To whom the epistle of Clement was precisely written — Corinth not a metropolitical church — Allowance of what by parity of reason may be deduced from what is of schism affirmed — Things required to make a man guilty of schism — Arbitrary definitions of schism rejected — That of Austin considered; as also that of Basil — The common use and acceptation of it in these days — Separation from any church in its own nature not schism — Aggravations of the evil of schism ungrounded — The evil of it from its proper nature and consequences evinced — Inferences from the whole of this discourse — The church of Rome, if a church, the most schismatical church in the world — The church of Rome no church of Christ; a complete image of the empire — Final acquitment of Protestants from schism on the principle evinced, peculiarly of them of the late reformation in England — False notions of schism the ground of sin and disorder.

THE thing whereof we treat being a disorder in the instituted worship of God, and that which is of pure revelation, I suppose it a modest request, to desire that we may abide solely by that discovery and description which is made of it in Scripture, — that that alone shall be esteemed schism which is there so called, or which hath the entire nature of that which is there so called. Other things may be other crimes; schism they are not, if in the Scripture they have neither the name nor nature of it attributed to them.

He that shall consider the irreconcilable differences that are among Christians all the world over about this matter, as also what hath passed concerning it in former ages, and shall weigh what prejudices the several parties at variance are entangled with in reference hereunto, will be ready to think that this naked appeal to the only common principle amongst us all is so just, necessary, and reasonable, that it will be readily on all hands condescended unto. But as this is openly opposed by the Papists, as a most destructive way of procedure, so I fear that when the tendency of it is discovered, it will meet with reluctancy from others. But let the reader know that as I have determined προτιμᾶν τὴν ἀλήθειαν, so to take the measure of it from the Scripture only. "Consuetudo sine veritate est vetustas erroris," Cyp. Ep. ad Pomp.; and the sole measure of evangelical truth is His word of whom it was said, Ὁ λόγος ὁ σὸς ἀλήθειά ἐστι. "Id verius quod prius, id prius quod ab initio, id ab initio quod ab apostolis," says Tertullian. It is to me a sufficient answer to that fond question, "Where was your religion before Luther? where was your religion in the days of Christ and his apostles?" My thoughts as to this particular are the same with Chrysostom's on the general account of truth, Ἔρχεται Ἕλλην καὶ λέγει, ὅτι βούλομαι γενέσθαι Χριστιανός· ἀλλὰ οὐκ οἶδα τίνι προσθῶμαι· μάχη παρ' ὑμῖν πολλὴ καὶ στάσις, πολὺς θόρυβος, ποῖον ἕλομαι δόγμα; τί αἱρήσομαι; ἕκαστος λέγει ὅτι ἐγὼ ἀληθεύω, τίνι πειθῶ μηδὲν ὅλως εἰδὼς ἐν ταῖς γραφαῖς; κἀκεῖνοι τὸ αὐτὸ προβάλλονται πάνυ γε τοῦτο ὑπὲρ ἡμῶν, εἰ μὲν γὰρ λογισμοῖς ἐλέγομεν πείθεσθαι εἰκότως ἐθορύβου, εἰ δὲ ταῖς γραφαῖς λέγομεν πιστεύειν, αὐταὶ δὲ ἁπλαῖ καὶ ἀληθεῖς, εὔκολόν σοι τὸ κρινόμενον, εἴτις ἐκείναις συμφωνεῖ οὗτος Χριστιανός· εἴτις μάχεται οὗτος πόρρω τοῦ κανόνος τούτου. Homil. iii. in Acta.[2]

But yet, lest this should seem too strait, as being, at first view, exclusive of the learned debates and disputes which we have had about this matter, I shall, after the consideration of the precise Scripture notion of the name and thing, wherein the conscience of a believer is alone concerned, — propose and argue also what by a parity of reason may thence be deduced as

---

2   We have not been able to discover the passage quoted in the homily referred to. We have ventured on some slight corrections from conjecture. — Ed.

to the ecclesiastical common use of them, and our concernment in the one and the other.

The word, which is metaphorical, as to the business we have in hand, is used in the Scripture both in its primitive native sense, in reference to things natural, as also in the tralatitious use of it, about things politic and spiritual, or moral. In its first sense we have the noun, Matt. ix. 16, Καὶ χεῖρον σχίσμα γίνεται, "And the rent" (in the cloth) "is made worse;" — and the verb, Matt. xxvii. 51, Καταπέτασμα τοῦ ναοῦ ἐσχίσθη, "The vail of the temple was rent;" Καὶ αἱ πέτραι ἐσχίσθησαν, "And the rocks were rent:" both denoting an interruption of continuity by an external power in things merely passive. And this is the first sense of the word, — a scissure or division of parts before continued, by force or violent dissolution. The use of the word in a political sense is also frequent: John vii. 43, Σχίσμα οὖν ἐν τῷ ὄχλῳ, "There was a division among the people," some being of one mind, some of another; John ix. 16, Καὶ σχίσμα ἦν ἐν αὐτοῖς, "There was a division among them;" and chap. x. 19 likewise. So Acts xiv. 4 Ἐσχίσθη δε τὸ πλῆθος τῆς πόλεως, "The multitude of the city was divided;" and chap. xxiii. 7, "There arose a dissension between the Pharisees and the Sadducees," καὶ ἐσχίσθη τὸ πλῆθος, "and the multitude was divided," some following one, some another of their leaders in that dissension. The same thing is expressed by a word answering unto it in Latin:— "Scinditur incertum studia in contraria vulgus." And in this sense, relating things, it is often used.[3]

This being the next posture of that word, from whence it immediately slips into its ecclesiastical use, expressing a thing moral or spiritual, there may some light be given into its importance when so appropriated, from its constant use in this state and condition to denote *differences of mind and judgment, with troubles ensuing thereon, amongst men met in some one assembly, about the compassing of a common end and design.*

In the sense contended about it is used only by Paul in his First Epistle to the Corinthians, and therein frequently: Chap. i. 10, "I exhort you, μὴ ᾖ ἐν ὑμῖν σχίσματα," — "that there be no schisms among you." Chap. xi. 18, "When ye come together in the church, ἀκούω σχίσματα ἐν ὑμῖν ὑπάρχειν," — "I hear

---

3   Οἱ τὴν Ῥώμην οἰκοῦντες διεμερίσθησαν εἰς τὰ μέρη, καὶ οὐκέτι ὠμονόησαν πρὸς ἀλλήλους· καὶ ἐγένετο μέγα σχίσμα.
— Chronic. Antioch Joh. Male. p. 98, A. MS. Bib. Bod.

that there be schisms among you." Chap. xii. 25, the word is used in reference to the natural body, but with an application to the ecclesiastical. Other words there are of the same importance, which shall also be considered, as Rom. xvi. 17, 18. Of schism in any other place, or in reference to any other persons, but only to this church of Corinth, we hear nothing.

Here, then, being the principal foundation, if it hath any, of that great fabric about schism which in latter ages hath been set up, it must be duly considered, that, if it be possible, we may discover by what secret engines or artifices the discourses about it, which fill the world, have been hence deduced, — being, for the most part, universally unlike the thing here mentioned, — or find out that they are built on certain prejudices and presumptions nothing relating thereto. The church of Corinth was founded by Paul, Acts xvii. 8–11; with him there were Aquila and Priscilla, verses 2, 18. After his departure, Apollos came thither, and effectually watered what he had planted, 1 Cor. iii. 6. It is probable that either Peter had been there also, or at least that sundry persons converted by him were come thither, for he still mentions Cephas and Apollos with himself, chap. i. 12, iii. 22. This church, thus watered and planted, came together for the worship of God, ἐπὶ τὸ αὐτό, chap. xi. 20, and for the administration of discipline in particular, chap. v. 4, 5. After a while, through the craft of Satan, various evils, in doctrine, conversation, and church-order crept in amongst them. As for *doctrine*, besides their mistake about eating things offered to idols, chap. viii. 4, some of them denied the resurrection of the dead, chap. xv. 12. In *conversation* they had not only the eruption of a scandalous particular sin amongst them, chap. v. 1, but grievous sinful miscarriages when they "came together" about holy admininistrations, chap. xi. 20, 21. These the apostle distinctly reproves in them. Their *church-order*, as to that love, peace, and union of heart and mind wherein they ought to have walked, was woefully disturbed with divisions and sidings about their teachers, chap. i. 12. And not content to make this difference the matter of their debates and disputes from house to house, even when they met for public worship, or that which they all met in and for, they were divided on that account, chap. xi. 18. This was the schism the apostle dehorts them from, charges them with, and shows them the evil thereof. They had differences amongst themselves about unnecessary things. On these they engaged in disputes and sidings even in their solemn assemblies, when they came all together for the same worship, about which they differed not. Probably, much vain jangling, alienation of affections, exasperation of spirit, with a neglect of due offices of love, ensued hereupon. All this appears from the entrance the apostle gives to his discourse on this subject: 1 Cor. i. 10, Παρακαλῶ ὑμᾶς, ἵνα τὸ αὐτὸ λέγητε πάντες, — "I beseech you that ye all speak the same thing." They were of various minds and opinions about their church affairs; which was attended with the confusion of disputings. "Let it not be so," saith the apostle; καὶ μὴ ᾖ ἐν ὑμῖν σχίσματα, "and let there be no schisms among you," which consist in such differences and janglings. He adds, Ἦτε δὲ κατηρτισμένοι ἐν τῷ αὐτῷ νοΐ καὶ ἐν τῇ αὐτῇ γνώμῃ, — "But that ye be perfectly joined together in the same mind and in the same judgment." They were joined together in the same church-order and fellowship, but he would have them so also in oneness of mind and judgment; which if they were not, though they continued together in their church-order, yet schisms would be amongst them. This was the state of that church, this the frame and carriage of the members of it, this the fault and evil whereon the apostle charges them with schism and the guilt thereof. The grounds whereon he manageth his reproof are their common interest in Christ, chap. i. 13; the nothingness of the instruments of preaching the gospel, about whom they contended, chap. i. 27, iii. 4, 5; their church-order instituted by God, chap. xii. 13: of which afterward.

This being, as I said, the principal seat of all that is taught in the Scripture about schism, we are here, or hardly at all, to learn what it is and wherein it doth consist. The arbitrary definitions of men, with their superstructions and inferences upon them, we are not concerned in: at least, I hope I shall have leave from hence to state the true nature of the thing, before it be judged necessary to take into consideration what, by parity of reason, may be deduced from it. In things purely moral and of natural equity, the most general notion of them is to be the rule, whereby all particulars claiming an interest in their nature are to be measured and regulated. In things of institution, the particular instituted is first and principally to be regarded; how far the general reason of it may be extended is of after-consideration. And as is the case in respect of duty, so it is in respect of the evils that are contrary thereto. True and false are indicated and tried by the same rule. Here, then, our foot is to be fixed; what compass may be taken to fetch in things of a like kin will in its proper place follow. Observe, then, —

1. That the thing mentioned is entirely in *one church*, amongst the members of *one particular* society. No mention is there in the least of one church divided against another, or separated from another or others, — whether all true or some true, some false or but pretended. Whatever the crime be, it lies wholly within the verge of one church, that met together for the worship of God and administration of the ordinances of the gospel; and unless men will condescend so to state it upon the evidence tendered, I shall not hope to prevail much in the process of this discourse.

2. Here is no mention of any *particular man's*, or any *number* of men's, separation from the holy assemblies of the whole church, or of subduction of themselves from its power: nor doth the apostle lay any such thing to their charge, but plainly declares that they continued all in the joint celebration of that worship and performance together of those duties which were required of them in their assemblies; only, they had groundless, causeless differences amongst themselves, as I shall show afterward. All the divisions of one church from another, or others, the separation of any one or more persons from any church or churches, are things of another nature, made good or evil by their circumstances, and not that at all which the Scripture knows and calls by the name of schism; and therefore there was no such thing or name as schism, in such a sense, known in the Judaical church, though in the former it abounded. All the different sects to the last still communicated in the same carnal ordinances; and those who utterly deserted them were apostates, not schismatics. So were the body of the Samaritans; they worshipped they knew not what, nor was salvation among them, John iv. 22.

3. Here is no mention of any *subtraction of obedience* from bishops or rulers, in what degree soever, no exhortation to regular submission unto them, — much leas from the pope or church of Rome. Nor doth the apostle thunder out against them, "You are departed from the unity of the catholic church, have rent Christ's seamless coat, set up 'altare contra altare,' have forsaken the visible head of the church, the fountain of all unity; you refuse due subjection to the prince of the apostles;"

nor, "You are schismatics from the national church of Achaia, or have cast off the rule of your governors;" with the like language of after days; — but, "When ye come together, ye have divisions amongst you." "Behold how great a matter a little fire kindleth!"

A condition not unlike to this befalling this very church of Corinth, sundry years after the strifes now mentioned were allayed by the epistle of the apostle, doth again exhibit to us the case and evil treated on. Some few unquiet persons among them drew the whole society (upon the matter) into division and an opposition to their elders. They who were the causes, μιαρᾶς καὶ ἀνοσίου στάσεως, as Clement tells them in the name of the church at Rome, were ὀλίγα πρόσωπα a few men acted by pride and madness; yet such power had those persons in the congregation, that they prevailed with the multitude to depose the elders and cast them out of office. So the same Clement tells them, Ὁρῶμεν ὅτι ἐνίους ὑμεῖς μετηγάγετε καλῶς πολιτευομένους ἐκ τῆς ἀμέμπτως αὐτοῖς τετιμημένης λειτουργίας. What he intends by his μετηγάγετε, etc., he declares in the words foregoing, where he calls the elders that were departed this life happy and blessed, as not being subject or liable to expulsion out of their offices: Οὐ γὰρ εὐλαβοῦνται μή τις αὐτοὺς μεταστήσῃ ἀπὸ τοῦ ἱδρυμένου αὐτοῖς τόπου. Whether these men who caused the differences and sedition against those elders that were deposed were themselves by the church substituted into their room and place, I know not. This difference in that church the church of Rome, in that epistle of Clement, calls everywhere schism, as it also expresses the same thing, or the evil frame of their minds and their actings, by many other words. Ζῆλος, ἔρις, στάσις, διωγμός, ἀκαταστασία, ἀλαζονεία, τύφος, πόλεμος, are laid to their charge. That there was any separation from the church, that the deposed elders, or any for their sakes, withdrew themselves from the communion of it, or ceased to assemble with it for the celebration of the ordinances of the gospel, there is not any mention; only the difference in the church is the schism whereof they are accused. Nor are they accused of schism for the deposition of the elders, but for their differences amongst themselves, which was the ground of their so doing.

It is alleged, indeed, that it is not the single church of Corinth that is here intended, but all the churches of Achaia, whereof that was the metropolis; which though, as to the nature of schism, it be not at all prejudiced to what hath been asserted, supposing such a church to be, yet, because it sets up in opposition to some principles of truth that must afterward be improved, I shall briefly review the arguments whereby it is attempted to be made good.

The title of the epistle, in the first place, is pretended to this purpose. It is: Ἡ ἐκκλησία Θεοῦ ἡ παροικοῦσα Ῥώμην τῇ ἐκκλησίᾳ τοῦ Θεοῦ παροικούσῃ Κόρινθον· "wherein" (as it is said) "on each part the παροικία, or whole province, as of Rome, so of Corinth, the region and territory that belonged to those metropolises is intended." But, as I have formerly elsewhere said, we are beholden to the frame and fabric of church affairs in after ages for such interpretations as these. The simplicity of the first knew them not. They who talked of the church of God that did παροικεῖν, at Rome little then thought of province or region. Ἐκκλησία παροικοῦσα Ῥώμην is as much as ἐκκλησία ἐν Ἱεροσολύμοις, Acts viii. 1. Πάροικος is a man that dwells at such a place, properly one that dwells in another's house or soil, or that hath removed from one place and settled in another; whence it is often used in the same sense with μέτοικος. He is such a inhabitant as hath yet some such consideration attending him as makes him a kind of a foreigner to the place where he is. So, Eph. ii. 19, πάροικοι and συμπολῖται are opposed. Hence is παροικία, which, as Budæus says, differs from κατοικία in that it denotes a temporary habitation, this a stable and abiding one. Παροικέω, is so to "inhabit" to dwell in a place, where yet something makes a man a kind of a stranger. So it is said of Abraham, Πίστει παρῴκησεν εἰς τὴν γῆν τῆς ἐπαγγελίας ὡς ἀλλοτρίαν, Heb. xi. 9; joined with παρεπίδημος, 1 Pet. ii. 11 (hence this word by the learned publisher of this epistle is rendered "peregrinatur, diversatur"); and more clearly Luke xxiv. 18, Σὺ μόνος παροικεῖς ἐν Ἱερουσαλήμ; which we have rendered, "Art thou only a stranger in Jerusalem?" Whether παροικία and "parœcia" is from hence or no by some is doubted. Πάροχος is "convivator," and παροχή "præbitio," Gloss. vetus; so that "parochiæ" may be called so from them who met together to break bread and to eat. Allow "parochia" to be barbarous, and our only word to be "parœcia," from παροικία then it is as much as the voisinage, men living near together for any end whatever. So says Budæus, πάροικοι are πρόσοικοι· thence churches were called παροικίαι, consisting of a number of them, who were πάροικοι or πρόσοικοι. The saints of God, expressing the place which they inhabited, and the manner, as strangers said of the churches whereof they were, Ἐκκλησία παροικοῦσα Ῥώμην, and Ἐκκλησία παροικοῦσα Κόρινθον. This is now made to denote a region, a territory, the adjacent region to a metropolis, and suchlike things as the poor primitive pilgrims little thought of. This will scarcely, as I suppose, evince the assertion we are dealing about. There may be a church of dwelling at Rome or Corinth, without any adjacent region annexed to it, I think. Besides, those who first used the word in the sense now supposed did not understand a province by παροικία, which with them (as originally) the charge of him that was a bishop, and no more. Ἐπαρχία was with them a province that belonged to a metropolitan, such as the bishop of Corinth is supposed to be. I do not remember where a metropolitan's province is called his παροικία, there being many of these in every one of them. But at present will not herein concern myself.

But it is said that this epistle of Clement was written to them whom Paul's epistles were written; which appears, as from the common title, so also from hence, that Clement advises them to whom he writes to take and consider that epistle which Paul had formerly wrote to them. Now, Paul's epistle was written to all the churches of Achaia, as it is said expressly in the second, "Unto the church of God which is at Corinth, with all the saints, which are in all Achaia," chap. i. 1. And for the former, that also is directed πᾶσι ἐπικαλουμένοις τὸ ὄνομα τοῦ Χριστοῦ ἐν παντὶ τόπῳ. And the same form is used at the close of this [Clement's]: Καὶ μετὰ πάντων πανταχῇ κεκλημένων ὑπὸ τοῦ Θεοῦ, wherein all places in Achaia (and everywhere therein) not absolutely are intended; for if they should, then this epistle would be a catholic epistle, and would conclude the things mentioned in it of the letter received by the apostle, etc., to relate to the catholic church.

Ans. It is confessed that the epistles of Paul and Clement have one common title; so that Τῇ ἐκκλησίᾳ παροικούσῃ Κόρινθον, which is Clement's expression, is the same with Τῇ ἐκκλησίᾳ τῇ οὔσῃ ἐν Κορίνθῳ, which is Paul's in both his epistles; which adds little strength to the former argument from the word ταροικοῦσα, οὔσῃ ἐν Κορίνθῳ, as I suppose, confining it thither. It is true, Paul's second epistle, after its inscription, Τῇ ἐκκλησίᾳ τῇ οὔσῃ ἐν Κορίνθῳ, adds, σὺν τοῖς ἁγίοις πᾶσι τοῖς οὖσιν ἐν ὅλῃ τῇ Ἀχαΐα. He mentions not anywhere any more churches in Achaia than that of Corinth and that at Cenchrea, nor doth he speak of any churches here in this salutation, but only of the saints; and he plainly makes Achaia and Corinth to be all one, 2 Cor. ix. 2: so that to me it appears that there were not as yet, any more churches brought into order in Achaia but that mentioned, with that other at Cenchrea, which, I suppose, comes under the same name with that of Corinth. Nor am I persuaded that it was a completed congregation in those days. Saints in Achaia that lived not at Corinth there were perhaps many, but, being scattered up and down, they were not formed into societies, but belonged to the church of Corinth, and assembled therewith, as they could, for the participation of ordinances. So that there is not the least evidence that this epistle of Paul was directed to any other church but that of Corinth. For the first, it can scarce be questioned. Paul writing an epistle for the instruction of the saints of God and disciples of Christ in all ages, by the inspiration of the Holy Ghost, salutes in its beginning and ending all them that on that general account are concerned in it. In this sense all his epistles were catholic, even those he wrote to single persons. The occasion of writing this epistle was, indeed, from a particular church, and the chief subject-matter of it was concerning the affairs of that church; hence it is in the first place particularly directed to them. And our present inquiry is not after all that by any means were or might be concerned in that which was then written, as to their present or future direction, but after them who administered the occasion to what was so written, and whose particular condition was spoken to. This, I say, was the single church of Corinth. That πάντες οἱ ἐπικαλούμενοι τὸ ὄνομα τοῦ Χριστοῦ ἐν παντὶ τόπῳ, "all in every place," should be all only in Achaia, or that Clement's μετὰ πάντων πανταχῇ τῶν κεκλημένων ὑπὸ τοῦ Θεοῦ, should be, "with them that are called in Achaia," I can yet see no ground to conjecture. Paul writes an epistle to the church of Ephesus, and concludes it, Ἡ χάρις μετὰ πάντων τῶν ἀγαπώντων τὸν Κύριον ἡμῶν Ἰησοῦν Χριστόν ἐν ἀφθαρσίᾳ, — the extent of which prayer is supposed to reach farther than Ephesus and the region adjacent. It doth not, then, as yet appear that Paul wrote his epistles particularly to any other but the particular church at Corinth. If concerning the latter, because of that expression, "with all the saints which are in all Achaia," it be granted there were more churches than that of Corinth, with its neighbour Cenchrea (which whether it were a stated distinct church or no I know not), yet it will not at all follow, as was said before, that Clement, attending the particular occasion only about which he and the church of Rome were consulted, did so direct his epistle, seeing he makes no mention in the least that so he did. But yet, by the way, there is one thing more that I would be willingly resolved about in this discourse, and that is this: seeing that it is evident that the apostle by his πάντες ἐν παντὶ τόπῳ, and Clement by his πάντων πανταχῇ κεκλημένων, intend an enlargement beyond the first and immediate direction to the church of Corinth, if by the church of Corinth, as it is pleaded, they intend to express that whole region of Achaia, what does either the apostle or Clement obtain by that enlargement, if restrained to that same place?

It is, indeed, said that at this time *there were many other episcopal sees* in Achaia; which, until it is attempted to be put upon some kind of proof, may be passed by. It is granted that Paul speaks of that which was done at Corinth to be done in Achaia, Rom. xv. 26, as what is done in London is without doubt done in England; but that which lies in expectation of some light or evidence to be given unto it is, that there was a metropolitical see at Corinth at this time, whereunto many episcopal sees in Achaia were in subordination, being all the παροικία of Corinth, all which are called the church of Corinth, by virtue of their subjection thereunto. When this is proved, I shall confess some principles I afterward insist on will be impaired thereby.

This, then, is added by the same author, "That the ecclesiastical estate was then conformed to the civil. Wherever there was a metropolis in a civil-political sense, there was seated also a metropolitical church. Now, that Corinth was a metropolis, the proconsul of Achaia keeping his residence there, in the first sense is confessed." And besides what follows from thence, by virtue of the principle now laid down, Chrysostom calls it a metropolis, relating to the time wherein Paul wrote his epistle to the church there, in the latter sense also.

The plea about metropolitical churches, I suppose, will be thought very impertinent to what I have now in hand, so it shall not at present be insisted on. That the state of churches in after ages was moulded and framed after the pattern of the civil government of the Roman empire is granted; and that conformity (without offence to any be it spoken) we take to be a fruit of the working of "the mystery of iniquity." But that there was any such order instituted in the churches of Christ by the apostles, or any intrusted with authority from their Lord and Ruler, is utterly denied; nor is any thing but very uncertain conjectures from the sayings of men of after ages produced to attest any such order or constitution. When the order, spirituality, beauty, and glory of the church of Christ shall return, and men obtain a light whereby they are able to discern a beauty and excellency in the inward, more noble, spiritual part, indeed life and soul, of the worship of God, these disputes will have an issue. Chrysostom says, indeed, that Corinth was the metropolis of Achaia; but in what sense he says not. The political is granted; the ecclesiastical not proved. Nor are we inquiring what was the state of the churches of Christ in the days of Chrysostom, but of Paul. But to return.

If any one now shall say, "Will you conclude, because this evil mentioned by the apostle is *schism*, therefore nothing else is so?"

I answer, that having before asserted this to be the chief and only seat of the doctrine of schism, I am inclinable so to do. And this I am resolved of, that unless any man can prove that something else is termed schism by some divine writer, or blamed on that head of account by the Holy Ghost elsewhere, and is not expressly reproved as another crime, I will be at liberty from admitting it so to be.

But yet for what may hence by a parity of reason be deduced, I shall close with and debate at large, as I have professed.

The schism, then, here described by the apostle, and blamed by him, consists in *causeless differences and contentions amongst the members of a particular church, contrary to that [exercise] of love, prudence, and forbearance, which are required of them to be exercised amongst themselves, and towards one another*; which is also termed στάσις, Acts xv. 2, and διχοστασία, Rom. xvi. 17. And he is a schismatic that is guilty of this sin of schism, — that is, who raiseth, or entertaineth, or persisteth in such differences. Nor are these terms used by the divine writers in any other sense.

That any men may fall under this guilt, it is required, —

1. That they be *members* of or belong to some *one church*, which is so by the institution and appointment of Jesus Christ.

And we shall see that there is more required hereunto than the bare being a believer or a Christian.

2. That they either *raise or entertain*, and persist in, causeless differences with others of that church, more or less, to the interruption of that exercise of love, in all the fruits of it, which ought to be amongst them, and the disturbance of the due performance of the duties required of the church in the worship of God; as Clement in the fore-mentioned epistle, Φιλόνεικοί ἐστε ἀδελφοὶ καὶ ζηλωταὶ περὶ μὴ ἀνηκόντων εἰς σωτηρίαν.

3. That these differences be *occasioned* by and do belong to some things, in a remoter or nearer distance, *appertaining to the worship of God*, Their differences on a civil account are elsewhere mentioned and reproved, 1 Epist. chap. vi.; for therein, also, there was, from the then state of things, an ἥττημα, verse 7.

This is that crime which the apostle rebukes, blames, condemns, under the name of schism, and tells them that were guilty of it that they showed themselves to be carnal, or to have indulged to the flesh, and the corrupt principle of self, and their own wills, which should have been subdued to the obedience of the gospel. Men's definitions of things are for the most part arbitrary and loose, fitted and suited to their several apprehensions of principles and conclusions, so that thing clear or fixed is generally to be expected from them; from the Romanists' description of schism, who violently, without the least colour or pretence, thrust in the pope and his headship into all that they affirm in church matters, least of all. I can allow men that they may extend their definitions of things unto what they apprehend of an alike nature to that which gives rise to the whole disquisition, and is the first thing defined; but at this I must profess myself to be somewhat entangled, that I could never yet meet with a definition of schism that did comprise, that was not exclusive of, that which alone in the Scripture is affirmed so to be.

Austin's definition contains the sum of what hath since been insisted on. Saith he, "Schisma ni fallor est eadem opinantem, et eodem ritu utentem solo congregationis delectari dissidio," Con. Faust lib. xx. Cap. 3. By "dissidium congregationis" he intends separation from the church into a peculiar congregation; a definition directly suited to the cause he had in hand and was pleading against the Donatists. Basil, in Epist. ad Amphiloch. Con. xliv., distinguisheth between αἵρεσις, σχίσμα, and παρασυναγωγή. And as he makes schism to be a division arising from some church controversies, suitable to what those days experienced, and in the substance true, so he tells us that παρασυναγωγή is when either presbyters, or bishops, or laics hold unlawful meetings, assemblies, or conventicles; which was not long since with us the only schism.

Since those days, schism in general hath passed for a *causeless separation from the communion and worship of any true church of Christ* ("The Catholic church," saith the Papist), with a relinquishment of its society, as to a joint celebration of the ordinances of the gospel. How far this may pass for schism, and what may be granted in this description of it, the process of our discourse will declare. In the meantime, I am most certain that a separation from some churches, true or pretended so to be, is commanded in the Scriptures; so that the withdrawing from or relinquishment of any church or society whatever, upon the plea of its corruption, be it true or false, with a mind and resolution to serve God in the due observation of church institutions, according to that light which men have received, is nowhere called schism, nor condemned as a thing of that nature, but is a matter that must be tried out, whether it be good or evil, by virtue of such general rules and directions as are given us in the Scriptures for our orderly and blameless walking with God in all his ways.

As for them who suppose all church power to be invested in some certain church officers originally (I mean that which they call of jurisdiction), who on that account are "eminenter" the church, the union of the whole consisting in a subjection to those officers, according to rules, orders, and canons of their appointment, whereby they are necessitated to state the business of schism on the rejection of their power and authority, I shall speak to them afterward at large. For the present, I must take leave to say, that I look upon the whole of such a fabric as a product of prudence and necessity.

I cannot but fear lest some men's surmisings may prompt them to say that the evil of schism is thus stated in a compliance with that and them which before we blamed, and seems to serve to raise slight and contemptible thoughts of it, so that men need not be shaken though justly charged with it. But besides that sufficient testimony which I have to the contrary, that will abundantly shelter me from this accusation, by an assurance that I have not the least aim δουλεύειν ὑποθέσει, I shall farther add my apprehension of the greatness of the evil of this sin, if I may first be borne with a little in declaring what usual aggravations of it I do either not understand or else cannot assent unto.

Those who say it is a *rending of the seamless coat of Christ* (in which metaphorical expression men have wonderfully pleased themselves) seem to have mistaken their aim, and, instead of an aggravation of its evil, by that figure of speech, to have extenuated it. A rent of the body well compacted is not heightened to any one's apprehension in its being called the rending of a seamless coat. But men may be indulged the use of the most improper and groundless expressions, so they place, no power of argument in them, whilst they find them moving their own, and suppose them to have an alike efficacy upon the affections of others. I can scarce think that any ever supposed that the coat of Christ was a type of his church, his church being clothed with him, not he with it. And, therefore, with commendation of his success who first invented that illusion, I leave it in the possession of them who want better arguments to evince the evil of this sin.

It is most usually said to be *a sin against charity*, as heresy is against faith. Heresy is a sin against faith, if I may so speak, both as it is taken for the doctrine of faith which is to be believed, and the assent of the mind whereby we do believe. He that is a heretic (I speak of him in the usual acceptation of the word, and the sense of them who make this comparison, in neither of which I am satisfied) rejects the doctrine of faith, and denies all assent unto it. Indeed, he doth the former by doing the latter. But is schism so a sin against charity? Doth it supplant and root love out of the heart? Is it an affection of the mind attended with an inconsistency therewith? I much question it.

The apostle tells us that "love is the bond of perfectness," Col. iii. 14, because, in the several and various ways whereby it exerts itself, it maintains and preserves, notwithstanding all hindrances and oppositions, that perfect and beautiful order which Christ hath pointed amongst his saints. When men by schism are kept off and withheld from the performance of any of those offices and duties of love which are useful or necessary for the preservation of the bond of perfection, then is it, or may in some sense be said to be, a sin against love.

Those who have seemed to aim nearest the apprehension of the nature of it in these days have described it to be an *open breach of love*, or charity. That that expression is warily to be understood is evident in the light of this single consideration: It is possible for a man to be all and do all that those were and did whom the apostle judges for schismatics, under the power of some violent temptation, and yet have his heart full of love to the saints of the communion disturbed by him. It is thus far, then, in its own nature a breach of love, in that in such men love cannot exert itself in its utmost tendency in wisdom and forbearance for the preservation of the perfect order instituted by Christ in his church. However, I shall freely say that the schoolmen's notion of it, who insist on this as its nature, that it is a sin against charity, as heresy is against faith, is fond and becoming them; and so will others also that shall be pleased to consider what they intend by charity.

Some say it is *a rebellion against the church*, — that is, the rulers and officers of the church. I doubt not but that there must be either a neglect in the church in the performance of its duty, or of the authority of it in so doing, wherever there is any schism, though the discovery of this also have innumerable entanglements attending it. But that to refuse the authority of the church is to rebel against the rulers or guides of it will receive farther light than what it hath done, when once a pregnant instance is produced, not where the church signifies the officers of it, but where it doth not signify the body of the congregation in contradistinction from them, or comprising them therein.

Add unto these those who dispute whether schismatics do belong to the church or no, and conclude in the negative, seeing, according to the discovery already made, it is impossible a man should be a schismatic unless he be a church member. Other crimes a man may be guilty of on other accounts; of schism, only in a church, What is the formal reason of any man's relation to a church, in what sense soever that word is used, must be afterward at large discussed.

But now this foundation being laid, that schism is a causeless difference or division amongst the members of any particular church that meet together, or ought so to do, for the worship of God and celebration of the same numerical ordinances, to the disturbance of the order appointed by Jesus Christ, and contrary to that exercise of love in wisdom and mutual forbearance which is required of them, it will be easy to see wherein the iniquity of it doth consist, and upon what considerations its aggravations do arise.

It is evidently a *despising of the authority of Jesus Christ*, the great sovereign Lord and Head of the church. How often hath he commanded us to forbear one another, to forgive one another, to have peace among ourselves, that we may be known to be his disciples, to bear with them that are in any thing contrary-minded to ourselves! To give light to this consideration, let that which at any time is the cause of such hateful divisions, rendered as considerable as the prejudices and most importune affections of men can represent it to be, be brought to the rule of love and forbearance in the latitude of it, as prescribed to us by Christ, and it will evidently bear no proportion thereunto; so that such differences, though arising on real miscarriages and faults of some, because they might otherwise be handled and healed, and ought to be so, cannot be persisted in without the contempt of the immediate authority of Jesus Christ. If it were considered that he "standeth in the congregation of the mighty," Ps. lxxxii. 1; that he dwells in the church in glory, "as in Sinai, in the holy place," Ps. lxviii. 17, 18, walking "in the midst of the candlesticks," Rev. i. 13, with his eyes upon us as a "flame of fire," verse 14, his presence and authority would, perhaps, be more prevalent with some than they seem to be.

Again; *His wisdom*, whereby he hath ordered all things in his church on set purpose that schism and divisions may be prevented, *is no less despised*. Christ, who is the wisdom of the Father, 1 Cor. i. 24, the stone on which are seven eyes, Zech. iii. 9, upon whose shoulder the government is laid, Isa. ix. 6, 7, hath, in his infinite wisdom, so ordered all the officers, orders, gifts, administrations of and in his church, as that this evil might take no place. To manifest this is the design of the Holy Ghost, Rom. xii. 3–9; 1 Cor. xii.; Eph. iv. 8–13. The consideration, in particular, of this wisdom of Christ, — suiting the officers of his church, in respect of the places they hold, the authority wherewith from him they are invested, the way whereby they are entered into their functions; distributing the gifts of his Spirit in marvellous variety unto several kinds of usefulness, and with such distance and dissimilitude in the particular members, as, in a due correspondency and proportion, give comeliness and beauty to the whole; disposing of the order of his worship, and sundry ordinances in especial, to be expressive of the highest love and union; pointing all of them against such causeless divisions; — might be of use, were that my present intendment.

The grace and goodness of Christ, whence he hath promised to give us one heart and one way, to leave us peace such as the world cannot give, with innumerable other promises of the like importance, are disregarded thereby. So also is his prayer for us. With what affection and zeal did he pour out his soul to his Father for our union in love! That seems to be the thing his heart was chiefly fixed on when he was leaving this world, John xvii.. What weight he laid thereon, how thereby we may be known to be his disciples, and the world be convinced that he was sent of God, is there also manifested.

How far the exercise of love and charity is obstructed by it hath been declared. The consideration of the *nature, excellency, property, effects, usefulness* of this grace in all the saints in all their ways, its especial *designation* by our Lord and Master to be the bond of union and perfection, in the way and order instituted for the comely celebration of the ordinances of the gospel, will add weight to this aggravation.

Its constant growing to farther evil, in some to apostasy itself, — its usual and certain ending in strife, variance, debate, evil surmisings, wrath, confusion, disturbances public and private, — are also to be laid all at its door. What farther of this nature and kind may be added (as much may be added) to evince the heinousness of this sin of schism, I shall willingly subscribe unto; so that I shall not trouble the reader in abounding in what on all hands is confessed.

It is incumbent upon him who would have me to go farther in the description of this evil than as formerly stated, to evince from Scripture another notion of the name or thing than that given; which when he hath done, he shall not find me refractory. In the meantime, I shall both consider what may be objected against that which hath been delivered, and also discuss the present state of our divisions on the usual principles and common acceptation of schism, if, first, I may have leave to make some few inferences or deductions from what hath already been spoken, and, as I hope, evinced.

On supposition that the church of Rome is a church of Christ, it will appear to be the most schismatical church in the world. I say on supposition that it is a church, and that there is such a thing as a schismatical church (as perhaps a church may from its intestine differences be not unfitly so denominated), that is the state and condition thereof. The pope is the head of their church; several nations of Europe are members of it. Have we not seen that head taking his flesh in his teeth, tearing his body and his limbs to pieces? Have some of them thought on any thing else but, "Arise, Peter, kill and eat," all their days? Have we not seen this goodly head, in disputes about Peter's patrimony and his own jurisdiction, wage war, fight, and shed blood, — the blood of his own members? Must we believe armies raised, and battles fought, towns fired, all in pure love and perfect church order? not to mention their old "altare contra altare," anti-popes, anti-councils. Look all over their church, on their potentates, bishops, friars, — there is no end of their variances. What do the chiefest, choicest pillars, eldest sons, and I know not what, of their church at this day? Do they not kill, destroy, and ruin each other, as they are able? Let them not say these are the divisions of the nations that are in their church, not of the church; for all these nations, on their hypothesis, are members of that one church. And that church which hath no means to prevent its members from designed, resolved on, and continued murdering one of another, nor can remove them from its society, shall never have me in its communion, as being bloodily schismatical. Nor is there any necessity that men should forego their respective civil interests by being members of one church. Prejudicate apprehensions of the nature of a church and its authority lie at the bottom of that difficulty. Christ hath ordained no church that inwraps such interests as on the account whereof the members of it may murder one another. Whatever, then, they pretend of unity, and however they make it a note of the true church (as it is a property of it), that which is like it amongst them is made up of these two ingredients, — *subjection to the pope, either for fear of their lives or advantage to their livelihood, and a conspiracy for the destruction and suppression of them that oppose their interests*; wherein they agree like those who maintained Jerusalem in its last siege by Titus, — they all consented to oppose the Romans, and yet fought out all other things among themselves. That they are not so openly clamorous about the differences at present as in former ages is merely from the pressure of Protestants round about them. However, let them at this day silence the Jesuits and Dominicans, especially the Baijans and the Jansenians on the one part, and the Molinists on the other; — take off the Gallican church from its schismatical refusal of the council of Trent; — cause the king of Spain to quit his claim to Sicily, that they need not excommunicate him every year; — compel the commonwealth of Venice to receive the Jesuits; stop the mouths of the Sorbonnists about the authority of a general council above the pope, and of all those whom, opposing the papal omnipetency, they call politicians; — quiet the contest of the Franciscans and Dominicans about the blessed Virgin; — burn Bellarmine's books, who almost on every controversy of Christian religion gives an account of their intestine divisions; branding some of their opinions as heretical, as that of Medina about bishops and presbyters; some as idolatrical, as that of Thomas about the worship of the cross with "latria," etc.; — and they may give a better colour to their pretences than any as yet they wear.

But what need I insist upon this supposition, when I am not more certain that there is any instituted church in the world, owned by Christ as such, than I am that the church of Rome is none, properly so called? Nor shall I be thought singular in this persuasion, if it be duly considered what this amounts unto. Some learned men of latter days in this nation, pleading in the justification of the church of England as to her departure from Rome, did grant that the church of Rome doth not err in fundamentals, or maintained no errors remedilessly pernicious and destructive of salvation. How far they entangled themselves by this concession I argue not. The foundation of it lies in this clear truth, that no church whatever, universal or particular, can possibly err in fundamentals; for by so doing it would cease to be a church. My denying, then, the synagogue of Rome to be a church, according to their principles, amounts to no more than this, — the Papists maintain, in their public confessions, fundamental errors; in which assertion it is known I am not alone.

But this is not the principle, at least not the sole or main principle, whereon I ground my judgment in this case; but this, that there was never any such thing, in any tolerable likeness or similitude, as that which is called the church of Rome, allowing the most skilful of its rabbis to give in the characters and delineations of it, instituted in reference to the worship of God by Jesus Christ. The truth is, the whole of it is but an imitation and exemplar of the old imperial government. One is set up in chief, and made ἀνυπεύθυνος in spirituals, as the emperors were in several things; from him all power flows to others. And as there was a communication of power by the emperors, in the civil state to prefects, proconsuls, vicars, presidents, governors of the lesser and greater nations, with those under them, in various civil subordinations, according to the dignity of the places where they did bear rule and preside; and in the military to generals, legates, tribunes, and the inferior officers; — so is there by the pope to patriarchs, archbishops, bishops, in their several subordinations, which are as his civil state; and to generals of religious orders, provincials, and their dependants, which are as his military. And it is by some (not in all things agreeing with them) confessed that the government pleaded for by them in the church was brought in and established in correspondency and accommodation to the civil government of the empire; which is undeniably evident and certain. Now, this being not thoroughly done till the empire had received an incurable wound, it seems to me to be the making of an image to the beast, giving life to it, and causing it to speak. So that the present Roman church is nothing else but an image or similitude of the Roman empire, set up, in its declining, among and over the same persons in succession, by the craft of Satan, through principles of deceit, subtlety, and spiritual wickedness, as the other was by force and violence, for the same ends of power, dominion, fleshliness, and persecution with the former.

The exactness of this correspondency in all things, both in respect of those who claim to be the stated body of his ecclesiastical commonwealth, and those who are merely dependent on his will, bound unto him professedly by a military sacrament, exempted from the ordinary rules and government of his fixed rulers in their several subordinations, under officers of their own, immediately commissionated by him, with his management of both these parties to balance and keep them mutually in quiet and in order for his service (especially confiding in his men of war, like the emperors of old), may elsewhere be farther manifested.

I suppose it will not be needful to add any thing to evince the vanity of the pretensions of the Romanists or others against all or any of us on the account of schism, upon a grant of the principles laid down, it lies so clear in them without need of farther deduction; and I speak with some confidence that I am not in expectation of any hasty confutation of them, — I mean, that which is so indeed. [As for] the earnestness of their clamours, importuning us to take notice of them, by the way, before I enter upon a direct debate of the cause, as it stands stated in reference to them, I shall only tell them, that, seeking to repose our consciences on the mind of God revealed in the Scriptures, we are not at all concerned in the noise they make in the world. For what have we done? Wherein doth our guilt consist? Wherein lies the peculiar concernment of these ἀλλοτριοεπίσκοποι? Let them go to the churches with whom we walk, of whom we are, and ask of them concerning our ways, our love, and the duties of it. Do we live in strife and variance? Do we not bear with each other? Do we not worship God without disputes and divisions? Have we differences and contentions in our assemblies? Do we break any bond of union wherein we are bound by the express institutions of Jesus Christ? If we have, let the righteous reprove us; we will own our guilt, confess we have been carnal, and endeavour reformation. If not, what have the Romanist, Italians, to do to judge us? Knew we not your design, your interest, your lives, your doctrines, your worship, we might possibly think that you might intermeddle out of love and mistaken zeal; but "ad populum phaleras," — you would be making shrines, and thence is this stir and uproar. "But we are schismatics, in that we have departed from the catholic church; and for our own conventicles, they are no churches, but sties of beasts." But this is most false. We abide in the catholic church, under all the bonds wherein, by the will of Christ, we stand related unto it; which if we prove not with as much evidence as the nature of such things will bear, though you are not at all concerned in it, yet we will give you leave to triumph over us. And if our own congregations be not churches, whatsoever we are, we are not schismatics; for schism is an evil amongst the members of a church, if St Paul may be believed. "But we have forsaken the church of Rome." But, gentlemen, show first how we were ever of it. No man hath lost that which he never had, nor hath left the place or station wherein he never was. Tell me when or how we were members of your church? We know not your language; you are barbarians to us. It is impossible we should assemble with you. "But your forefathers left that church, and you persist in their evil." Prove that our forefathers were ever of your church in any communion instituted by Christ, and you say somewhat. To desert a man's station and relation, which he had on any other account, good or bad, is not schism, as shall farther be manifested.

Upon the same principle, a plea for freedom from the charge of any church, real or pretended, as *national*, may be founded and confirmed. Either we are of the national church of England (to give that instance) or we are not; — if we are not, and are exempted by our protestation as before, whatever we are, we are not schismatics; if we are fatally bound unto it, and must be members of it whether we will or no, being made so we know not how, and continuing so we know not why, show us, then, what duty or office of love is incumbent on us that we do not perform. Do we not join in external acts of worship in peace with the whole church? Call the whole church together, and try what we will do. Do we not join in every congregation in the nation? This is not charged on us, nor will any say that we have right so to do without a relation to some particular church in the nation. I know where the sore lies. A national officer or officers, with others acting under them in several subordinations, with various distributions of power, are the church intended. A non-submission to their rules and constitutions is the schism we are guilty of "Quem das finem, rex magne, laborum!"

But this pretence shall afterward be sifted to the utmost. In the meantime, let any one inform me what duty I ought to perform towards a national church, on supposition there is any such thing by virtue of an institution of Jesus Christ, that is possible for me to perform, and I shall, σὺν Θεῷ, address myself unto it.

To close these considerations with things of more immediate concernment: Of the divisions that have fallen out amongst us in things of religion since the last revolutions of this nation, there is no one thing hath been so effectual a promotion (such is the power of tradition and prejudice, which even bear all before them in human affairs) as the mutual charging one another with the guilt of schism. That the notion of schism whereon this charge is built by the most, if not all, was invented by some of the ancients, to promote their plea and advantage with them with whom they had to do, without due regard to the simplicity of the gospel, at least in a suitableness to the present state of the church in those days, is too evident; for on very small foundations have mighty fabrics and μορμωλυκεῖα in religion been raised. As an ability to judge of the present posture and condition of affairs, with counsel to give direction for their order and management towards any end proposed, — not an ability to contrive for events, and to knit on one thing upon another, according to a probability of success, for continuance, which is almost constantly disturbed by unexpected providential interveniences, leaving the contrivers at a perplexing loss, — will be found to be the sum of human wisdom; so it will be our wisdom, in the things of God, not to judge according to what by any means is made present to us, and its principles on that account rendered ready to exert themselves, but ever to recoil to the original and first institution. When a man first falls into some current, he finds it strong and almost impassable; trace it to its fountain, and it is but a dribbling gutter. Paul tells the members of the church of Corinth that there were divisions amongst them, breaches of that love and order that ought to be observed in religious assemblies. Hence there is a sin of schism raised; which, when considered as now stated, doth no more relate to that treated on by the apostle than "Simon, son of Jonas, lovest thou me?" doth to the pope's supremacy; or Christ saying to Peter of John, "If I will that he tarry till I come, what is that to thee?" did to the report that afterward went abroad, "that that disciple should not die." When God shall have reduced his churches to their primitive purity and institution, when they are risen and have shaken themselves out of the dust, and things of religion return to their native simplicity, it is scarce possible to imagine what vizards will fall off, and what a contrary appearance many things will have to what they now walk up and down in.

I wish that those who are indeed really concerned in this business, — namely, the members of particular churches who have voluntarily given up themselves to walk in them according to the appointment of Christ, — would seriously consider what evil lies at the door if they give place to causeless differences and divisions amongst themselves. Had this sin of schism been rightly stated, as it ought, and the guilt of it charged in its proper place, perhaps some would have been more careful in their deportment, in their relations. At present the dispute in the world relating hereunto is about *subjection to the pope* and the church of Rome, as it is called; and this managed on the principles of edicts and of councils, with the practices of princes and nations, in the days long ago past, with the like considerations, wherein the concernment of Christians is doubtless very small; or of obedience and conformity to metropolitan and diocesan bishops in their constitutions and ways of worship, jointly or severally prescribed by them. In more ancient times, that which was agitated under the same name was about persons or churches renouncing the communion and society of saints with all other churches in the world, yet consenting with them in the same confession of faith, for the substance of it. And these differences respectively are handled in reference to what the state of things was and is grown unto in the days wherein they are managed. When Paul wrote his epistle, there was no occasion given to any such controversies, nor foundation laid making them possible. That the disciples of Christ ought everywhere to abound in love and forbearance towards one another, especially to carry all things in union and peace in those societies wherein they were joined for the worship of God, were his endeavours and exhortations: of these things he is utterly silent. Let them who aim to recover themselves into the like state and condition consider his commands, exhortations, and reproofs. Things are now generally otherwise stated, which furnisheth men with objections against what hath been spoken; to whose removal, and farther clearing of the whole matter, I shall now address myself.

Chapter III.

Objections against the former discourse proposed to consideration — Separation from any church in the Scripture not called schism — Grounds of such separation; apostasy, irregular walking, sensuality — Of separation on the account of reformation — Of commands for separation — No example of churches departing from the communion of one another — Of the common notion of schism, and the use made of it — Schism a breach of union — The union instituted by Christ.

"THAT which lies obvious to every man against what hath been delivered, and which is comprehensive of what particular objections it seems liable and obnoxious to, is, that according to this description of schism, separation of any man or men from a true church, or of one church from others, is not schism, seeing that is an evil only amongst the members of one church, whilst they continue so to be; which is so contrary to the judgment of the generality of Christians in this business that it ought to be rejected as fond and absurd."

Of what hath been the judgment of most men in former ages, what it is in this, what strength there is in an argument deduced from the consent pretended, I am not as yet arrived to the consideration. Nor have I yet manifested what I grant of the general notion of schism, as it may be drawn, by way of analogy or proportion of reason, from what is delivered in the Scriptures concerning it.

I am upon the precise signification of the word and description of the thing, as used and given by the Holy Ghost. In this sense I deny that there is any relinquishment, departure, or separation from any church or churches mentioned or intimated in the Scriptures, which is or is called schism, or agreeth with the description by them given us of that term. Let them that are contrary minded attempt the proof of what they affirm. As far as a negative proposition is capable of evidence from any thing but the weakness of the opposition made unto it, that laid down will receive it by the ensuing considerations: —

All blamable departure from any church or churches, or relinquishment of them mentioned in the gospel, may be reduced to one of these three heads or causes: — 1. *Apostasy*; 2. *Irregularity of walking*; 3. *Professed sensuality*.

1. Apostasy or falling away from the faith of the gospel, and thereupon forsaking the congregations or assemblies for the worship of God in Jesus Christ, is mentioned, Heb. x. 25, Μὴ ἐγκαταλείποντες τὴν ἐπισυναγωγὴν ἑαυτῶν, — "Not wholly deserting the assembling ourselves, as is the manner of some." A separation from and relinquishment of the communion of that church or those churches with whom men have assembled for the worship of God is the guilt here charged on some by the apostle. Upon what account they so separated themselves is declared, verse 26, They "sinned wilfully, after they had received the knowledge of the truth;" thereby slipping out their necks from the yoke of Christ, verse 38, and "drawing back unto perdition," verse 39; — that is, they departed off to Judaism. I much question whether any one would think fit to call these men schismatics, or whether we should so judge or so speak of any that in these days should forsake our churches and turn Mohammedans; such departure makes men apostates, not schismatics. Of this sort many are mentioned in the Scriptures. Nor are they not at all accounted schismatics because the lesser crime is swallowed up and drowned in the greater, but because their sin is wholly of another nature.

Of some who withdraw themselves from church communion, at least for a season, by their disorderly and irregular walking, we have also mention. The apostle calls them, ἄτακτοι, 1 Thess. v. 14, "unruly," or "disorderly" persons, not abiding in obedience to the order prescribed by Christ in and unto his churches, and says they walked ἀτάκτως, 2 Thess. iii. 6, out of all church order; whom he would have warned and avoided: so also, ἀτόπους, verse 2, persons that abide quietly in no place or station, but wander up and down; whom, whatever their profession be, he denies to have faith. That there were many of this sort in the primitive times, who, through a vain and slight spirit, neglected and fell off from church assemblies, when yet they would not openly renounce the faith of Christ, is known. Of such disorderly persons we have many in our days wherein we live, whom we charge not with schism, but vanity, folly, disobedience to the precepts of Christ in general.

Men also separated themselves from the churches of Christ upon the account of sensuality, that they might freely indulge to their lusts, and live in all manner of pleasure all their days: Jude 19, "These be they who separate themselves, sensual, having not the Spirit." Who are these? They that "turn the grace of our God into lasciviousness," and that "deny the only Lord God, and our Saviour Jesus Christ," verse 4; that "defile the flesh," after the manner of Sodom and Gomorrah, verses 7, 8; that "speak evil of things they know not," and in "things they know naturally, as brute beasts, they corrupt themselves," verses 10, — sinning openly, like beasts, against the light of nature: so verses 12, 13, 16. "These," saith the apostle, "be they who separate themselves," men given over to work all uncleanness with delight and greediness in the face of the sun, abusing themselves, and justifying their abominations with a pretence of the grace of God.

That there is any blamable separation from or relinquishment of any church or churches of Christ mentioned in the Scripture, but what may be referred to one of those heads, I am yet to learn. Now, whether the men of these abominations are to be accounted schismatics, or their crime in separating themselves to be esteemed schism, it is not hard to judge. If, on any of these accounts, any persons have withdrawn themselves from the communion of any church of Christ; if they have on any motives of fear or love apostatized from the faith of the gospel; if they do it by walking disorderly and loosely in their conversations; if they give themselves up to sensuality and uncleanness, and so be no more able to bear the society of them whom God hath called to holiness and purity of life and worship, — they shall assuredly bear their own burden.

But none of these instances are comprehensive of the case inquired after; so that, for a close of them, I say, for a man to withdraw or withhold himself from the communion external and visible of any church or churches, on the pretension and plea, be it true or otherwise, that the worship, doctrine, or discipline, instituted by Christ is corrupted among them, with which corruption he dares not defile himself, it is nowhere in the Scripture called schism. Nor is that case particularly exemplified or expressly supposed whereby a judgment may be made of the fact at large; but we are left upon the whole matter to the guidance of such general principles and rules as are given us for that end and purpose.

What may regularly, on the other hand, be deduced from the commands given to "turn away from them who have only a form of godliness," 2 Tim. iii. 5; to "withdraw from them that walk disorderly," 2 Thess. iii. 6; not to bear nor endure in communion men of corrupt principles and wicked lives, Rev. ii. 14; but positively to separate from an apostate church, chap. xviii. 4, that in all things we may worship Christ according to his mind and appointment; what is the force of these commands Ἀποτρέπεσθαι, μὴ συναναμίγνυσθαι, παραπίπτεσθαι, ἐκκλίνειν, μὴ κοινωνεῖν, μὴ λέγειν χαίρειν, φεύγειν, and the like, — is without the compass of what I am now treating about.

Of one particular church departing from that communion with another or others, be it what it will, which it ought to hold, unless in the departing of some of them in some things from the common faith, which is supposed not to relate to schism, in the Scripture we have no example. Diotrephes, assuming an authority over that church wherein he was placed, 3 John 9, 10, and for a season hindering the brethren from the performance of the duty incumbent upon them toward the great apostle and others, makes the nearest approach to such a division, but yet in such a distance that it is not at all to our purpose in hand. When I come to consider that communion that churches have, or ought to have, among themselves, this will be more fully discussed. Neither is this my sense alone, that there is no instance of any such separation as that which is the matter of our debate to be found in the Scripture; it is confessed by others differing from me in and about church affairs. To "leave all ordinary communion in any church with dislike, where opposition or offence offers itself, is to separate from such a church in the Scripture sense; such separation was not in being in the apostles' time," say they, Pap. Accom. p. 55. But how they came to know exactly the sense of the Scriptures in and about things not mentioned in them, I know not. As I said before, were I unwilling, I do not as yet understand how I may be compelled to carry on the notion of schism any farther. Nor is there need of adding any thing to demonstrate how little the conscience of a godly man, walking peaceably in any particular church-society, is concerned in all the clamorous disputes of this age about it, these being built on false hypotheses, presumptions, and notions, no other way considerable but as received by tradition from our fathers.

But I shall, for the sake of some, carry on this discourse to a fuller issue. There is another common notion of schism, which pleads for an original from that spoken expressly of it by a parity of reason; which, tolerable in itself, hath been, and is, injuriously applied and used, according as it hath fallen into the hands of men who needed it as an engine to fix or improve them in the station wherein they are or were, and wherewith they are pleased. Indeed, being invented for several purposes, there is nothing more frequent than for men who are scarce able to keep off the force of it from their own heads, whilst managed against them by them above, at the same time vigorously to apply it for the oppression of all under them. What is on all hands consented unto as its general nature I shall freely grant, that I might have liberty and advantage thence to debate the restriction and application of it to the several purposes of men prevailing themselves thereon.

Let, then, the general demand be granted, that schism is διαίρεσις τῆς ἑνότητος, "the breach of union," which I shall attend with one reasonable postulatum, — namely, that this union be a union of the appointment of Jesus Christ. The consideration, then of what or what sort of union in reference to the worship of God, according to the gospel, is instituted and appointed by Jesus Christ, is the proper foundation of what I have farther to offer in this business. Let, the breach of this, if you please, be accounted schism; for being an evil, I shall not contend by what name or title it be distinguished. It is not pleaded that any kind of relinquishment or desertion of any church or churches is presently schism, but only such a separation as breaks the bond of union instituted by Christ.

Now, this union being instituted in the church, according to the various acceptations of that word, so is it distinguished. Therefore, for a discovery of the nature of that which is particularly to be spoken to, and also its contrary, I must show, —

1. The several *considerations of the church* wherein and with which union is to be preserved.

2. What that *union* is, and wherein it doth consist, which, according to the mind of Christ, we are to keep and observe with the church, under the several notions of it respectively.

3. And *how that union is broken*, and what is that sin whereby it is done.

In handling this triple proposal, I desire that it may not be expected that I should much insist on any thing that falls in my way, though never so useful to my end and purpose, which hath been already proved and confirmed by others beyond all possibility of control; and such will many, if not most, of the principles that I proceed upon appear to be.

Chapter IV.

Several acceptations in the Scripture of the name "church" — Of the church catholic, properly so called — Of the church visible — Perpetuity of particular churches — A mistake rectified — The nature of the church catholic evinced — Bellarmine's description of the church catholic — Union of the church catholic, wherein it consists — Union by way of consequence — Unity of faith, of love — The communion of the catholic church in and with itself — The breach of the union of the church catholic, wherein it consisteth — Not morally possible — Protestants not guilty of it — The papal world out of interest in the church catholic — As partly profane — Miracles no evidence of holiness — Partly ignorant — Self-justiciaries — Idolatrous — Worshippers of the beast.

To begin with the first thing proposed: The church of Christ living in this world, as to our present concernment, is taken in Scripture three ways:—

1. For the *mystical body* of Christ, his elect, redeemed, justified, and sanctified ones throughout the world; commonly called *the church catholic militant*.

2. For the *universality* of men throughout the world *called* by the preaching of the word, visibly professing and yielding obedience to the gospel; called by some *the church catholic visible*.

3. For a *particular church* of some place, wherein the instituted worship of God in Christ is celebrated according to his mind.

From the rise and nature of the things themselves doth this distinction of the signification of the word "church" arise: for whereas the church is a society of men called out of the world, it is evident there is mention of a twofold call in Scripture; — one *effectual*, according to the purpose of God, Rom. viii. 28; the other only *external*. The church must be distinguished according to its answer and obedience to these calls, which gives us the first two states and considerations of it. And this is confessed by the ordinary gloss, ad Rom. viii. "Vocatio exterior fit per prædicatores, et est communis bonorum et malorum, interior vero tantum est electorum." And whereas there are laws and external rules for joint communion given to them that are called, which is confessed, the necessity of churches in the last acceptation, wherein obedience can alone be yielded to those laws, is hereby established.

In the first sense the church hath, as such, the properties of *perpetuity, invisibility, infallibility*, as to all necessary means of salvation, attending of it; not as notes whereby it may be known, either in the whole or any considerable part of it, but as certain adjuncts of its nature and existence. Neither are there any signs of less or more certainty whereby the whole may be discerned or known as such, though there are of the individuals whereof it doth consist.

In the second, the church hath *perpetuity, visibility*, and *infallibility*, as qualified above, in a secondary sense, — namely, not as such, not as visible and confessing, but as comprising the individuals whereof the catholic church doth consist; for all that truly believe profess, though, all that profess do not truly believe.

Whether Christ hath had always a church, in the last sense and acceptation of the word, in the world, is a most needless inquiry; nor are we concerned in it any farther than in other matters of fact that are recorded in story: though I am apt to believe that although very many, in all ages, kept up their station in and relation to the church in the two former acceptations, yet there was in some of them scarce any visible society of worshippers, so far answering the institution of Christ as to render them fit to be owned and joined withal as a visible particular church of Christ. But yet, though the notions of men were generally corrupt, the practice of all professors throughout the world, whereof so little is recorded, and least of them that did best, is not rashly to be determined of. Nor can our judgment be censured in this by them who think that when Christ lay in the grave there was no believer left but his mother, and that the church was preserved in that one person. So was Bernard minded, Tractat. de Pass. Dom. "Ego sum vitis," cap. ii., "[B. Virgo] sola per illud triste sabbathum stetit in fide, et salvata fuit ecclesia in ipsâ solâ." Of the same mind is Marsilius in Sent., quæst. 20, art. 3; as are also others of that sort of men: see Bannes, in 2, 2; Thom., quæst. 1, art. 10. I no way doubt of the perpetual existence of innumerable believers in every age, and such as made the profession that is absolutely necessary to salvation, one way or other, though I question a regular association of men for the celebration of instituted worship, according to the mind of Christ. The seven thousand in Israel, in the days of Elijah, were members of the church of God, and yet did not constitute a church-state among the ten tribes. But these things must be farther spoken to.

I cannot but by the way remind a learned person,[4] with whom I have formerly occasionally had some debate in print about episcopacy and the state of the first churches, of a mistake of his, which he might have prevented with a little inquiry into the judgment of them whom he undertook to confute at a venture. I have said that "there was not any ordinary church-officer instituted in the first times, relating to more churches in his office, or to any other church, than a single particular congregation." He replies, that "this is the very same which his memory suggested to him out of the 'Saints' Belief,' printed twelve or fourteen years since, where, instead of that article of the apostolic symbol, 'The holy catholic church,' this very hypothesis was substituted." If he really believed that, in professing I owned no instituted church with officers of one denomination in Scripture beyond a single congregation, I renounced the catholic church, or was any way necessitated so to do, I suppose he may, by what hath now been expressed, be rectified in his apprehension. If he was willing only to make use of the advantage, wherewith he supposed himself accommodated by that expression, to press the persuasion owned on the minds of ignorant men, who could not but startle at the noise of denying the catholic church, it may pass at the same rate that most of the repartees in such discourses are to be allowed at. But to proceed:—

I. In the first sense the word is used Matt. xvi. 18, "Upon this rock I will build my church, and the gates of hell shall not prevail against it." This is the *church of the elect*, redeemed, justified, sanctified ones, that are so built on Christ, and these only; and all these are interested in the promise made to the church. There is no promise made to the church, as such in any sense, but is

---

4 Dr Hammond, with whom Owen had some controversy in regard to the sentiments of Grotius, and the divine authority of episcopal government. See Owen's preface to his work on "The Perseverance of the Saints," his "Vindiciæ Evangelicæ" and "Review of the Annotations of Grotius." — Ed.

peculiarly made therein to every one that is truly and properly a part and member of that church. Who, and who only, are interested in that promise Christ himself declares, John vi. 40, x. 27-29, xvii. 20, 24. They that will apply this to the church in any other sense must know that it is incumbent on them to establish the promise made to it unto every one that is a true member of the church in that sense; which, whatever be the sense of the promise, I suppose they will find difficult work of. Eph. v. 25-27, "Christ loved the church, and gave himself for it, that he might sanctify and cleanse it with the washing of water by the word, that he might present it to himself a glorious church, not having spot, or wrinkle, or any such thing." He speaks only of those whom Christ loved antecedently to his dying for them, whereof his love to them was the cause: who they are is manifest, John x. 15, xvii. 17, even those on whom, by his death, he accomplished the effects mentioned, by washing, cleansing, and sanctifying, bringing them into the condition promised to the "bride, the Lamb's wife," Rev. xix. 8, which is the "new Jerusalem," xxi. 2, of elected and saved ones, verse 27. Col. i. 18 contains an expression of the same light and evidence, "Christ is the head of the body, the church;' not only a governing head, to give it rules and laws, but, as it were, a natural head unto the body, which is influenced by him with a new spiritual life; — which Bellarmine protesteth against as any requisite condition to the members of the catholic church, which he pleaded for. In that same sense, verse 24, saith the apostle, "I fill up that which is behind of the afflictions of Christ in my flesh, for his body's sake, which is the church;" which assertion is exactly parallel to that of 2 Tim. ii. 10, "Therefore I endure all things for the elect's sakes, that they may obtain salvation" So that the *elect* and the *church* are the same persons under several considerations. And therefore even a particular church, on the account of its participation of the nature of the catholic, is called "elect," 1 Pet. v. 13; and so the church, Matt. xvi. 18, is expounded by our Saviour himself, chap. xxiv. 24. But to prove at large, by a multiplication of arguments and testimonies, that the catholic church, or mystical body of Christ, consists of the whole number of the elect, as redeemed, justified, sanctified, called, believing, and yielding obedience to Christ throughout the world (I speak of it as militant in any age), and of them only, were as needlessly "actum agere" as a man can well devise. It is done already, and that to the purpose uncontrollably, "terque quaterque." And the substance of the doctrine is delivered by Aquinas himself, p. 3, q. 8, a 3. In brief, the sum of the inquiry upon this head is concerning the matter of that church concerning which such glorious things are spoken in Scripture, — namely, that it is "the spouse, the wife, the bride, the sister, the only one of Christ, his dove, his undefiled, his temple, elect, redeemed, his Zion, his body, his new Jerusalem;" concerning which inquiry the reader knows where he may abundantly find satisfaction.

That the asserting the catholic church in this sense is no new apprehension is known to them who have at all looked backward to what was past before us. "Omnibus consideratis," saith Austin, "puto me non temere dicere, alios ita esse in domo Dei, ut ipsi etiam sint eadem domus Dei, quæ dicitur ædificari supra petram, quæ unica columba appellatur, quæ sponsa pulchra sine macula, et ruga, et hortus conclusus, fons signatus, puteus aquæ vivæ, paradisus cum fructu pomorum, alios autem ita constat esse in domo, ut non pertineant ad compagem domûs, sed sicut esse palea dicitur in frumentis," De Bapt., lib. i. cap. 51; who is herein followed by not a few of the Papists. Hence saith Biel., "Accipitur etiam ecclesia pro tota multitudine prædestinatorum," in Canon. Miss. Lec. 22. In what sense this church is visible was before declared. Men elected, redeemed, justified, as such, are not visible, for that which makes them so is not; but this hinders not but they may be so upon the other consideration, sometimes to more, sometimes to fewer, yea, they are so always to some. Those that are may be seen; and when we say they are visible, we do not intend that they are actually seen by any that we know, but that they may be so.

Bellarmine gives us a description of this catholic church (as the name hath of late been used at the pleasure of men, and wrested to serve every design that was needful to be carried on) to the interest which he was to contend for, but in itself perfectly ridiculous. He tells us, out of Austin, that the church is a *living body*, wherein is a body and a soul. Thence, saith he, the *soul is* the *internal graces* of the Spirit, faith, hope, and love; the *body* is the *eternal profession* of faith. Some are of the soul and body, perfectly united to Christ by faith and the profession of it; some are of the soul that are not of the body, as the catechumeni, which are not as yet admitted to be members of the visible church, but yet are true believers; some, saith he, are of the body that are not of the soul, who having no true grace, yet, out of hope or temporal fear, do make profession of the faith, and these are like the hair, nails, and ill humours in a human body. Now, saith Bellarmine, our definition of a church compriseth only the last sort, whilst they are under the head the pope; — which is all one as if he had defined a man to be a dead creature, composed of hair, nails, and ill humours, under a hat. But of the church in this sense so far.

It remaineth, then, that we inquire what is the union which the church in this sense hath from the wisdom of its head, Jesus Christ. That it is one, that it hath a union with its head and in itself, is not questioned. It is one sheepfold, one body, one spouse of Christ, his "only one" as unto him; and that it might have oneness in itself, with all the fruits of it, our Saviour prays, John xvii. 19-23. The whole of it is described, Eph. iv. 15, 16, "May grow up into him in all things, which is the head, even Christ: from whom the whole body fitly joined together and compacted by that which every joint supplieth, according to the effectual working in the measure of every part, maketh increase of the body unto the edifying itself in love." And of the same importance is that of the same apostle, Col. ii. 19, "Not holding the Head, from which all the body by joints and bands having nourishment ministered, and knit together, increaseth with the increase of God."

Now, in the union of the church, in every sense, there is considerable both the "formalis ratio" of it, whence it is, what it is, and the way and means whereby it exerts itself and is useful and active in communion. The first, in the church as now stated, consists in its joint holding the Head, and growing up into him by virtue of the communication of supplies unto it therefrom for that end and purpose. That which is the formal reason and cause of the union of the members with the head is the formal reason and cause of the union of the members with themselves. The original union of the members is in and with the head; and by the same have they union with themselves as one body. Now, the inhabitation of the same Spirit in him and them is that which makes Christ personal and his church to be one Christ mystical, 1 Cor. xii. 12, 13. Peter tells us that we are by the promises "made partakers of the divine nature," 2 Pet. i. 4. We are θείας κοινωνοὶ φύσεως, — we have communion with it. That θεία φύσις is no more but καινὴ κτίσις, I cannot easily consent. Now, it is in the person of the Spirit, whereof we are by the promise made partakers. He is the "Spirit of promise," Eph. i. 13; promised by God to Christ, Acts ii. 33, Ἐπαγγελίαν τοῦ ἁγίου Πνεύματος λαβὼν παρὰ τοῦ Πατρός, and by him to us, John xiv. 16, 17; being of old the great promise of the covenant, Isa. lix. 21; Ezek. xi. 19, xxxvi. 26, 27. Now, in the participation of the divine nature consists the union of the saints with Christ. John vi. 56, our Saviour tells us that it arises from eating his flesh and drinking his blood: "He that eateth my flesh, and drinketh my blood, dwelleth in me, and I in him" This he expounds, verse 63: "It is the Spirit that quickeneth; the flesh profiteth nothing." By the quickening Spirit, inhabitation in Christ, and Christ in it, is intended. And the same he manifests in his prayer, that his church may be one in the Father and the Son, as the Father is in him and he in the Father, John xvii. 21: for the Spirit being the love of the Father and of the Son, is "vinculum Trinitatis;" and so here of our union in some resemblance.

The unity of members in the body natural with one head is often chosen to set forth the union of the church, 1 Cor. xii. 12, xi. 3; Eph. v. 23; Col. i. 18. Now, every man can tell that union of the head and members whereby they become all one body, that and not another, is oneness of soul, whereby the whole is animated; which makes the body, be it less or greater, to be one body. That which answers hereunto in the mystical body of Christ is the animation of the whole by his Spirit, as the apostle fully [states], 1 Cor. xv. 45. The union between husband and wife is also chosen by the Holy Ghost to illustrate the union between Christ and his church: "For this cause shall a man leave his father and mother, and shall be joined unto his wife, and they two shall be one flesh. This is a great mystery: but I speak concerning Christ and the church," Eph. v. 31, 32. The union between man and wife we have, Gen. ii. 24; "They are no more twain, but one flesh," Matt. xix. 6; — of Christ and his church, that they are one spirit, "He that is joined unto the Lord is one spirit," 1 Cor. vi. 17. See also another similitude of the same importance, John xv. 5; Rom. xi. 16, 17. This, I say, is the *fountain-radical* union of the church catholic in itself, with its head and formal reason of it.

Hence flows a double consequential union that it hath also:—

1. Of *faith*, All men united to Christ by the inhabitation of the same Spirit in him and them, are by it, from and according

to the word, "taught of God," Isa. liv. 13; John vi. 45: so taught, every one of them, as to come to Christ, verse 47; that is, by believing, by faith. They are so taught of God as that they shall certainly have that measure of knowledge and faith which is needful to bring them to Christ, and to God by him. And this they have by the unction or Spirit which they have received, 1 John ii. 20, 27, accompanying the word, by virtue of God's covenant with them, Isa. lix. 21. And hereby are all the members of the church catholic, however divided in their visible profession by any differences among themselves, or differenced by the several measures of gifts and graces they have received, brought to the perfection aimed at, to the "unity of the faith, and to the acknowledgment of the Son of God, unto a perfect man, unto the measure of the stature of the fulness of Christ," Eph. iv. 13. Nor was this hidden from some of the Papists themselves: "Ecclesia sancta corpus est Christi uno Spiritu vivificata, unita fide unâ, et sanctificata," saith Hugo de Victore, de Sacram., lib. ii., as he had said before in the former chapter: "Sicut scriptum est, qui non habet Spiritum Christi, hic non est ejus; qui non habet Spiritum Christi, non est membrum Christi. In corpore uno Spiritus unus, nihil in corpore mortuum, nihil extra corpus vivum." See to the same purpose, Enchirid. Concil. Colon. in Symbol.

2. With peculiar reference to the members themselves, there is another necessary consequence of the union mentioned, and that is the *mutual love* of all those united in the head, as before, towards one another, and of every one towards the whole, as so united in the head, Christ Jesus. There is an "increase made of the body to the edifying itself in love," Eph. iv. 16; and so it becomes the bend of perfectness to this body of Christ, I cannot say that the members or parts of this church have their union in themselves by love, because they have that with and in Christ whereby they are one in themselves, John xvii. 21, 23; they are one in God, even in Christ, where their life is hid, Col. iii. 3; — but it is the next and immediate principle of that communion which they severally have one with another, and the whole body in and with itself. I say, then, that the communion which the catholic church, the mystical body of Christ, hath with and in itself, springing from the union which it hath in and with Christ, and in itself thereby, consists in love exerting itself in inexpressible variety, according to the present state of the whole, its relation to Christ, to saints and angels, with the conditions

and occasions of the members of it respectively, 1 Cor. xii. 26, 27.

What hath been spoken concerning the union and communion of this church will not, I suppose, meet with any contradiction. Granting that there is such a church as that we speak of, "cœtus prædestinatorum credentium," the Papists themselves will grant that Christ alone is its head, and that its union ariseth from its subjection to him and dependence on him. Their modesty makes them contented with constituting the pope in the room of Christ, as he is, as it were, a political head for government. They have not as yet directly put in their claim to his office as a mystical head, influencing the body with life and motion; though by their figment of the sacraments communicating grace, "ex opere operato," and investing the original power of dispensing them in the pope only, they have contended fair for it. But if any one can inform me of any other union or communion of the church, described as above, than these laid down, I shall willingly attend unto his instructions. In the meantime, to carry on the present discourse unto that which is aimed at, it is manifest that the breach of this union must consist in these two things:—

1. *The casting out, expelling, and losing that Spirit which, abiding in us, gives us this union.*

2. *The loss of that love* which thence flows into the body of Christ, and believers as parts and members thereof.

This being the state of the church under the first consideration of it, certainly it would be an extravagancy scarcely to he paralleled for any one to affirm a breach of this union, as such, to be schism, under that notion of it which we are inquiring after. But because there is very little security to be enjoyed in an expectation of the sobriety of men in things wherein they are, or suppose they may be, concerned, that they may know beforehand what is farther incumbent on them if, in reference to us, they would prevail themselves of any such notion, I here inform them that our persuasion is, that this union was never utterly broken by any man taken into it, nor ever shall be to the end of the world; and I suppose they esteem it vain to dispute about the adjuncts of that which is denied to be.

But yet this persuasion being not common to us with them with whom we have to do in this matter, I shall not farther make use of it as to our present defence. That any other union of the catholic church, as such, can possibly be fancied or imagined by any (as to the substance of what hath been pleaded), leaving him a plea for the ordinary soundness of his intellectuals, is denied.

Let us see now, then, what is our concernment in this discourse: Unless men can prove that we have not the Spirit of God, that we do not savingly believe in Jesus Christ, that we do not sincerely love all the saints, his whole body, and every member of it, they cannot disprove our interest in the catholic church. It is true, indeed, men that have so great a confidence of their own abilities, and such a contempt of the world, as to undertake to dispute men out of conclusions from their natural senses about their proper objects, in what they see, feel, and handle, and will not be satisfied that they have not proved there is no motion, whilst a man walks for a conviction under their eye, may probably venture to disprove us in our spiritual sense and experience also, and to give us arguments to persuade us that we have not that communion with Christ which we know we have every day. Although I have a very mean persuasion of my own abilities, yet I must needs say I cannot think that any man in the world can convince me that I do not love Jesus Christ in sincerity, because I do not love the pope, as he is so. Spiritual experience is a security against a more cunning sophister than any Jesuit in the world, with whom the saints of God have to deal all their lives, Eph. vi. 12. And, doubtless, through the rich grace of our God, help will arise to us, that we shall never make a covenant with these men for peace, upon conditions far worse than those that Nahash would have exacted on the men of Jabesh-gilead; which were but the loss of one eye, with an abiding reproach; they requiring of us the deprivation of whatsoever we have to see by, whether as men or Christians, and that with a reproach never to be blotted out.

But as we daily put our consciences upon trial as to this thing, 2 Cor. xiii. 5, and are put unto it by Satan, so are we ready at all times to give an account to our adversaries of the hope that is in us. Let them sift us to the utmost, it will be to our advantage. Only let them not bring frivolous objections, and such as they know are of no weight with us, speaking (as is their constant manner) about the pope and their church, — things utterly foreign to what we are presently about, miserably begging the thing in question. Let them weigh, if they are able, the true nature of union with Christ, of faith in him, of love to the saints; consider them in their proper causes, adjuncts, and effects, with a spiritual eye, laying aside their prejudices and intolerable impositions; — if we are found wanting as to the truth and sincerity of these things, if we cannot give some account of our translation from death to life, of our implantation into Christ, and our participation of the Spirit, we must bear our own burden. If otherwise, we stand fast on the most noble and best account of church-union whatever; and whilst this shield is safe, we are less anxious about the issue of the ensuing contest. Whatever may be the apprehensions of other men, I am not in this thing solicitous. (I speak not of myself, but assuming for the present the person of one concerning whom these things may be spoken). Whilst the efficacy of the gospel accomplisheth in my heart all those divine and mighty effects which are ascribed unto it as peculiarly its work towards them that believe; whilst I know this one thing, that whereas I was blind, now I see, — whereas I was a servant of sin, I am now free to righteousness, and at liberty from bondage unto death, and instead of the fruits of the flesh, I find all the fruits of the Spirit brought forth in me, to the praise of God's glorious grace; whilst I have an experience of that powerful work of conversion and being born again, which I am able to manage against all the accusations of Satan, having peace with God upon justification by faith, with the love of God shed abroad in my heart by the Holy Ghost, investing me in the privileges of adoption, — I shall not certainly be moved with the disputes of men that would persuade me I do not belong to the catholic church, because I do not follow this, or that, or any party of men in the world.

"But you will say, this you will allow to them also with whom you have to do, that they may be members of the catholic church?" I leave other men to stand or fall to their own master. Only, as to the papal multitude, on the account of several inconsistencies between them and the members of this church, I shall place some swords in the way, which will reduce their number to an invisible scantling. I might content myself by affirming at once, that, upon what hath been spoken, I must exclude from the catholic church all and every one whom Bellarmine intends to include in it as such, — namely, those who belong to the church as hairs and ill humours to the body of a man. But I add in particular, —

1. *All wicked and profane persons*, of whom the Scripture speaks expressly that they shall not enter into the kingdom of God, are indisputably cut off. Whatever they pretend in show at any time, in the outward duties of devotion, they have neither faith in Christ nor love to the saints; and so have part and fellowship neither in the union nor communion of the catholic church.

How great a proportion of that synagogue whereof we are speaking will be taken off by this sword, — of their popes, princes, prelates, clergy, votaries, and people, — and that not by a rule of private surmises, but upon the visible issue of their being servants to sin, haters of God and good men, is obvious to all. Persons of really so much as reformed lives amongst them are like the berries after the shaking of an olive tree, 1 Cor. vi. 7–10; Rev. xxii. 15.

I find some persons of late appropriating holiness and regeneration[5] to the Roman party on this account, that among them only miracles are wrought; "which is," say they, "the only proof of true holiness." But these men err as their predecessors, "not knowing the Scriptures, nor the power of God." Amongst all the evidences that are given in Scripture of regeneration, I suppose they will scarcely find this to be one. And they who have no other assurance that they are themselves born of God, but that some of their church work miracles, had need maintain also that no man can be assured thereof in this life. They will find that a broken reed,[6] if they lean upon it. Will it evince all the members of their church to be regenerate, or only some? If they say all, I ask then what becomes of Bellarmine's church, which is made up of them who are not regenerate? If some only, I desire to know on what account the miracles of one man may be an evidence to some in his society that they are regenerate, and not to others? or whether the foundation of that distinction must not lie in themselves? But the truth is, the miracles now pretended are an evidence of a contrary condition to what these men are willing to own, 2 Thess. ii. 8–12.

---

5 "Ille cœtus Christianorum qui solus in orbe claret regeneratis est ecclesia; solus cœtus Christianorum papæ subditorum claret regeneratis; apud illos solos sunt qui miracula faciunt. ergo." — Val. Mag.

6 Deut. xiii. 1–3; Matt. vii. 22, 23; Exod. viii. 7.

2. All *ignorant* persons, into whose hearts God hath not shined, "to give them the knowledge of his glory in the face of Jesus Christ," are to be added to the former account. There is a measure of knowledge of absolute and indispensable necessity to salvation, whereof how short the most of them are is evident. Among the open abominations of the papal combination, for which they ought to be an abhorrency to mankind, their professed design of keeping the people in ignorance is not the least, Hos. iv. 6. That it was devotion to themselves, and not to God, which they aimed to advance thereby, is by experience sufficiently evinced; but that whose reverence is to be preserved by its being hid is in itself contemptible. What other thoughts wise men could have of Christian religion, in their management of it, I know not. Woe to you, Romish clergy! "for ye have taken away the key of knowledge; ye entered not in yourselves, and them that were entering in ye hindered." The people have perished under your hands, for want of knowledge: Zech. xi. 15–17. The figment of an implicit faith, as managed by these men, to charm the spirits and consciences of poor perishing creatures with security in this life, will be found as pernicious to them in the issue as their purgatory, invented on the same account, will be useless.

3. Add to these all *hypocritical self-justiciaries*, who seek for a righteousness as it were by the works of the law, which they never attain to, Rom. ix. 31, 32, though they take pains about it, chap. x. 2; Eph. ii. 8–10. By this sword will fall the fattest cattle of their herd. How the hand of the Lord on this account sweeps away their devotionists, and therein takes down the pride of their glory, the day will discover. Yet, besides these, there are two other things that will cut them down as the grass falls before the scythe of the mower.

4. The first of these is *idolatry*: "Be not deceived; no idolaters shall inherit the kingdom of God," 1 Cor. vi. 9, 10; "Without are idolaters," Rev. xxii. 15. This added to their lives hath made Christian religion, where known only as by them professed, to be an abomination to Jews and Gentiles. Some will one day, besides himself, answer for Averroës thus determining of the case as to his soul: "Quoniam Christiani adorant quod comedunt, anima mea sit cum philosophis." Whether they are idolaters or no, whether they yield the worship due to the Creator to the creature, hath been sifted to the utmost, and the charge of its

evil, which the jealous God doth of all things most abhor, so fastened on them, beyond all possibility of escape, that one of the wisest of them hath at length fixed on that most desperate and profligate refuge, that some kind of idolatry is lawful, because Peter mentions "abominable idolatries," 1 Pet. iv. 3; who is therein so far from distinguishing of several sorts and kinds of it to any such purpose, as that he aggravates all sorts and kinds of it with the epithet of "nefarious" or "abominable."

A man may say, What is there almost that they have not committed lewdness in this kind withal? On every hill, and under every green tree, is the filth of their abomination found. Saints and angels in heaven, images of some that never were, of others that had been better they never had been, bread and wine, cross and nails, altars, wood, and iron, and the pope on earth, are by them adored. The truth is, if we have any assurance left us of any thing in the world, that we either see or hear, feel or taste, and so, consequently, that we are alive, and not other men, the poor Indians who worship a piece of red cloth are not more gross idolaters than they are.

5. *All that worship the beast set up by the dragon*, all that receive his mark in their hand or forehead, are said not to have their names written in the book of life of the Lamb, Rev. xiii. 8, 16; which what aspect it bears towards the visible Roman church, time will manifest.

All these sorts of persons we except against, as those that have no interest in the union of the catholic church, — all profane, ignorant, self-justiciaries, all idolaters, worshippers, or adorers of the papal power. If any remain among them, not one way or other visibly separated from them, who fall not under some one or more of these exceptions, as we grant they may be members of the catholic church, so we deny that they are of that which is called the Roman. And I must needs inform others by the way, that whilst the course of their conversation, ignorance of the mystery of the gospel, hatred of good men, contempt of the Spirit of God, his gifts and graces, do testify to the consciences of them that fear the Lord that they belong not to the church catholic, it renders their rebuking of others for separating from any instituted church, national (as is pretended), or more restrained, very weak and contemptible. All discourses about motes have a worm at the root, whilst there is a beam lies in the eye. Do men suppose that a man who hath tasted how gracious the Lord is, and hath by grace obtained communion with the Father and his Son Jesus Christ, walking at peace with God, and in a sense of his love all his days, filled with the Holy Ghost, and by him with joy unspeakable and glorious in believing, is not strengthened against the rebukes and disputes of men whom he sees and knows by their fruits to be destitute of the Spirit of God, uninterested in the fellowship of the gospel and communion thereof?

Chapter V.

Of the catholic church visible — Of the nature thereof — In what sense the universality of professors is called a church — Amyraldus' judgment in this business — The union of the church in this sense, wherein it consists — Not the same with the union of the church catholic, nor that of a particular instituted church — Not in relation to any one officer, or more, in subordination to one another — Such a subordination not provable — Τὰ ἀρχαῖα of the Nicene synod — Of general councils — Union of the church visible not in a general council — The true unity of the universality of professors asserted — Things necessary to this union — Story of a martyr at Bagdad — The apostasy of churches from the unity of the faith — Testimony of Hegesippus vindicated — Papal apostasy — Protestants not guilty of the breach of this unity — The catholic church, in the sense insisted on, granted by the ancients — Not a political body.

II. THE second general notion of the church, as it is usually taken, signifies the *universality of men professing the doctrine of the gospel and obedience to God in Christ*, according to it, throughout the world. This is that which is commonly called the visible catholic church, which now, together with the union which it hath in itself, and how that unity is broken, falls under consideration.

That all professors of the gospel throughout the world, called to the knowledge of Christ by the word, do make up and constitute his visible kingdom, by their professed subjection to him, and so may be called his church, I grant. That they are precisely so called in Scripture is not unquestionable. What relation it stands in to all particular churches, whether as a genus to its species, or as a *totum* to its parts, hath lately by many been discussed. I must crave leave to deny that it is capable of filling up or of being included in any of these denominations and relations. The universal church we are speaking of is not a thing that hath, as such, a specificative form, from which it should be called a universal church, as a particular hath for its ground of being so called. It is but a collection of all that are duly called Christians in respect of their profession. Nor are the several particular churches of Christ in the world so parts and members of any catholic church as that it should be constituted or made up by them and of them for the order and purpose of an instituted church, — that is, the celebration of the worship of God and institutions of Jesus Christ according to the gospel; which to assert were to overthrow a remarkable difference between the economy of the Old Testament and the New. Nor do I think that particular congregations do stand unto it in the relation of species unto a genus, in which the whole nature of it should be preserved and comprised; which would deprive every one of membership in this universal church which is not joined actually to some particular church or congregation, than which nothing can be more devoid of truth. To debate the thing in particular is not my present intention, nor is needful to the purpose in hand.

The sum is, The *universal church* is not so called upon the same account that a *particular church* is so called. The formal reason constituting a particular church to be a particular church is, that those of whom it doth consist do join together, according to the mind of Christ, in the exercise of the same numerical ordinances for his worship. And in this sense the universal church cannot be said to be a church, as though it had such a particular form of its own; which that it hath, or should have, is not only false but impossible. But it is so called because all Christians throughout the world (excepting some individual persons, providentially excluded) do, upon the enjoyment of the same preaching of the world, the same sacraments administered in *specie, profess one common faith and hope.* But, to the joint performance of any exercise of religion, that they should hear one sermon together, or partake of one sacrament, or have one officer for their rule and government, is ridiculous to imagine; nor do any profess to think so, as to any of the particulars mentioned, but those only who have profit by the fable. As to the description of this church, I shall acquiesce in that lately given of it by a very learned man. Saith he, "Ecclesia universalis, est communio, seu societas omnium cœtuum" (I had rather he had said, and he had done it more agreeably to principles by himself laid down, "Omnium fidem Christianam profitentium sive illi ad ecclesias aliquas particulares pertineant, sive non pertineant"), "qui religionem Christianam profitentur, consistens in eo, quod tametsi neque exercitia pietatis uno numero frequentent, neque sacramenta eadem numero participent, neque uno eodemque omnino ordine regantur et gubernentur, unum tamen corpus in eo constituunt, quod eundem Christum servatorem habere se profitentur, uno in evangelio propositum, iisdem promissionibus comprehensum, quas obsignant et confirmant sacramenta, ex eadem institutione pendentia," Amyrald. Thes. de Eccles. Nom. et. Defin. Thes. 29.

There being, then, in the world a great multitude, which no man can number, of all nations, kindreds, people, and language, professing the doctrine of the gospel, not tied to mountains or hills, John iv. 21, 23, but worshipping ἐν παντὶ τόπῳ, 1 Cor. i. 2, 1 Tim. ii. 8, let us consider what union there is amongst them as such, wrapping them all in the bond thereof by the will and appointment of Jesus Christ, and wherein the breach of that union doth consist, and how any man is or may be guilty thereof:

1. I suppose this will be granted, that only elect believers belong to the church, in this sense considered, is a chimera feigned in the brains of the Romanists, and fastened on the reformed divines. I wholly assent to Austin's dispute on this head against the Donatists. And the whole entanglement that hath been about this matter hath arisen from obstinacy in the Papists in not receiving the catholic church in the sense mentioned before; which to do they know would be injurious to their interest, This church being visible and professing, and being now considered under that constituting difference, that the union of it cannot be the same with that of the catholic church before mentioned, it is clear from hence that multitudes of men belong unto it who have not the relation mentioned before to Christ and his body, which is required in all comprehended in that union, seeing "many are called, but few are chosen."

2. Nor can it consist in a joint assembly, either ordinary or extraordinary, for the celebration of the ordinances of the gospel, or any one of them, as was the case of the church of the Jews, which met at set times in one place for the performance of that worship which was then required, nor could otherwise be accomplished: for as it is not at all possible that any such thing should ever be done, considering what is and shall be the estate of Christ's visible kingdom to the end of the world, so it is not (that I know of) pleaded that Christ hath made any such appointment; yea, it is on all hands confessed, at least can-

not reasonably be denied, that there is a *supersedeas* granted to all supposals of any such duty incumbent on the whole visible church, by the institution of particular churches, wherein all the ordinances of Christ are duly to be administered.

I shall only add, that if there be not an institution for the joining in the same numerical ordinances, the union of this church is not really a church-union, — I mean of an instituted church, which consists therein, — but something of another nature. Neither can that have the formal reason of an instituted church as such, which as such can join in no one act of the worship of God instituted to be performed in such societies. So that he that shall take into his thoughts the condition of all the Christians in the world, their present state, what it hath been for fifteen hundred years, and what it is like to be ἕως τῆς συντελείας τοῦ αἰῶνος, will easily understand what church-state they stand in and relate unto.

3. It cannot Possibly have its union by a *relation to any one officer* given to the whole, such a one as the Papists pretend the pope to be; for though it be possible that one officer may have relation to all the churches in the world, as the apostles severally had (when Paul said the care of all the churches lay on him), who, by virtue of their apostolical commission, were to be received and submitted to in all the churches in the world, being antecedent in office to them, yet this neither did nor could make all the churches one church, no more than if one man were an officer or magistrate in every corporation in England, this would make all those corporations to be one corporation. I do not suppose the pope to be an officer to the whole church visible as such, which I deny to have a union or order capable of any such thing. But suppose him an officer to every particular church, no union of the whole would thence ensue. That which is one church must join at least in some one church act, numerically one. So that though it should be granted that the pope were a general officer unto all and every church in the world, yet this would not prove that they all made one church, and had their church-union in subjection to him who was so an officer to them all; because to the constitution of such a union, as hath been showed, there is that required which, in reference to the universal society of Christians, is utterly and absolutely impossible. But the non-institution of any such officer ordinarily to bear rule in and over all the churches of God hath been

so abundantly proved by the divines of the reformed churches, and he who alone puts in his claim to that prerogative so clearly manifested to be quite another thing, that I will not needlessly go over that work again. Something, however, shall afterward be remarked as to his pretensions, from the principles whereon I proceed in the whole business.

There is, indeed, by some pleaded a subordination of officers in this church, tending towards a union on that account; as that ordinary ministers should be subjected to diocesan bishops, they to archbishops or metropolitans, they again to patriarchs, where some would bound the process, though a parity of reason would call for a pope: nor will the arguments pleaded for such a subordination rest until they come to be centred in some such thing.

But, first, before this plea be admitted, it must be proved that all these officers are appointed by Jesus Christ, or it will not concern us, who are inquiring solely after his will, and the settling of conscience therein. To do this with such an evidence [as] that the consciences of all those who are bound to yield obedience to Jesus Christ may appear to be therein concerned, will be a difficult task, as I suppose. And, to settle this once for all, I am not dealing with the men of that lazy persuasion, that church affairs are to be ordered by the prudence of our civil superiors and governors; and so seeking to justify a non-submission to any of their constitutions in the things of this nature, or to evidence that the so doing is not schism. Nor do I concern myself in the order and appointment of ancient times, by men assembled in synods and councils; wherein, whatever was the force of their determinations in their own seasons, we are not at all concerned, knowing of nothing that is obligatory to us, not pleading from sovereign authority or our own consent: but it is after things of pure institution that I am inquiring. With them who say there is no such thing in these matters, we must proceed to other principles than any yet laid down.

Also, it must be proved that all these officers are given and do belong to the catholic church as such, and not to the particular churches of several measures and dimensions to which they relate; which is not as yet, that I know of, so much as pretended by them that plead for this order. They tell us, indeed, of various arbitrary distributions of the world, or rather of the Roman empire, into patriarchates, with the dependent jurisdictions mentioned, and that all within the precincts of those patriarchates must fall within the lines of the subordination, subjection, and communication before described; but as there is no subordination between the officers of one denomination in the inferior parts, no more is there any between the superior themselves, but they are independent of each other. Now, it is easily discernible that these patriarchates, how many or how few soever they are, are particular churches, not any one of them the catholic, nor altogether comprising all that are comprehended in the precincts of it (which none will say that ever they did); and, therefore, this may speak something as to a combination of those churches, nothing as to the union of the catholic as such, which they are not.

Supposing this assertion to the purpose in hand, which it is not at all, it would prove only a combination of all the officers of several churches, consisting in the subordination and dependence mentioned, not of the whole church itself, though all the members of it should be at once imagined or fancied (as what shall hinder men from fancying what they please?) to be comprised within the limits of those distributions, unless it be also proved that Christ hath instituted several sorts of particular churches, parochial, diocesan, metropolitical, patriarchal (I use the words in the present vulgar acceptation, their signification having been somewhat otherwise formerly; "parœcia" being the care of a private bishop, "provincia" of a metropolitan, and "diœcesis" of a patriarch), in the order mentioned, and hath pointed out which of his churches shall be of those several kinds throughout the world; which that it will not be done to the disturbance of my principles whilst I live, I have some present good security.

And because I take the men of this persuasion to be charitable men, that will not think much of taking a little pains for the reducing any person whatever from the error of his way, I would entreat them that they would inform me what patriarchate, according to the institution of Christ, I (who by the providence of God live here at Oxon) do "de jure" belong unto; that so I may know how to preserve the union of that church, and to behave myself therein. And this I shall promise them, that if I were singly, or in conjunction with any others, so considerable, that those great officers should contend about whose subjects we should be (as was done heretofore about the Bulgarians), that it should not at all startle me about the truth and excellency of Christian religion, as it did those poor creatures; who, being newly converted to the faith, knew nothing of it but what they received from men of such principles.

But that this constitution is human, and the distributions of Christians, in subjection unto church-officers, into such and such divisions of nations and countries, prudential and arbitrary, I suppose will not be denied. The τὰ ἀρχαῖα of the Nicene synod intend no more; nor is in any thing of institution, nor so much as of apostolical tradition, pleaded therein. The following ages were of the same persuasion. Hence in the council of Chalcedon, the archiepiscopacy of Constantinople was advanced into a patriarchate, and many provinces cast in subjection thereunto; wherein the primates of Ephesus and Thrace were cut short of what they might plead τὰ ἀρχαῖα for, and sundry other alterations were likewise made in the same kind, Socrat. lib. v. cap. 8: the ground and reason of which procedure the fathers assembled sufficiently manifest in the reason assigned for the advancement of the bishops of Constantinople; which was for the city's sake: Διὰ τὸ εἶναι αὐτὴν νέαν Ῥώμην, Can. iii., Con. Constan. And what was the judgment of the council of Chalcedon upon this matter may be seen in the composition and determination of the strife between Maximus bishop of Antioch and Juvenalis of Jerusalem, Ac. vii. Con. Cal., with translation of provinces from the jurisdiction of one to another. And he that shall suppose that such assemblies as these were instituted by the will and appointment of Christ in the gospel, with church-authority for such dispositions and determinations, so as to make them of concernment to the unity of the church, will, if I mistake not, be hardly bestead in giving the ground of that his supposal.

4. I would know of them who desire to be under this law, whether the power with which Jesus Christ hath furnished the officers of his church come forth from the supreme mentioned patriarchs and archbishops, and is by them communicated to the inferiors, or "vice versa;" or whether all have their power in an equal immediation from Christ? If the latter be granted, there will be a greater independency established than most men are aware of (though the Papalins[7] understood it in the council of

---

7   See Paul Sarpi's History of the Council of Trent, book vii., sect. xi., xii. In the course of a dispute respecting the superiority of

Trent), and a wound given to successive episcopal ordination not easily to be healed. That power is communicated from the inferiors to the superiors will not be pleaded. And seeing the first must be insisted on, I beseech them not to be too hasty with men not so sharp-sighted as themselves, if, finding the names they speak of barbarous and foreign as to the Scriptures, and the things themselves not at all delineated therein, ἐπέχουσι.

5. The truth is, the whole subordination of this kind, which "de facto" hath been in the world, was so clearly a human invention or a prudential constitution, as hath been showed (which being done by men professing authority in the church, gave it, as it was called "vim ecclesiasticam"), that nothing else, in the issue, is pleaded for it. And now, though I shall, if called thereunto, manifest both the unreasonableness and unsuitableness to the design of Christ for his worship under the gospel, and the comparative novelty and mischievous issue, of that constitution, yet, at the present, being no farther concerned but only to evince that the union of the general visible church doth not therein consist, I shall not need to add any thing to what hath been spoken.

The Nicene council, which first made towards the confirmation of something like somewhat of what was afterward introduced in some places, pleaded only, as I said before, the τὰ ἀρχαῖα, old usage for it; which it would not have done could it have given a better original thereunto. And whatever the antiquities then pretended might be, we know that ἀπ' ἀρχῆς οὐ γέγονεν οὕτω. And I do not fear to say, what others have done before me, concerning the canons of that first and best general council, as it is called, they are all hay and stubble. Nor yet doth the laying this custom on τὰ ἀρχαῖα, in my apprehension, evince their judgment of any long prescription. Peter, speaking of a thing that was done a few years before, says that it was done ἀφ' ἡμερῶν ἀρχαίων, Acts xv. 7. Somewhat a greater antiquity

---

bishops over priests, the Spanish bishops held the institution and superiority of bishops to be "de jure divino," and not merely "de jure pontificio." The legates and their party, — since this implied that the bishops were independent of the pope, — maintained that the pope only was a bishop of divine institution, and the other bishops were merely his delegates and vicars. The latter party bear the name of Panalins in Sarpi's History. — Ed.

than that by him intended, I can freely grant to the custom by the fathers pretended.

But a general council is pleaded with the best colour and pretence for a bond of union to this general and visible church. In consideration hereof I shall not divert to the handling of the rise, right use, authority, necessity, of such councils; about all which somewhat in due time towards satisfaction may be offered to those who are not in bondage to names and traditions; — nor shall I remark what hath been the management of the things of God in all ages in those assemblies; many of which have been the stains and ulcers of Christian religion; — nor yet shall I say with what little disadvantage to the religion of Jesus Christ I suppose a loss of all the canons, of all councils that ever were in the world since the apostles' days, with their acts and contests (considering what use is made of them), might be undergone; — nor yet shall I digress to the usefulness of the assemblies of several churches in their representatives, to consider and determine about things of common concernment to them, with their tendency to the preservation of that communion which ought to be amongst them; — but as to the present instance only offer, —

1. That such general councils, being things purely extraordinary and occasional, as is confessed, cannot be *an ordinary standing bond of union to* the catholic church. And if any one shall reply, that though in themselves and in their own continuance they cannot be so, yet in their authority, laws, and canons they may; I must say, that besides the very many reasons I have to call into question the power of law-making for the whole society of Christians in the world, in all the general councils that have been or possibly can be on the earth, the disputes about the title of those assemblies which pretend to this honour, which are to be admitted, which excluded, are so endless; the rules of judging them so dark, lubricous, and uncertain, framed to the interest of contenders on all hands; the laws of them, which "de facto" have gone under that title and name, so innumerable, burdensome, uncertain, and frivolous, in a great part so grossly contradictory to one another, — that I cannot suppose that any man upon second thoughts can abide in such an assertion. If any shall, I must be bold to declare my affection to the doctrine of the gospel maintained in some of those assemblies for some hundreds of years, and then to desire him to prove that any

general council, since the apostles fell asleep, hath been so convened and managed as to be enabled to claim that authority to itself which is or would be due to such an assembly instituted according to the mind of Christ.

That it hath been of advantage to the truth of the gospel, that godly learned men, bishops of churches, have convened and witnessed a good confession in reference to the doctrine thereof, and declared their abhorrence of the errors that are contrary thereunto, is confessed. That any man or men is, are, or ever were, intrusted by Christ with authority so to convene them, as that thereupon and by virtue thereof they should be invested with a new authority, power, and jurisdiction, at such a convention, and thence should take upon them to make laws and canons that should be ecclesiastically binding to any persons or churches, as theirs, is not as yet, to me, attended with any convincing evidence of truth. And seeing at length it must be spoken, I shall do it with submission to the thoughts of good men that are any way acquainted with these things, and in sincerity therein commend my conscience to God, that I do not know any thing that is extant bearing clearer witness to the sad degeneracy of Christian religion in the profession thereof, nor more evidently discovering the efficacy of another spirit than what was poured out by Christ at his ascension, nor containing more hay and stubble, that is to be burned and consumed, than the stories of the acts and laws of the councils and synods that have been in the world.

2. But, to take them as they are, as to that alone wherein the first councils had any evidence of the presence of the Holy Ghost with them, — namely, in the declaring the doctrine of the gospel, — it falls in with that which I shall give in for the bend of union unto the church in the sense pleaded about.

3. Such an assembly arising cumulative out of particular churches, as it is evident that it doth, it cannot first and properly belong to the church generally as such; but it is only a means of communion between those particular churches as such, of whose representatives (I mean virtually, for formally the persons convening for many years ceased to be so) it doth consist.

4. There is nothing more ridiculous than to imagine a general council that should represent the whole catholic church, or so much as all the particular churches that are in the world. And let him that is otherwise minded, that there hath been such a

one, or that it is possible there should be such a one, prove by instance that such there hath been since the apostles' times, or by reason that such may be in the present age, or be justly expected in those that are to succeed, and we will, as we are able, crown him for his discovery.

5. Indeed, I know not how any council, that hath been in the world these thirteen hundred years and somewhat upwards, could be said to represent the church in any sense, or any churches whatever. Their convention, as is known, hath been always by imperial or papal authority, the persons convened such, and only they who, as was pretended and pleaded, had right of suffrage, with all necessary authority, in such conventions, from the order, degree, and office which personally they held in their several churches. Indeed, a pope or bishop sent his legate or proxy to represent, or rather personate, him and his authority. But that any of them were sent or delegated by the church wherein they did preside is not so evident.

I desire, then, that some man more skilled in laws and common usages than myself would inform me on what account such a convention could come to be a church-representative, or the persons of it to be representatives of any churches. General grounds of reason and equity, I am persuaded, cannot be pleaded for it. The lords in parliament in this nation, who, being summoned by regal authority, sat there in their own personal right, were never esteemed to represent the body of the people. Supposing, indeed, all church power in any particular church, of whatever extract or composition, to be solely vested in one single person, a collection of those persons, if instituted, would bring together the authority of the whole; but yet this would not make that assembly to be a church-representative, if you will allow the name of the church to any but that single person. But for men who have but a partial power and authority in the church, and perhaps, separated from it, none at all, without any delegation from the churches, to convene, and in their own authority to take upon them to represent these churches, is absolute presumption.

These several pretensions being excluded, let us see wherein the unity of this church, — namely, of the great society of men professing the gospel, and obedience to Christ according to it, throughout the world, — doth consist. This is summed up by the apostle, Eph. iv. 5, "One Lord, one faith, one baptism." It is the unity of the doctrine of faith which men profess, in subjection to one Lord, Jesus Christ, being initiated into that profession by baptism. I say, the saving doctrine of the gospel of salvation by Jesus Christ, and obedience through him to God, as professed by them, is the bond of that union whereby they are made one body, are distinguished from all other societies, have one head, Christ Jesus, which as to profession they hold; and whilst they do so they are of this body, in one professed hope of their calling.

1. Now, that this union be preserved, it is required that all those *grand and necessary truths of the gospel*, without the knowledge whereof no man can be saved by Jesus Christ, be so far believed as to be outwardly and visibly professed, in that variety of ways wherein they are or may be called out thereunto. There is a "proportion of faith," Rom. xii. 6; a "unity of faith, and of the knowledge of the Son of God," Eph. iv. 13; a measure of saving truths, the explicit knowledge whereof in men, enjoying the use of reason within and the means of grace without, is of indispensable necessity to salvation, — without which it is impossible that any soul, in an ordinary way, should have communion with God in Christ, having not light sufficient for converse with him, according to the tenor of the covenant of grace. These are commonly called fundamentals, or first principles; which are justly argued by many to be clear, perspicuous, few, lying in an evident tendency to obedience. Now, look what truths are savingly to be believed to render a man a member of the church catholic invisible, — that is, whatever is required in any one, unto such a receiving of Jesus Christ as that thereby he may have power given to him to become the son of God, — the profession of those truths is required to instate a man in the unity of the church visible.

2. That *no other internal principle of the mind*, that hath an utter inconsistency with the real belief of the truths necessary to be professed, be manifested by professors. Paul tells us of some who, though they would be called Christians, yet they so walked as that they manifested themselves to be "enemies of the cross of Christ," Phil. iii. 18. Certainly those who on one account are open and manifest enemies of the cross of Christ, are not on any members of his church. There is "one Lord" and "one faith" required, as well as "one baptism;" and a protestation contrary to evidence of fact is in all law null. Let a man

profess ten thousand times that he believes all the saving truths of the gospel, and, by the course of a wicked and profane conversation, evidence to all that he believes no one of them, shall his protestation be admitted? Shah he be accounted a servant in and of my family who will call me master, and come into my house only to do me and mine a mischief, not doing any thing I require of him, but openly and professedly the contrary? Paul says of such, Tit. i. 16, "They profess that they know God, but in works they deny him, being abominable, and disobedient, and unto every good work reprobate;" which, though peculiarly spoken of the Jews, yet contains a general rule, that men's profession of the knowledge of God, contradicted by a course of wickedness, is not to be admitted as a thing giving any privilege whatever.

3. That no *thing, opinion, error, or false doctrine, everting* or overthrowing any of the necessary saving truths professed as above, be added in and with that profession, or deliberately be professed also. This principle the apostle lays down and proves, Gal. v. 3, 4. Notwithstanding the profession of the gospel, he tells the Galatians that if they were bewitched to profess also the necessity of circumcision and keeping of the law for justification, Christ or the profession of him would not profit them. On this account the ancients excluded many heretics from the name of Christians: so Justin Martyr of the Marcionites, and others, Ὧν οὐδενὶ κοινωνοῦμεν οἱ γνωρίζοντες ἀθέους καὶ ἀσεβεῖς, καὶ ἀδίκους, καὶ ἀνόμους αὐτοὺς ὑπάρχοντας, καὶ ἀντὶ τοῦ τὸν Ἰησοῦν σέβειν, ὀνόματι μόνον ὁμολογεῖν, καὶ Χριστιανοὺς ἑαυτοὺς λέγουσιν, ὃν τρόπον οἱ ἐν τοῖς ἔθνεσι τὸ ὄνομα τοῦ Θεοῦ ἐπιγράφουσι τοῖς χειροποιήτοις.

We are at length, then, arrived at this issue: The belief and profession of all the necessary saving truths of the gospel, without the manifestation of an internal principle of the mind inconsistent with the belief of them, or adding of other things in profession that are destructive to the truths so professed, is the bond of the unity of the visible professing church of Christ. Where this is found in any man, or number of men, though otherwise accompanied with many failings, sins, and errors, the unity of the faith is by him or them so far preserved as that they are thereby rendered members of the visible church of Christ, and are by him so esteemed.

Let us suppose a man, by a bare reading of the Scriptures, brought to him by some providence of God (as finding the Bible on the highway), and evidencing their authority by their own light, instructed in the knowledge of the truths of the gospel, who shall thereupon make profession of them amongst them with whom he lives, although he be thousands of miles distant from any particular church wherein the ordinances of Christ are administered, nor perhaps knows there is any such church in the world, much less hath ever heard of the pope of Rome (which is utterly impossible he should, supposing him instructed only by reading of the Scriptures); — I ask whether this man, making open profession of Christ according to the gospel, shall be esteemed a member of the visible church in the sense insisted on, or no?

That this may not seem to be such a fiction of a case as may involve in it any impossible supposition, which, being granted, will hold a door open for other absurdities, I shall exemplify it, in its most material "postulata," by a story of unquestionable truth.

Elmacinus, who wrote the story of the Saracens, being secretary to one of the caliphs of Bagdad, informs us that in the year 309 of their hegira (about the year 921 of our account), Muctadinus the caliph of Bagdad, by the counsel of his wise men, commanded one Huseinus, the son of Mansor, to be crucified for certain poems, whereof some verses are recited by the historian, and are thus rendered by Erpenius:—

"Laus ei qui manifestavit humilitatem suam, celavit inter nos divinitatem suam permeantem donec cœpit in creatura sua apparere sub specie edentis et bibentis.

"Jamque aspexit eum creatura ejus, sicuti supercilium obliquum respiciat spercilium."

From which remnant of his work it is easy to perceive that the crime whereof he was accused, and for which he was condemned and crucified, was the confession of Jesus Christ, the Son of God. As he went to the cross he added, says the same author, these that follow:

"Compotor meus nihil plane habet in se iniquitatis, bibendum mihi dedit simile ejus quod bibit, fecit hospitem in hospite."

And so he died constantly (as it appears) in the profession of the Lord Jesus.

Bagdad was a city built not long before by the Saracens, wherein, it is probable, there were not at that time any Christians abiding. Add now to this story what our Saviour speaks, Luke xii. 8, "I say unto you, Whosoever shall confess me before men, him shall the Son of man also confess before the angels of God;' and consider the unlimitedness of the expression as to any outward consideration, and tell me whether this man, or any other in the like condition, be not to be reckoned as a subject of Christ's visible kingdom, a member of his church in the world?

Let us now recall to mind what we have in design. Granting, for our process' sake, that schism is the breach of any unity instituted and appointed by Christ, in what sense soever it is spoken of, our inquiry is, whether we are guilty in any kind of such a breach, or the breach of such a unity. This, then, now insisted on being the union of the church of Christ, as visibly professing the Word, according to his own mind, when I have laid down some general foundations of what is to ensue, I shall consider whether we are guilty of the breach of this union, and argue the several pretensions of men against us, especially of the Romanists, on this account.

1. I confess that this union of the general visible church was once comprehensive of all the churches in the world, the faith once delivered to the saints being received amongst them. From this unity it is taken also for granted that a separation is made, and it continues not as it was at the first institution of the churches of Christ, though some small breaches were made upon it immediately after their first planting. The Papists say, as to the European churches (wherein their and our concernment principally lies), this breach was made in the days of our forefathers, by their departure from the common faith in those ages, though begun by a few some ages before. We are otherwise minded, and affirm that this secession was made by them and their predecessors in apostasy, in several generations, by several degrees; which we manifest by comparing the present profession and worship with that in each kind which we know was at first embraced, because we find it instituted. At once, then, we say this schism lies at their doors, who not only have deviated from the common faith themselves, but do also actually cause and attempt to destroy temporally and eternally all that will not join with them therein; for as the "mystery of iniquity" began

to work in the apostles' days, so we have a testimony beyond exception in the complaint of those that lived in them, that not long after, the operation of it became more effectual, and the infection of it to be more diffused in the church. This is that of Hegesippus in Eusebius, Eccles. Hist. lib. iv. cap. 22; who affirms that the church remained a virgin (whilst the apostles lived), — pure and uncorrupted; but when that sacred society had ended its pilgrimage, and the generation that heard and received the word from them were fallen asleep, many false doctrines were preached and divulged therein.

I know who hath endeavoured to elude the sense of this complaint, as though it concerned not any thing in the church, but the *despisers and persecutors of it, the Gnostics*: but yet I know, also, that no man would so do but such a one as hath a just confidence of his own ability to make passable at least any thing that he shall venture to say or utter; for why should that be referred by Hegesippus to the ages after the apostles and their hearers were dead, with an exception against its being so in their days, when, if the person thus expounding this testimony may be credited, the Gnostics were never more busy nor prevalent than in that time which alone is excepted from the evil here spoken of? Nor can I understand how the opposition and persecution of the church should be insinuated to be the deflouring and violating of its chastity, which is commonly a great purifying of it. So that, speaking of that broaching and preaching of errors, which was not in the apostles' times, nor in the time of their hearers, — the chiefest time of the rage and madness of the Gnostics, — such as spotted the pure and uncorrupted virginity of the church, which nothing can attain unto that is foreign unto it, and that which gave original unto sedition in the church, I am of the mind, and so I conceive was Eusebius that recited those words, that the good man intended corruptions in the church, not out of it, nor oppositions to it.

The process made in after ages in a deviation from the unity of the faith, till it arrived to that height wherein it is now stated in the papal apostasy, hath been the work of others to declare. Therein, then, I state the rise and progress of the present schism (if it may be so called) of the visible church.

2. As to our concernment in this business, they that will make good a charge against us, that we are departed from the unity of the church catholic, it is incumbent on them to evi-

dence, — (1.) That we either do not believe and make profession of all the truths of the gospel indispensably necessary to be known, that a man may have a communion with God in Christ and be saved; or, —

(2.) That doing so, in the course of our lives we manifest and declare a principle that is utterly inconsistent with the belief of those truths which outwardly we profess; or, —

(3.) That we add unto them, in opinion or worship, that or those things which are in very deed destructive of them, or do any way render them insufficient to be saving unto us.

If neither of these three can be proved against a man, he may justly claim the privilege of being a member of the visible church of Christ in the world, though he never in all his life be a member of a particular church; which yet, if he have fitting opportunity and advantage for it, is his duty to be.

And thus much be spoken as to the state and condition of the visible catholic church, and in this sense we grant it to be, and the unity thereof. In the late practice of men, that expression of the "catholic church hath been an "individuum vagum," few knowing what to make of it; a "cothurnus," that every one accommodated at pleasure to his own principles and pretensions. I have no otherwise described it than did Irenæus of old. Said he, "Judicabit omnes eos, qui sunt extra veritatem, id est, extra ecclesiam," lib. iv. cap. 62. And on the same account is a particular church sometimes called by some the catholic: "Quandoque ego Remigius episcopus de hac luce transiero, tu mihi hæres esto, sancta et venerabilis ecclesia catholica urbis Remorum," Flodoardus, lib. i.

In the sense insisted on was it so frequently described by the ancients.

So again Irenæus: "Etsi in mundo loquelæ dissimiles sunt, sed tamen virtus traditionis una et eadem est, et neque hæ quæ in Germania sunt fundatæ ecclesiæ aliter credunt, aut aliter tradunt; neque hæ quæ in Hiberis sunt, neque hæ quæ in Celtis, neque hæ quæ in Oriente, neque hæ quæ in Ægypto, neque hæ quæ in Libya, neque hæ quæ in medio mundi constitutæ. Sed sicut sol, creatura Dei, in universo mundo unus et idem est, sic et lumen, prædicatio veritatis ubique lucet," lib. i. cap. 10. To the same purpose Justin Martyr: Οὐδὲ ἕν γὰρ ὅλως ἐστὶ τὸ γένος ἀνθρώπων εἴτε Βαρβάρων, εἴτε Ἑλλήνων, εἴτε ἁπλῶς ὡτινιοῦν ὀνόματι προσαγορευομένων, ἢ ἁμαξοβίων, ἢ ἀσίκων καλουμένων, ἢ ἐν σκηναῖς κτηνοτρόφων οἰκούντων, ἐν οἷς μὴ διὰ τοῦ ὀνόματος τοῦ σταυρωθέντος Ἰησοῦ εὐχαὶ καὶ εὐχαριστίαι τῷ πατρὶ καὶ ποιητῇ τῶν ὅλων γίνωται. Dialog. cum Tryphone.

The generality of all sorts of men worshipping God in Jesus Christ is the church we speak of whose extent in his days Tertullian thus related: "In quem alium crediderunt gentes universæ, nisi in ipsum, qui jam venit? Cui enim aliæ gentes crediderunt, Parthi, Medi et Elamitæ, et qui habitant Mesopotamiam, Armeniam, Phrygiam, et incolentes Ægyptum et regionem Africæ quæ est trans Cyrenem, Romani et incolæ; tunc et in Hierusalem Judæi, et gentes cæteræ, ut jam Gætulorum varietates, et Maurorum multi fines, Hispaniarum omnes termini, et Galliarum diversæ nationes, et Brittanorum inaccessa Romanis loca, Christo vero subdita; et Sarmatarum et Dacorum et Germanorum et Scytharum et abditarum multarum gentium et provinciarum et insularum multarum nobis ignotarum, et quæ enumerare non possumus? In quibus omnibus locis Christi nomen, qui jam venit, regnat ad Judæos." [Adver. Jud., cap. vii.]

Some have said, and do yet say, that the church in this sense is a *visible, organic, political body*. That it is visible is confessed; both its mater and form bespeak visibility, as an inseparable adjunct of is subsisting. That it is a body also in the general sense wherein that word the same faith, is ambiguous term; the use of it is plainly metaphorical, taken from the members, instruments, and organs of a natural body. Because Paul hath said that in "one body there are many members, as eyes, feet, hands, yet the body is but one, so is the church," it hath been usually said that the church is an organical body. What church Paul speaks of in that place is not evident, but what he alludes unto is. The difference he speaks of in the individual persons of the church is not in respect of office, power, and authority, but gifts or graces, and usefulness on that account. Such an organical body we confess the church catholic visible to be. In it are persons endued with variety of gifts and graces for the benefit and ornament of the whole.

An organical political body is a thing of another nature. A politic body or commonwealth united under some form of rule or government, whose supreme and subordinate administration is committed to several persons, according to the tenor of such laws and customs as that society hath or doth consent unto. This also is said to be organical on a metaphorical account, — because the officers and members that are in it and over it hold proportion to the more noble parts of the body. Kings are said to be heads; counsellors, ὀφθαλμοὶ βασιλέων. To the constitution of such a commonwealth distinctly, as such, it is required that the whole hath the same laws, but not that only. Two nations most distinct and different, on account of other ends and interests, may yet have the same individual laws and customs for the distribution of justice and preservation of peace among themselves. An entire form of regimen and government peculiar thereunto is required for the constitution of a distinct political body. In this sense we deny the church whereof we speak to be an organical, political body, as not having indeed any of the requisites thereunto, not one law of order. The same individual moral law, or law of moral duties, it hath; but a law given to the whole as such, for order, polity, rule, it hath not. All the members of it are obliged to the same law of order and polity in their several societies; but the whole, as such, hath no such law. It hath no such head or governor, as such. Nor will it suffice to say that Christ is its head; for if, as a visible political body, it hath a political head, that head also must be visible. The commonwealth of the Jews was a political body; of this God was the head and king; hence their historian saith their government was Θεοκρατία. And when they would choose a king, God said they rejected him who was their political head, to whom a shekel was paid yearly as tribute, called the "shekel of the sanctuary." Now, they rejected him, not by asking a king simply, but a king after the manner of the nations. Yet, that it might be a visible political body, it required a visible supreme magistrate to the whole; which when there was none, all polity was dissolved amongst them, Judges xxi. 25. Christ is the head of every particular church, its lawgiver and ruler; but yet, to make a church a visible, organical, political body, it is required that it hath visible governors and rulers, and of the whole. Nor can it be said that it is a political body that hath a supreme government and order in it, as it is made up and constituted of particular churches, and that in the representatives convened doth the supreme visible power of it consist; for such a convention in the judgment of all ought to be extraordinary only, in ours is utterly impossible, and "de facto" was not among the churches for three hundred years, — yea, never. Besides, the visible catholic church is not made up of particular churches, as such; for if so, then no man can be member of it but by virtue of his being a member of some visible church, which is false. Profession of the truth, as before stated, is the formal reason and cause of any person's relation to the church visible; which he hath thereby, whether he belong to any particular church or no.

Let it be evidenced that the universal church whereof we speak hath any law or rule of order and government, as such, given unto it; or that it is in possibility, as such, to put any such law or rule into execution; that it hath any homogeneous ruler or rulers, that have the care of the administration of the rule and government of the whole, as such, committed to him or them by Jesus Christ; that as it hath the same common spiritual and known orders and interest, and the same specifical ecclesiastical rule given to all its members, so it hath the same political interest, order, and conversation, as such; or that it hath any one cause constitutive of a political body, whereby it is such, or hath at all the form of an instituted church, or is capable of any such form, — and they that do so shall be farther attended to.

Chapter VI.

Romanists' charge of schism on the account of separation from the church, catholic proposed to consideration — The importance of this plea on both sides — The sum of their charge — The church of Rome not the church catholic; not a church in any sense — Of antichrist in the temple — The catholic church, how intrusted with interpretation of Scripture — Of interpretation of Scripture by tradition — The interest of the Roman church herein discharged — All necessary truths believed by Protestants — No contrary principle by them manifested — Profane persons no members of the church catholic — Of the late Roman proselytes — Of the Donatists — Their business reported and case stated — The present state of things unsuited to that of old — Apostasy from the unity of the church catholic charged on the Romanists — Their claim to be that church sanguinary, false — Their plea to this purpose considered — The blasphemous management of their plea by some of late — The whole dissolved — Their inferences on their plea practically prodigious — Their apostasy proved by instances — Their grand argument in this cause proposed; answered — Consequences of denying the Roman church to be a church of Christ weighed.

LET us see now what as to conscience can be charged on us, Protestants I mean, who are all concerned herein as to the breach of this union. The Papists are the persons that undertake to manage this charge against us. To lay aside the whole plea "subesse Romano pontifici," and all those fears wherewith they juggled when the whole world sat in darkness, which they do now use at the entrance of their charge, the sum of what they insist upon, firstly, is: The catholic church is intrusted with the interpretation of the Scripture, and declaration of the truths therein contained; which being by it so declared, the not receiving of them implicitly or explicitly, — that is, the disbelieving of them as so proposed and declared, — cuts off any man from being a member of the church, Christ himself having said that he that hears not the church is to be as a heathen man and a publican;

which church they are, that is certain. It is all one, then, what we believe or do not believe, seeing that we believe not all that the catholic church proposeth to be believed, and what we do believe we believe not on that account.

Ans. Their insisting on this plea so much as they do is sufficient to evince their despair of making good by instance our failure, in respect of the way and principles by which the unity of the visible church may be lost or broken. Fail they in this, they are gone; and if they carry this plea, we are all at their disposal. The sum of it is, The catholic church is intrusted with the sole power of delivering what is truth, and what is necessary to be believed: this catholic church is the church of Rome, — that is, the pope, or what else may in any juncture of time serve their interest. But, as it is known, —

1. *We deny their church, as it is styled, to be the catholic church,* or as such any part of it, as particular churches are called or esteemed; so that, of all men in the world, they are least concerned in this assertion. Nay, I shall go farther. Suppose all the members of the Roman church to be sound in the faith as to all necessary truths, and no way to prejudice the advantages and privileges which accrue to them by the profession thereof, whereby the several individuals of it would be true members of the catholic church, yet I should not only deny it to be the catholic church, but also, — abiding in its present order and constitution, being that which by themselves it is supposed to be, — to be any particular church of Christ at all, as wanting many things necessary to constitute them so, and having many things destructive utterly to the very essence and being of that order that Christ hath appointed in his churches.

The best plea that I know for their church-state is, that Antichrist sits in the temple of God. Now, although we might justly omit the examination of this pretence until those who are concerned in it will professedly own it as their plea, yet as it lies in our way in the thoughts of some, I say to it that I am not so certain that καθίσαι εἰς τὸν ναὸν τοῦ Θεοῦ, signifies "to sit in the temple of God;" seeing a learned man long ago thought it rather to be a "setting up against the temple of God," Aug. de Civitate Dei, lib. x. cap. 59. But grant the sense of the expression to be as it is usually received, it imports no more but that the man of sin shall set up his power against God in the midst of them who, by their outward visible profession, have right to be called his temple; which entitles him and his copartners in apostasy to the name of the church as much as changing of money and selling of cattle were ordinances of God under the old temple, when, by some men's practising of them in it, it was made a den of thieves.

2. Though as to the plea of them and their interest with whom we have to do, we have nothing requiring our judgments in the case, yet, "ex abundanti," we add, that *we deny that, by the will and appointment of Jesus Christ, the catholic church visible is in any sense intrusted with such an interpretation of Scripture* as that her declaration of truth should be the measure of what should be believed; or that, as such, it is intrusted with any power of that nature at all, or is enabled to propose a rule of faith to be received, as so proposed, to the most contemptible individual in the world; or that it is possible that any voice of it should be heard or understood, but only this, "I believe the necessary saving truths contained in the Scripture;" or that it can be consulted withal, or is, as such, intrusted with any power, authority, or jurisdiction; nor shall we ever consent that the office and authority of the Scriptures be actually taken from it on any pretence. As to that of our Saviour, of telling the church, it is so evidently spoken of a particular church, that may immediately be consulted in case of difference between brethren, and does so no way relate to the business in hand, that I shall not trouble the reader with a debate of it. But do we not receive the Scripture itself upon the authority of the church? I say, if we did so, yet this concerns not Rome, which we account no church at all. That we have received the Scriptures from the church of Rome at first, — that is, so much as the book itself, — is an intolerable figment, But it is worse to say that we receive and own their authority from the authority of any church, or all the churches in the world. It is the expression of our learned Whitaker, "Qui Scripturam non credit esse divinam, nisi propter ecclesiæ vocem, Christianus non est." To deny that the Scripture hath immediate force and efficacy to evince its own authority is plainly to deny it, On that account, being brought unto us by the providence of God (wherein I comprise all subservient helps of human testimony), we receive them, and on no other.

But is not the Scripture to be interpreted according to the tradition of the catholic church? and are not those interpretations so made to be received?

I say, among all the figments that these latter ages have invented, — I shall add, amongst the true stories of Lucian, — there is not one more remote from truth than this assertion, that any one text of Scripture may be interpreted according to the universal tradition of the catholic church, and be made appear so to be; any farther than that, in general, the catholic church hath not believed any such sense to be in any portion of Scripture, which to receive were destructive of salvation. And, therefore, the Romanists tell us that the present church (that is, theirs) is the keeper and interpreter of these traditions; or rather, that its power, authority and infallibility, being the same that it hath been in former ages, what it determines is to be received to be the tradition of the catholic church. For the trial whereof, whether it be so or no, there is no rule but its own determination; which if they can persuade us to acquiesce in, I shall grant that they have acquired such an absolute dominion over us and our faith, that it is fit that we should be, soul and body, at their disposal.

It being, then, the work of the Scripture to propose the saving truths of Christ (the belief and profession whereof are necessary to make a man a member of the church) so as to make them of indispensable necessity to be received, if they can from them convince us that we do not believe and profess all and every one of the truths or articles of faith so necessary as expressed, we shall fall down under the authority of such conviction; if not, we profess our consciences to be no more concerned in the authority of their church than we judge their church to be in the privileges of the church catholic.

But, secondly, it may be we are chargeable with manifesting some *principles of profaneness*, wherewith the belief of the truth we profess hath an absolute inconsistency. For those who are liable and obnoxious to this charge, I say, let them plead for themselves; for let them profess what they will, and cry out ten thousand times that they are Christians, I shall never acknowledge them for other than visible enemies of the cross, kingdom, and church of Christ. Traitors and rebels are not, "de facto," subjects of that king or ruler in reference to whom they are so. Of some, who said they were Jews, Christ said they lied, and were not, but "the synagogue of Satan," Rev. ii. 9. Though such as these say they are Christians, I will be bold to say they lie, "they are not, but slaves of Satan." Though they live within the pale, as they call it, of the church (the catholic church being an enclosure as to profession, not place), yet they are not within it nor of it any more than a Jew or Mohammedan within the same precinct. Suppose they have been baptized, yet if their belly be their god, and their lives dedicated to Satan, all the advantage they have thereby is, that they are apostates and renegadoes.

That we have added any thing of our own, making profession of any thing in religion absolutely destructive to the fundamentals we profess, I know not that we are accused, seeing our crime is asserted to consist in detracting, not adding. Now, unless we are convinced of failing on one of these three accounts, we shall not at all question but that we abide in the unity of the visible catholic church.

It is the common cry of the Romanists that we are *schismatics*. Why so? Because we have separated ourselves from the communion of the catholic church. What this catholic church is, and how little they are concerned in it, hath been declared. How much they have prevailed themselves with ignorant souls by this plea, we know. Nor was any other success to be expected in respect of many whom they have won over to themselves; who, being persons ignorant of the righteousness of God and the power of the faith they have professed, not having had experience of communion with the Lord Jesus under the conduct of them, have been, upon every provocation and temptation, a ready prey to deceivers.

Take a little view of their late proselytes, and it will quickly appear what little cause they have to boast in them. With some, by the craft and folly of some relations, they are admitted to treat, when they are drawing to their dissolution. These, for the most part, having been persons of dissolute and profligate lives, never having tasted the power of any religion, whatever they have professed, in their weakness and disturbed dying thoughts, may be apt to receive any impression that with confidence and violence is imposed upon them. Besides, it is a far easier proposal to be reconciled to the church of Rome, and so by purgatory to get to heaven, than to be told of regeneration, repentance, faith, and the covenant of grace, things of difficulty to such poor creatures. Others that have been cast down from their hopes and expectations, or out from their enjoyments, by the late revolution in these nations, have by their discontent or necessity made themselves an easy prey to their zeal. What hath been the residue of their proselytes? What one who hath ever manifested himself to share in the power of our religion, or was not prepared by principles of superstition almost as deep as their own, have they prevailed on? But I shall not farther insist on these things. To return:—

Our communion with the visible catholic church is in the unity of the faith only. The breach of this union, and therein a relinquishment of the communion of the church, lies in a relinquishment of, or some opposition to, some or all of the saving, necessary truths of the gospel; now, this is not schism, but heresy or apostasy; — or it is done by an open profligateness of life: so that, indeed, this charge is nothing at all to the purpose in hand; though, through grace, in a confidence of our own innocency, we are willing to debate the guilt of the crime under any name or title whatever.

Unto what hath been spoken, I shall only add the removal of some common objections, with a recharge on them with whom principally we have as yet had to do, and come to the last thing proposed. The case of some of old, who were charged with schism for separating from the catholic church on an account wholly and clearly distinct from that of a departure from the faith, is an instance of the judgment of antiquity lying in an opposition to the notion of departure from the church now delivered. "Doth not Augustine, do not the rest of his orthodox contemporaries, charge the Donatists with schism because they departed from the catholic church? and doth not the charge rise up with equal efficacy against you as them? at least, doth it not give you the nature of schism in another sense than is by you granted?"

The reader knows sufficiently, if he hath at all taken notice of these things, where to find this cloud scattered, without the least annoyance or detriment to the Protestant cause, or of any concerned in that name, however by lesser differences diversified among themselves. I shall not repeat what by others hath been at large insisted on. In brief, put the whole church of God into that condition of liberty and soundness of doctrine which it was in when the great uproar was made by the Donatists, and we shall be concerned to give in our judgments concerning them.

To press an example of former days, as binding unto duty or convincing of evil, in respect of any now, without stating the whole "substratum" of the business and complete cause, as it was in the days and seasons wherein the example was given, we judge it not equal. Yet, although none can with ingenuity press me with the crime they were guilty of, unless they can prove themselves to be instated in the very same condition as they were against whom that crime was committed, — which I am fully assured none in the world can, the communion of the catholic church then pleaded for being, in the judgment of all, an effect of men's free liberty and choice, now pressed as an issue of the tyranny of some few, — I shall freely deliver my thoughts concerning the Donatists; which will be comprehensive also of those others that suffer with them in former and after ages under the same imputation.

1. Then, I am persuaded that in the matter of fact the Donatists[8] were some of them *deceived*, and others of them did *deceive*, in charging Cæcilianus to be ordained by "traditores;" which they made the main ground of their separation, however they took in other things (as is usual) into their defence afterward. Whether any of themselves were ordained by such persons, as they are recharged, I know not.

2. On supposition that he was so, and they that ordained him were known to him to have been so, yet he being not guilty of the crime, renouncing communion with them therein, and themselves repenting of their sin, as did Peter, whose sin exceeded theirs, this was no just cause of casting him out of communion, he walking and acting in all other things suitably to principles by themselves acknowledged.

3. That on supposition they had just cause hereupon to renounce the communion of Cæcilianus, which, according to the principles of those days, retained by themselves, was most false, — yet they had no ground of separating from the church of Carthage, where were many elders not obnoxious to that charge. Indeed, to raise a jealousy of a fault in any man, which is denied by him, which we are not able to prove, which if it were proved were of little or no importance, and on pretence thereof to separate from all who will not believe what we surmise, is a wild and unchristian course of proceeding.

---

8   Owen had occasion afterwards to consider more fully the case of the Donatists, so far as it bears on the charge of schism brought against the Nonconformists. See his "Inquiry concerning Evangelical Churches," vol. xv. p. 369. — Ed.

4. Yet grant, farther, that men of tender consciences, regulated by the principle then generally received, might be startled at the communion of that church wherein Cæcilianus did preside, yet nothing but the height of madness, pride, and corrupt fleshly interest, could make men declare hostility against all the churches of Christ in the world who would communicate with or did not condemn that church; which were to regulate all the churches in the world by their own fancy and imagination.

5. Though men, out of such pride and folly, might judge all the residue of Christians to be faulty and guilty in this particular, of not condemning and separating from the church of Carthage, yet to proceed to cast them out from the very name of Christians, and so disannul their privileges and ordinances that they had been made partakers of, as manifestly they did, by rebaptizing all that entered into their communion, was such unparalleled Pharisaism and tyranny as was wholly to be condemned and intolerable.

6. The divisions, outrages, and enthusiastical furies and riots that befell them, or they fell into, in their way, were, in my judgment, tokens of the hand of God against them; so that, upon the whole matter, their undertaking and enterprise was utterly undue and unlawful.

I shall farther add, as to the management of the cause by their adversaries, that there is in their writings, especially those of Austin, for the most part, a sweet and gracious spirit breathing, full of zeal for the glory of God, peace, love, union among Christians: and as to the issue of the cause under debate, it is evident that they did sufficiently foil their adversaries on principles then generally confessed and acknowledged on all hands, though some of them seem to have been considering, learned, and dexterous men.

How little we are at this day, in any contests that are managed amongst us about the things of God, concerned in those differences of theirs, these few considerations will evince; yet, notwithstanding all this, I must take liberty to profess, that although the fathers justly charged the Donatists with disclaiming of all the churches of Christ as a thing wicked and unjust, yet many of the principles whereon they did it were such as I cannot assent to. Yea, I shall say, that though Austin was sufficiently clear on the nature of the invisible church catholic, yet his frequent confounding it with a mistaken notion of the visible general church hath given no small occasion of stumbling and sundry unhappy entanglements to divers in after ages. His own book, "De Unitate Ecclesiæ," which contains the sum and substance of what he had written elsewhere, or disputed against the Donatists, would afford me instances enough to make good my assertion, were it now under consideration or proof.

Being, then, thus come off from this part of our charge and accusation of schism, for the relinquishment of the catholic visible church, — which as we have not done, so to do is not schism, but a sin of another nature and importance, — according to the method proposed, a recharge on the Romanists in reference to their present condition, and its unsuitableness to the unity of the church evinced, must briefly ensue.

Their claim is known to be no less than that they are this catholic church, out of whose communion there is no salvation (as the Donatists' was of old); also, that the union of this church consists in its subjection to its head, the pope, and worshipping of God according to his appointment, in and with his several qualifications and attendancies. Now, this claim of theirs, to our apprehension and consciences, is, —

1. *Cruel* and *sanguinary*, condemning millions to hell that invocate and call on the name of the Lord Jesus Christ, believing all things that are written in the Old and New Testaments; for no other cause in the world but because they are not convinced that it is their duty to give up reason, faith, soul, and all, to him and his disposal whom they have not only unconquerable presumptions against as an evil and wicked person, but are also resolved and fully persuaded in their consciences that he is an enemy to their dear Lord Jesus Christ, out of love to whom they cannot bear him. Especially will this appear to be so if we consider their farther improvement of this principle to the killing, hanging, torturing to death, burning of all that they are able, who are in the condition before mentioned. This, upon the matter, is the great principle of their religion. All persons that will not be subject (at least in spiritual things) to the pope are to be hanged or burned in this world, or by other means destroyed, and damned for ever hereafter. This is the substance of the gospel they preach, the centre wherein all the lines of their writings do meet; and to this must the holy, pure word of God be wrested to give countenance. Blessed be the God of our salvation! who as he never gave merciless men power over the souls and

eternal condition of his saints, so he hath begun to work a deliverance of the outward condition of his people from their rage and cruelty, which, in his good time, he will perfect in their irrecoverable ruin. In the meantime, I say, the guilt of the blood of millions of innocent persons, yea, saints of God, lies at their door. And although things are so stated in this age that in some nations they have left none to kill, in others are restrained, that they can kill no more, yet retaining the same principles with their forefathers, and justifying them in their paths of blood, I look upon them all as guilty of murder, and so not to have "eternal life abiding in them;" being of that wicked one, as Cain, who slew his brother. I speak not of individuals, but of those in general that constitute their governing church.

2. *Most false,* and such as nothing but either judiciary hardness from God, sending men strong delusions that they might believe a lie, or the dominion of cursed lusts, pride, ambition, covetousness, desire of rule, can lie at the bottom of; for, —

(1.) It is false that the union of the catholic church, in the notion now under consideration, *consists in subjection to any officer* or officers; or that it hath any peculiar form, constituting one church in relation to them, or in joint participation of the same individual ordinances whatever, by all the members of it; or that any such oneness is at all possible, or any unity whatever, but that of the faith which by it is believed, and of the truth professed.

(2.) It is most ridiculous that they are *this catholic church,* or that their communion is comprehensive of it in its latitude. He must be blind, uncharitable, a judge of what he cannot see or know, who can once entertain a thought of any such thing. Let us run a little over the foundations of this assertion.

First, "*Peter was the prince of the apostles.*" It is denied; arguments lie clear against it. The Gospel, the Acts of the Apostles, all confute it. The express testimony of Paul lies against it; our Saviour denies that it was so, gives order that it should not be so. The name and thing are foreign to the times of the apostles. It was a ministry, not a principality, they had committed to them; therein they were all equal. It is from that spirit whence they inquired after a kingdom and dominion, before they had received the Spirit of the gospel, as it was dispensed after Christ's ascension, that such assertions are now insisted on. But let that be supposed, what is next? "*He had a universal monarchical jurisdiction committed to him over all Christians*; for Christ said, 'Tu es Petrus, tibi dabo claves, et pasce oves meas.'" But these terms are barbarous to the Scripture. Monarchy is not the English of, "Vos autem non sic." Jurisdiction is a name of a right, for the exercise of *civil* power. Christ hath left no such thing as jurisdiction, in the sense wherein it is now used, to Peter or his church. Men do but make sport, and expose themselves to the contempt of considering persons, who talk of the institutions of our Lord in the language of the last ages, or expressions suitable to what was in practice in them. He that shall compare the fraternal church admonition and censures of the primitive institution, with the courts, powers, and jurisdictions set up in pretence and colour of them in after ages, will admire at the likeness and correspondency of the one with the other. The administration of ecclesiastical jurisdiction in the Papacy, and under the Prelacy here in England, had no more relation to any institution of Christ (unless it be that it effectually excluded the exercise of his institutions) than other civil courts of justice among Christians have. Peter had the power and authority of an apostle in and over the churches of Christ, to teach, to instruct them, to ordain elders in them by their consent, wherever he came; so had the rest of the apostles. But as to this monarchy of Peter over the rest of the apostles, let them show what authority he ever exercised over them while he and they lived together. We read that he was once reproved by one of them, not that he ever reproved the meanest of them. If Christ made the grant of pre-eminency to him when he said, "Tu es Petrus," why did the apostles inquire afterward who among them should be greatest? And why did not our Saviour, on that dispute, plainly satisfy them that Peter was to be chief, but chose rather to so determine the question as to evince them of the vanity of any such inquiry? And yet the determination of it is that that lies at the bottom of the papal monarchy. And why doth Paul say that he was in nothing inferior to any of the apostles, when (if these gentlemen say true) he was in many things inferior to Peter? What special place hath the name of Peter in the foundation of the new Jerusalem? Rev. xxi. 14. What exaltation hath his throne among the twelve, whereon the apostles judge the world and house of Israel? Matt. xix. 28. What eminency of commission had he for teaching all nations or forgiving sins? What had his keys more than those of the rest of the apostles? What was peculiar in that triple command of feeding the sheep of Christ, but his triple denial that preceded? John xxi. 15–17. Is an injunction for the performance of duty a grant of new authority? But that we may make some progress, suppose this also," Why, *this power, privilege, and jurisdiction of Peter, was to be transferred to his successors, when the power of all the other apostles, as such, died with them.*" But what pretence or colour of it is there for this assertion? What one tittle or ἰῶτα is there in the whole book of God giving the least countenance to this imagination? What distinction between Peter and the rest of the apostles on this account is once made, or in any kind insinuated? Certainly, this was a thing of great importance to the churches to have been acquainted with it. When Paul so sadly tells the church, that after his departure grievous wolves would spoil the flock, and many among themselves would arise, speaking perverse things, to draw disciples after them, why did he not give them the least direction to make their address to him that should succeed Peter in his power and office, for relief and redress? Strange, that it should be of necessity to salvation to be subject to him in whom this power of Peter was to be continued; that he was to be one in whom the saints were to be consummated; that in relation to him the unity of the catholic church, to be preserved under pain of damnation, should consist; — and yet not a word spoken of him in the whole word of God!

But they say, "*Peter had not only an apostolical power with the rest of the apostles, but also an ordinary power, that was to be continued in the church.*" But the Scripture being confessedly silent of any such thing, let us hear what proof is tendered for the establishment of this uncouth assertion. Herein, then, thus they proceed: "It will be confessed that Jesus Christ ordained his church wisely, according to his infinite wisdom, which he exercised about his body. Now, to this wisdom of his, for the prevention of innumerable evils, it is agreeable that he should appoint some one person with that power of declaring truth, and of jurisdiction to enforce the receiving of it, which we plead for; for this was in Peter, as is proved from the texts of Scripture before mentioned: therefore, it is continued in them that succeed him." And here lies the great stress of their cause, — that, to prevent evils and inconveniencies, it became the wisdom of Jesus Christ to appoint a person with all that authority, power, and infallibility, to continue in his church to the end of the world. And this plea they manage variously, with much sophistry, rhetoric, and testimonies of antiquity. But suppose all this should be granted, yet I am full well assured that they can never bring it home to their concernment by any argument, but only the actual claim of the pope, wherein he stands singly now in the world; which that it is satisfactory, to make it good "de fide" that he is so, will not easily be granted. The truth is, of all the attempts they make against the Lord Jesus Christ, this is one of the greatest, wherein they will assert that it became his wisdom to do that which by no means they can prove that he hath done; which is plainly to tell us what in their judgment he ought to have done, though he hath not, and that, therefore, it is incumbent on them to supply what he hath been defective in. Had he taken the care he should of them and their master, that he and they might have ruled and revelled over and in the house of God, he would have appointed things as now they are; which they affirm to have become his wisdom. He was a king that once cried, "Si Deo in creatione adfuissem, mundum melius ordinassem." But every friar or monk can say of Jesus Christ, had they been present at his framing the world to come (whereof we speak), they would have told him what had become his wisdom to do. Our blessed Lord hath left sufficient provision against all future emergencies and inconveniencies in his word and Spirit, given and promised to his saints. And the one remedy which these men have found out, with the contempt and blasphemy of him and them, hath proved worse than all the other evils and diseases for whose prevention he made provision; which he hath done also for that remedy of theirs, but that some are hardened through the righteous judgment of God and deceitfulness of sin.

The management of this plea by some of late is very considerable. Say they, "Quia non de verbis solum Scripturæ, sed etiam de sensu plurima controversia est, si ecclesiæ interpretatio non est certa intelligendi norma, ecquis erit istiusmodi controversiæ judex? Sensum enim suum pro sua virili quisque defendet; quod si in explorandâ verbi Dei intelligentiâ nullus est certus judex, audemus dicere nullam rempublicam fuisse stultius constitutam. Sin autem apostoli tradiderunt ecclesiis verbum Dei sine intelligentia verbi Dei, quomodo prædicârunt evangelium omni creaturæ? quomodo docuerunt omnes gentes servare quæcunque illis fuerunt a Christo commendata. Non est puerorum aut psittacorum prædicatio, qui sine mente dant, accipiuntque sonum," Walemburg, Con. 4, Num. 26.

It is well that at length these men speak out plainly. If the pope be not a visible supreme judge in and over the church, Christ hath, in the constitution of his church, dealt more foolishly than ever any did in the constitution of a commonwealth! If he have not an infallible power of determining the sense of the Scripture, the Scripture is but an empty, insignificant word, like the speech of parrots or popinjays! Though Christ hath, by his apostles, given the Scripture to make the man of God wise unto salvation, and promised his Spirit unto them that believe, by whose assistance the Scripture gives out its own sense to them, yet all is folly if the pope be not supreme and infallible! The Lord rebuke them who thus boldly blaspheme his word and wisdom! But let us proceed.

"*This Peter, thus invested in power that was to be traduced to others, went to Rome, and preached the gospel there.*" It is most certain, nor will themselves deny it, that if this be not so, and believed, their whole fabric will fall to the ground. But can this be necessary for all sorts of Christians, and every individual of men among them, to believe, when there is not the least insinuation of any such thing in the Scripture? Certainly, though it be only a matter of fact, yet being of such huge importance and consequence, and such a doctrine of absolute and indispensable necessity to be believed, as is pretended, depending upon it, if it were true, and true in reference to such an end and purpose as is pleaded, it would not have been passed over in silence there, where so many things of inconceivably less concernment to the church of God (though all in their respective degrees tending to edification) are recorded. As to what is recorded in story, the order and series of things, with the discovery afforded us of Peter's course and place of abode in Scripture, do prevail with me to think steadfastly that he was never there, against the self-contradicting testimonies of some few, who took up vulgar reports then when the mystery of iniquity had so far operated, at least, that it was judged meet that the chief of the apostles should have lived in the chief city of the world.

But that we may proceed, grant this also, that Peter was at Rome, which they shall never be able to prove, and that he did preach the gospel there, — yet so he did, by their own confession, at other places, making his residence at Antioch for some years, — what will this avail towards the settling of the matter under consideration? "There Christ appointed him to fix his chair, and make that church the place of his residence," — λῆροι!

Of his meeting Simon Magus at Rome, who in all probability was never there (for Semo Sangus was not Simon Magus, nor Sanctus, nor Deus Magnus), of the conquest made of him and his devils, of his being instructed of Christ not to go from Rome, but tarry there and suffer, something may be said from old legends; but of his chair, and fixing of it at Rome, of his confinement, as it were, to that place, in direct opposition to the tenor of his apostolical commission, who first told the story I know not. But this I know, they will one day be ashamed of their chair, thrones, and sees, and jurisdictions, wherein they now so please themselves.

But what is next to this? "*The bishop of Rome succeeds Peter in all that power, jurisdiction, infallibility, with whatsoever else was fancied before in him, as the ordinary lord of the church; and therefore the Roman church is the catholic,*" "quod erat demonstrandum." Now, though this inference will no way follow upon these principles, though they should all be supposed to be true, whereof not one is so much as probable, and though this last assertion be vain and ridiculous, nothing at all being pleaded to ground this succession, no institution of Christ, no act of any council of the church, no will or testament of Peter, but only it is so fallen out, as the world was composed of a casual concurrence of atoms; yet seeing they will have it so, I desire a little farther information in one thing that yet remains, and that is this: The charter, patents, and grant of all this power, and right of succession unto Peter, in all the advantages, privileges, and jurisdiction before mentioned, being wholly in their own keeping, whereof I never saw letter or tittle, nor ever conversed with any one, no not of themselves, that did, I would be gladly informed whether this grant be made to him absolutely, without any manner of condition whatever, so that whoever comes to be pope of Rome, and possessed of Peter's chair there, by what means soever he is possessed of it, whether he believe the gospel or no, or any of the saving truths therein contained, and so their church must be the catholic church, though it follow him in all abominations; or whether it be made on any condition to him, especially that of cleaving to the doctrine of Christ revealed in the gospel? If they say the first, that it is an absolute grant that is made to him, without any condition expressed or necessarily to be understood, I am at an issue, and have nothing to add but my desire that the grant may be produced; for whilst we are at this variance, it is against all law and equity that the parties litigant should be admitted to plead bare allegations without proof. If the latter, though we should grant all the former monstrous suppositions, yet we are perfectly secure against all their pretensions, knowing nothing more clearly and evidently than that he and they have broken all conditions that can possibly be imagined, by corrupting and perverting almost the whole doctrine of the gospel.

And whereas it may be supposed that the great condition of such a grant would consist in his diligent attendance to the Scriptures, the word of God, herein doth the filth of their abominations appear above all other things. The guilt that is in that society or combination of men in locking up the Scripture in an unknown tongue; forbidding the people to read it; burning some men to death for the studying of it, and no more; disputing against its power to make good its own authority; charging it with obscurity, imperfection, insufficiency; frightening men from the perusal of it, with the danger of being seduced and made heretics by so doing; setting up their own traditions in an equality with it, if not exalting them above it; studying by all means to decry it as useless and contemptible, at least comparatively with themselves; will not be purged from them for ever.

But you will say, "This is a simple question, for the pope of Rome hath a promise that he shall still be such a one as is fit to be trusted with the power mentioned, and not one that shall defend Mohammed to be the prophet of God sent into the world, or the like abominations; at least, that be he what he will, placed in the chair, he shall not err nor mistake in what he delivereth for truth." Now, seeing themselves, as was said, are the sole keepers of this promise and grant also, which they have not as yet showed to the world, I am necessitated to ask, once more, whether it be made to him merely upon condition of mounting into his chair, or also upon this condition, that he use the means appointed by God to come to the knowledge of the truth? If they say the former, I must needs say, that it is so remote from my apprehension that God, who will be worshipped in spirit and in truth only, should now, under the gospel, promise to any persons, that be they never so wicked and abominable, never so openly and evidently sworn enemies of him and his Anointed, whether they use any means or not by him appointed, they shall always in all things speak the truth, which they hate, in love, which they have not, with that authority which all his saints must bow unto, especially not having intimated any one word of any such promise in the Scripture, that I know not whatever I heard of in my life that I cannot as soon believe. If they say the latter, we close then as we did our former inquiry.

Upon the credit and strength of these sandy foundations and principles, which neither severally nor jointly will bear the weight of a feather, in a long-continued course of apostasy, have men conquered all policy, religion, and honesty, and built up that stupendous fabric, coupled together with subtle and scarce discernible joints and ligaments, which they call the catholic church.

(1.) In despite of policy, they have not only enslaved kings, kingdoms, commonwealths, nations, and people to be their vassals and at their disposal; but also, contrary to all rules of government, beyond the thoughts and conjectures of all or any that ever wrote of or instituted a government in the world, they have in most nations of Europe set up a *government*, authority, and jurisdiction, within another government and authority, settled on other accounts, the one independent of the other, and have brought these things to some kind of consistency: which that it might be accomplished never entered into the heart of any wise man once to imagine, nor had ever been by them effected without such advantages as none in the world ever had in such a continuance but themselves, unless the Druids of old in some nations obtained some such thing.[9]

---

9   "Si quis, aut privatus aut publicus, eorum decreto non stetit, sacrificiis interdicunt. Hæc pœna apud eos est gravissima. Quibus ira est interdictum, ii numero impiorum et sceleratorum habentur: iis omnes decedunt, aditum eorum sermonemque defugiunt, ne quid ex contagione incommodi accipiant; neque iis petentibus jus redditur, neque honos ullus communicatur. His autem omnibus Druidibus præest unus, qui summam inter eos habet authoritatem. Hoc mortuo, si quis ex reliquis excellit dignitate, succedit: at si sunt plures pares, suffragio Druidum allegitur, nonnunquam etiam armis de principatu contendunt." — Cæs. lib. vi. 13, de Bell. Gall.

(2.) In despite of religion itself, they have made a *new creed*, invented new ways of worship, given a whole sum and system of their own, altogether alien from the word of God, without an open disclaiming of that word, which in innumerable places bears testimony to its own perfection and fulness.

(3.) Contrary to common honesty, the first principles of reason, with violence to the evident dictates of the law of nature, they will, in confidence of these principles, have the word and sentence of a pope, though a beast, a witch, a conjuror (as by their own confession many of them have been), to be implicitly submitted to in and about things which he neither knoweth, nor loveth, nor careth for, being yet such in themselves as immediately and directly concern the everlasting condition of the souls of men. And this is our second return to their pretence of being the catholic church; to which I add, —

3. That their plea is so far from truth, that they are, and they only, the catholic church, that indeed they belong not to it, because they keep not the *unity of the faith*, which is required to constitute any person whatever a member of that church, but fail in all the conditions of it; for, —

(1.) To proceed, by way of instance, they do not profess nor believe *a justification distinct from sanctification*, and acceptance thereof; the doctrine whereof is of absolute and indispensable necessity to the preservation of the unity of the faith; and so fail in the first condition of professing all necessary truths. I know what they say of justification, what they have determined concerning it in the council of Trent, what they dispute about it in their books of controversies; but I deny that which they contend for to be a justification. So that they do not deny only justification by faith, but positively, over and above, the infusion of grace, and the acceptance of the obedience thence arising; — that there is any justification at all, consisting in the free and full absolution of a sinner, on the account of Christ.

(2.) *They discover principles corrupt and depraved*, utterly inconsistent with those truths and the receiving of them which in general, by owning the Scriptures, they do profess. Herein, to pass by the principles of atheism, wickedness, and profaneness, that effectually work and manifest themselves in the generality of their priests and people, that of self-righteousness, that is in the best of their devotionists, is utterly inconsistent with the whole doctrine of the gospel, and all saving truths concerning the mediation of Jesus Christ therein contained.

(3.) That in their doctrine of the *pope's supremacy, of merits, satisfaction, the mass, the worshipping of images*, they add such things to their profession as enervate the efficacy of all the saving truths they do profess, and so fail in the third condition. This hath so abundantly been manifested by others, that I shall not need to add any thing to give the charge of it upon them any farther evidence or demonstration.

Thus it is unhappily fallen out with these men, that what of all men they most pretend unto, that of all men they have the least interest in. Athenæus tells us of one Thrasilaus an Athenian, who being frenetically distempered, whatever ships came into the Piræus he looked on them and thought them his own, and rejoiced as the master of so great wealth, when he was not the owner of so much as a boat. Such a distemper of pride and folly hath in the like manner seized on these persons with whom we have to do, that wherever in Scripture they meet with the name *church*, presently, as though they were intended by it, they rejoice in the privileges of it, when their concernment lies not at all therein.

To close this whole discourse, I shall bring the grand argument of the Romanists (with whom I shall now, in this treatise, have little more to do), wherewith they make such a noise in the world, to an issue. Of the many forms and shapes whereinto by them it is cast, this seems to be the most perspicuously expressive of their intention:—

"Voluntarily to forsake the communion of the church of Christ is schism, and they that do so are guilty of it;

"You have voluntarily forsaken the communion of the church of Christ:

"Therefore, you are guilty of the sin of schism."

I have purposely omitted the interposing of the term *catholic*, that the reason of the argument might run to its length: for upon the taking in of that term we have nothing to do but only to deny the minor proposition, seeing the Roman church, be it what it will, is not the church catholic; but as it is without that limitation called the church of Christ indefinitely, it leaves place for a farther and fuller answer.

To this, by way of inference, they add, "That schism, as it is declared by St Austin and St Thomas of Aquin, being so great and damnable a sin, and whereas it is plain that out of the church, which, as Peter says, is as Noah's ark, 1 Pet. iii. 20, 21, there is no salvation, it is clear you will be damned." This is the sum of their plea.

Now, as for the fore-mentioned argument, some of our divines answer to the minor proposition, and that both as to the terms of "voluntary forsaking," and that also of the "communion of the church." For the first, they say they did not *voluntarily* forsake the communion of the church that then was, but being necessitated by the command of God to reform themselves in sundry things, they were driven out by bell, book, and candle, cursed out, killed out, driven out by all manner of violence, ecclesiastical and civil; which is a strange way of men's becoming schismatic.

Secondly, That they forsook not the *communion* of the church, but the *corruptions* of it, or the communion of it in its corruption, not in other things wherein it was lawful to continue communion with it.

To give strength to this answer they farther add, that though they grant the church of Rome to have been at the time of the first separation a true church of Christ, yet they deny it to be the catholic church, or only visible church then in the world, the churches in the east claiming that title by as good a right as she. So they. Others principally answer to the major proposition, and tell you that separation is either causeless, or upon just ground and cause; that it is a causeless separation only from the church of Christ that is schism; that there can be no cause of schism, for if there be a cause of schism materially, it ceaseth to be schism formally. And so, to strengthen their answer "in hypothesi," they fall upon the idolatries, heresies, tyranny, and apostasy of the church of Rome as just causes of separation from her. Nor will their plea be shaken to eternity; so that being true and popular, understood by the meanest, though it contain not the whole truth, I shall not in the least impair it.

For them who have found out new ways of justifying our separation from Rome, on principles of limiting the jurisdiction of the bishop of Rome to a peculiar patriarchate, and granting a power to kings or nations to erect patriarchs or metropolitans within their own territories, and the like, the protestant cause is not concerned in their plea; the whole of it on both hands being foreign to the Scripture, relating mostly to human constitutions, wherein they may have liberty to exercise their wits and abilities.

Not receding from what hath by others solidly been pleaded on the answers above mentioned, in answer to the principles I have hitherto evinced, I shall proceed to give my account of the argument proposed.

That we mistake not, I only premise that I take schism in this argument in the notion and sense of the Scripture precisely, wherein alone it will reach the conscience, and bear the weight of inferring damnation from it.

1. Then, I wholly deny the major proposition as utterly false, in what sense soever that expression," True church of Christ," is taken. Take it for the catholic church of Christ, I deny that any one who is once a true member of it can utterly forsake its communion. No living member of that body of Christ can perish; and on supposition it could do so, it would be madness to call that crime schism. Nor is this a mere denial of the assertion, but such as is attended with an invincible truth for its maintenance.

Take it for the *general visible church* of Christ; the voluntary forsaking of its communion, which consists in the profession of the same faith, is not schism but apostasy, and the thing itself is to be removed from the question in hand. And as for apostates from the faith of the gospel, we question not their damnation; it sleepeth not. Who ever called a Christian that turned Jew or Mohammedan a schismatic?

Take it for a *particular church* of Christ, I deny, —

(1.) That separation from a particular church, as such, as merely separation, is schism, or ought to be so esteemed; though, perhaps, such separation may proceed from schism, and be also attended with other evils.

(2.) That, however, separation upon just cause and ground from any church is no schism, this is granted by all persons living. Schism is causeless, say all men, however concerned. And herein is a truth uncontrollable: Separation upon just cause is a duty, and therefore cannot be schism, which is always a sin. Now, there are five hundred things in the church of Rome, whereof every one, grafted as they are there into the stock and principle of imposition on the practice and confession of men, is a sufficient cause of separation from any particular church in the world, yea, from all of them, one after another, should they all consent unto the same thing, and impose it in the same manner, if there be any truth in that maxim, "It is better to obey God than man."

2. I wholly deny the minor proposition also, if spoken in reference to the church of Rome, though I willingly acknowledge our separation to be voluntary from them, no more being done than I would do over again this day, God assisting me, were I called unto it. But separation, in the sense contended about, must be from some state and condition of Christ's institution, from communion with a church which we held by his appointment; otherwise it will not be pleaded that it is a schism, at least not in a gospel sense. Now, though our forefathers, in the faith we profess, lived in subjection to the pope of Rome, or his subordinate engines, yet they were not so subject to them in any way or state instituted by Christ; so that the relinquishment of that state can possibly be no such separation as to be termed schism: for I wholly deny that the Papacy, exercising its power in its supreme and subordinate officers, which with them is their church, is a church at all of Christ's appointment, or any such thing; and when they prove it is so, I will be of it. So that when our forefathers withdrew their neck from his tyrannical yoke, and forsook the practice of his abominations in the worship of God, they forsook no church of Christ's institution, they relinquished no communion of Christ's appointment. A man may possibly forsake Babylon, and yet not forsake Zion.

[As] for the aggravations of the sin of schism from some ancient writers, — Austin and Optatus, men interested in the contests about it; Leo and Innocent, gaining by the notion of it then growing in the world; Thomas Aquinas, and such vassals of the Papacy; we are not concerned in them: what the Lord speaks of it, that we judge concerning it. It is true of the catholic church always, that out of it is no salvation, it being the society of them that shall be saved; and of the visible church in general, in some sense and cases, seeing "with the heart man believeth unto righteousness, and with the mouth confession is made unto salvation; but of a particular church in no sense, unless that of contempt of a known duty, — and to imagine Peter to speak of any such thing is a fancy.

The consequence of this divesting the Roman synagogue of the privileges of a true church in any sense, arising in the thoughts of some to a denial of that *ministry* which we have at this day in England, must, by the way, a little be considered. For my part (be it spoken without offence), if any man hath nothing to plead for his ministry but merely that successive ordination which he hath received through the church of Rome, I cannot see a stable bottom of owning him so to be; I do not say, if he will plead nothing else, but if he hath nothing else to plead. He may have that which indeed constitutes him a minister, though he will not own that so it doth. Nor doth it come here into inquiry, whether there were not a true ministry in some all along under the Papacy, distinct from it, as were the thousands in Israel in the days of Elijah, when in the ten tribes, as to the public worship, there was no true ministry at all. Nor is it said that any have their ministry from Rome; as though the office, which is an ordinance of Christ, were instituted by Antichrist. But the question is, Whether this be *a sufficient and good basis and foundation* of any man's interest in the office of the ministry, that he hath received ordination in a succession, through the administration of, not the woman flying into the wilderness under the persecution of Antichrist, not of the two witnesses prophesying all along under the Roman apostasy, not from them to whom we succeed in doctrine, as the Waldenses, but the beast itself, the persecuting church of Rome, the pope and his adherents, who were certainly administrators of the ordination pleaded for; so that in *doctrine* we should succeed the *persecuted woman*, and in *office* the *persecuting beast*. I shall not plead this at large, professedly disclaiming all thoughts of rejecting those ministers as papal and antichristian who yet adhere to this ordination, being many of them eminently gifted of God to dispense the word, and submitted unto by his people in the administration of the ordinances, and are right worthy ministers of the gospel of Christ; but, —

I shall only remark something on the plea that is insisted on by them who would (if I mistake not) keep up in this particular what God would have pulled down. They ask us, "Why not ordination from the church of Rome as well as the Scripture?" in which inquiry I am sorry that some do still continue. We are so far from having the Scriptures from the church of Rome, by any authority of it as such, that it is one cause of daily praising God, that by his providence he kept them from being either corrupted or destroyed by them. It is true, the Bible was kept among the people that lived in those parts of the world where the pope prevailed; so was the Old Testament by the Jews; the whole by the eastern Christians; by none so corrupted as by those of the papal territory. God forbid we should say we had the Scriptures from the church of Rome, as such! If we had, why do we not keep them as she delivered them to us, in the Vulgar translation, with the apocryphal additions? The ordination pleaded for is from the authority of the church of Rome, as such. The Scriptures were by the providence of God preserved under the Papacy for the use of his people; and had they been found by chance, as it were, like the law of old, they had been the same to us that now they are. So that of these things there is not the same reason.

It is also pleaded that the granting true ordination to the church of Rome doth not prove that to be a *true* church. This I profess I understand not. They who ordained had no power so to do but as they were officers of that church. As such they did it; and if others had ordained who were not officers of that church, all would confess that action to be null. But they who will not be contented that Christ hath appointed the office of the ministry to be continued in his churches; that he continues to dispense the gifts of his Spirit for the execution of that office when men are called thereunto; that he prepares the hearts of his people to desire and submit unto them in the Lord; that as to the manner of entrance upon the work, they may have it according to the mind of Christ to the utmost, in all circumstances, so soon as his churches are shaken out of the dust of Babylon with his glory shining on them, and the tabernacle of God is thereby once more placed with men, — shall have leave, for me, to derive their interest in the ministry through that dark passage, wherein I cannot see one step before me. If they are otherwise qualified and accepted as above, I shall ever pay them that honour which is due to elders labouring in the word and doctrine.

Chapter VII.

Of a particular church; its nature — Frequently mentioned in Scripture — Particular congregations acknowledged the only churches of the first institution — What ensued on the multiplication of churches — Some things premised to clear the unity of the church in this sense — Every believer ordinarily obliged to join himself to some particular church — Many things in instituted worship answering a natural principle — Perpetuity of the church in this sense — True churches at first planted in England — How they ceased so to be — How churches may be again re-erected — Of the union of a particular church in itself — Foundation of that union twofold — The union itself — Of the communion of particular churches one with another — Our concernment in this union.

III. I NOW descend to the last consideration of a church, in the most usual acceptation of that name in the New Testament, — that is, of a *particular instituted church*. A church in this sense I take to be *a society of men called by the word to the obedience of the faith in Christ, and joint performance of the worship of God in the same individual ordinates, according to the order by Christ prescribed*. This general description of it exhibits its nature so far as is necessary to clear the subject of our present disquisition. A more accurate definition would only administer farther occasion of contesting about things not necessary to be determined as to the inquiry in hand. Such as this was the church at Jerusalem that was persecuted, Acts viii. 1, — the church whereof Saul made havoc, verse 3, — the church that was vexed by Herod, chap. xii. 1. Such was the church at Antioch, which assembled together in one place, chap. xiv. 27; wherein were sundry prophets, chap. xiii. 1, as that at Jerusalem consisted of elders and brethren, chap. xv. 22, — the apostles, or some of them, being there then present, which added no other consideration to that church than that we are now speaking of. Such were those many churches wherein elders were ordained by Paul's appointment, chap. xiv.

23; as also the church of Cæsarea, chap. xviii. 22, and at Ephesus, chap. xx. 17, 28; as was that of Corinth, 1 Cor. i. 2, vi. 4, xi. 18, xiv. 4, 5, 12, 19, 2 Cor. i. 1; and those mentioned, Rev. i., ii., iii.; — all which Paul calls the "churches of the Gentiles," Rom. xvi. 4, in contradistinction to those of the Jews; and calls them indefinitely "the churches of Christ," verse 16; or "the churches of God," 2 Thess. i. 4; or "the churches," 1 Cor. vii. 17, 2 Cor. viii. 18, 19, 23, 24, and in sundry other places. Hence we have mention of many churches in one country, — as in Judea, Acts ix. 31; in Asia, 1 Cor. xvi. 19; in Macedonia, 2 Cor. viii. 1; in Galatia, Gal. i. 2; the seven churches of Asia, Rev. i. 11; and unto τὰς πόλεις, Acts xvi. 4, αἱ ἐκκλησίαι answers, verse 5, in the same country.

I suppose that, in this description of a particular church, I have not only the consent of them of all sorts with whom I have now to do as to what remains of this discourse, but also their acknowledgment that these were the only kinds of churches of the first institution. The reverend authors of the Jus Divinum Ministerii [Evangelici] Anglicani, p. 2, cap. vi.,[10] tell us that "in the beginning of Christianity the number of believers, even in the greatest cities, was so few as that they might all meet ἐπὶ τὸ αὐτό, in one and the same place; and these are called the church of the city; and the angel of such a city was congregational, not diocesan;" — which discourse exhibits that state of a particular church which is now pleaded for, and which shall afterward be evinced, allowing no other, no not in the greatest cities. In a rejoinder to that treatise, so far as the case of episcopacy is herein concerned, by a person well known by his labours in that cause, this is acknowledged to be so. "Believers," saith he, "in great cities were not at first divided into parishes, whilst the number of Christians was so small that they might well assemble in the same place," Ham. Vind., p. 16.[11] Of the believers of one city meeting in one place, being one church, we have the like grant, p. 18. "In this particular church," he says, "there was one bishop, which had the rule of it, and of the believers in the villages adjacent to that city; which as it sometimes was not so, Rom.

---

10 A work published by the Provincial Assembly of London, in 4to, 1654. — Ed.

11 Dr Hammond's Vindication of the Dissertations concerning Episcopacy. — Ed.

xvi. 5, so for the most part it seems to have been the case: and distinct churches, upon the growth of the number of believers, were to be erected in several places of the vicinage."

And this is the state of a particular instituted church which we plead for. Whether in process of time, believers multiplying, those who had been of one church met in several assemblies, by a settled distribution of them, to celebrate the same ordinances specifically, and so made many churches, or met in several places in parties, still continuing one body, and were governed in common by the elders, whom they increased and multiplied in proportion to the increase of believers; or whether that one or more officers, elders, or bishops, of that first single congregation, taking on him or them the care of those inhabiting the city wherein the church was first planted, designed and sent some fitted for that purpose, upon their desire and choice, or otherwise, to the several lesser companies of the region adjacent, which, in process of time, became dependent on and subject to the officer or officers of that first church from whence they came forth, — I dispute not. I am satisfied that the first plantation of churches was as hath been pleaded; and I know what was done afterward, on the one hand or the other, must be examined, as to our concernment, by what ought to have been done. But of those things afterward.

Now, according to the course of procedure hitherto insisted on, a declaration of the unity of the church in this sense, what it is, wherein it doth consist, with what it is to be guilty of the breach of that unity, must ensue; and this shall be done after I have premised some few things previously necessary thereunto.

I say, then, —

1. A man may be a member of the catholic church of Christ, be united to him by the inhabitation of his Spirit, and participation of life from him, who, upon the account of some providential hinderance, is never joined to any particular congregation, for the participation of ordinances, all his days.

2. In like manner may he be a member of the church considered as professing visibly, seeing that he may do all that is of him required thereunto without any such conjunction to a visible particular church. But yet, —

3. I willingly grant that every believer is obliged, as in a part of his duty, to join himself to some one of those churches of Christ, that therein he may abide, in "doctrine and fellowship,

and in breaking of bread, and in prayers," according to the order of the gospel, if he have advantage and opportunity so to do; for,

(1.) There are some duties incumbent on us which cannot possibly be performed but on a supposition of this duty being previously required and submittal unto, Matt. xviii. 15–17.

(2.) There are some ordinances of Christ, appointed for the good and benefit of those that believe, which they can never be made partakers of if not related to some such society; as public admonition, excommunication, participation of the sacrament of the Lord's supper.

(3.) The care that Jesus Christ hath taken that all things be well ordered in these churches, — giving no direction for the performance of any duty of worship merely and purely of sovereign institution, but only in them and by them who are so joined, — sufficiently evinces his mind and our duty herein, Rev. ii. 7, 11, 29, iii. 6, 13, 22; 1 Cor. xi..

(4.) The gathering, planting, and settling of such churches by the apostles, with the care they took in bringing them to perfection, leaving none whom they converted out of that order, where it was possible for them to be reduced unto it, is of the same importance, Acts xiv. 23; Tit. i. 5.

(5.) Christ's institution of officers for them, Eph. iv. 11, 1 Cor. xii. 28; calling such a church his "body," verse 27; exactly assigning to every one his duty in such societies, in respect of the place he holds in them; with his care for their preservation from confusion and for order, — evince from whom they are, and what is our duty in reference unto them.

(6.) The judging and condemning them by the Holy Ghost as disorderly, blamable persons, who are to be avoided, who walk not according to the rules and order appointed in these churches; his care that those churches be not scandalized or offended; with innumerable other considerations, — evince their institution to be from heaven, not of men, or any prudential considerations of them whatever.

That there is an instituted worship of God, to be continued under the New Testament until the second coming of Christ, I suppose needs not much proof. With those with whom it doth so I am not now treating, and must not make it my business to give it evidence by the innumerable testimonies which might be alleged to that purpose. That for the whole of his worship, matter, or manner, or any part of it, God hath changed his way of proceeding, and will now allow the will and prudence of man to be the measure and rule of his honour and glory therein, contrary to what he did or would allow under the law, is so prejudicial to the perfection of the gospel, infinite wisdom and all-sufficiency of Christ, and so destructive to the whole obligation of the second commandment, having no ground in the Scripture, but being built merely on the conceit of men, suited to one carnal interest or other, I shall unwillingly debate it. That, as to this particular under consideration, there were particular churches instituted by the authority of Jesus Christ, owned and approved by him; that officers for them were of his appointment, and furnished with gifts from him for the execution of their employment; that rules, cautions, and instructions for the due settlement of those churches were given by him; that those churches were made the only seat of that worship which in particular he expressed his will to have continued until he came, — is of so much light in Scripture that he must wink hard that will not see it.

1. That either he did not originally appoint these things, or he did not give out the gifts of his Spirit in reference to the right ordering of them, and exalting of his glory in them; or that having done so then, yet that his institutions have an end, being only for a season, and that it may be known when the efficacy of any of his institutions ceaseth; or that he doth not now dispense the gifts and graces of his Spirit to render them useful, — is a difficult task for any man to undertake to evince.

There is, indeed, in the institutions of Christ, much that answers a *natural principle* in men, who are on many accounts formed and fitted for society. A confederation and consultation to carry on any design wherein the concernment of the individuals doth lie, within such bounds and in such order as lie in a ready way to the end aimed at, is exceeding suitable to the principles whereby we are acted and guided as men. But he that would hence conclude that there is no more but this, and the acting of these principles, in this church-constitution whereof we speak, and that therefore men may be cast into any prudential form, or appoint other ways and forms of it than those mentioned in the Scripture as appointed and owned, takes on himself the demonstrating that all things necessarily required to the constitution of such a church-society are commanded by the law of nature, and therefore allowed of and approved only by Christ, and so to be wholly moral, and to have nothing of instituted worship in them. And also, he must know that when, on that supposition, he hath given a probable reason why never any persons in the world fixed on such societies in all essential things as those, seeing they are natural, that he leaves less to the prudence of men, and to the ordering and disposing of things concerning them, than these who make them of pure institution, all whose circumstances cannot be derived from themselves, as those of things purely moral may. But this is not of my present consideration.

2. Nor shall I consider whether *perpetuity* be a property of the church of Christ in this sense; that is, not whether a church that was once so may cease to be so, — which it is known I plead for in the instance of the church of Rome, not to mention others, but whether, by virtue of any promise of Christ, there shall always be somewhere in the world a visible church, visibly celebrating his ordinances. Luke i. 33, "He shall reign over the house of Jacob for ever, and of his kingdom there shall be no end," is pleaded to this purpose; but that any more but the spiritual reign of Christ in his catholic church is there intended is not proved. Matt. xvi. 18, "Upon this rock will I build my church," is also urged; but to intend any but true believers, and that as such, in that promise, is wholly to enervate it, and to take away its force and efficacy. Matt. xviii. 19, 20, declares the presence of Christ with his church wherever it be, not that a church in the regard treated of shall be. To the same purpose are other expressions in the Scripture. As I will not deny this in general, so I am unsatisfied as to any particular instance for the making of it good.

It is said that *true churches were at first planted* in England. How, then, or by what means, did they cease so to be? how, or by what act, did God unchurch them? They did it themselves meritoriously, by apostasy and idolatry; God legally, by his institution of a law of rejection of such churches. If any shall ask, "How, then, is it possible that any such churches should be raised anew?" I say, that the catholic church mystical and that visibly professing being preserved entire, he that thinketh there needs a miracle for those who are members of them to join in such a society as those now spoken of, according to the institution of Christ, is a person delighting in needless scruples.

Christ hath promised that where two or three are gathered together in his name, he will be in the midst of them, Matt. xviii. 20. It is now supposed, with some hope to have it granted, that the Scripture, being the "power of God unto salvation," Rom. i. 16, hath a sufficient efficacy and energy in itself, as to its own kind, for the conversion of souls; yea, let us, till opposition be made to it, take it for granted that by that force and efficacy it doth mainly and principally evince its own divinity, or divine original. Those who are contented, for the honour of that word which God delighteth to magnify, to grant this supposition, will not, I hope, think it impossible that though all church-state should cease in any place, and yet the Scripture by the providence of God be there in the hand of individuals preserved, two or three should be called, converted, and regenerated by it. For my part, I think he that questions it must do it on some corrupt principle of a secondary dependent authority in the word of God as to us; with which sort of men I do not now deal. I ask whether these converted persons may not possibly come together, or assemble themselves, in the name of Jesus? May they not, upon his command, and in expectation of the accomplishment of his promise, so come together with resolution to do his will, and to exhort one another thereto? Zech. iii. 10; Mal. iii. 16. Truly, I believe they may, in what part of the world soever their lot is fallen. Here lie all the difficulties, whether, being come together in the name of Christ, they may do what he hath commanded them or no? whether they may exhort and stir up one another to do the will of Christ? Most certain it is that Christ will give them his presence, and therewithal his authority, for the performance of any duty that he requireth at their hands. Were not men angry, troubled, and disappointed, there would be little difficulty in this business. But of this elsewhere.

3. Upon this supposition, that particular churches are *institutions of Jesus Christ*, which is granted by all with whom I have to do, I proceed to make inquiry into their union and communion, that so we may know wherein the bonds of them do consist.

There is a *double foundation*, fountain, or cause of the union of such a church, — the one *external*, procuring, commanding; the other *internal*, inciting, directing, assisting. The first is the institution of Jesus Christ, before mentioned, requiring peace and order, union, consent, and agreement, in and among all the members of such a church; all to be regulated, ordered, and bounded by the rules, laws, and prescripts, which from him they have received for their walking in those societies. The latter is that love without dissimulation which always is, or which always ought to be, between all the members of such a church, exerting itself in their respective duties one towards another in that holy combination whereunto they are called and entered for the worship of God, whether they are those which lie in the level of the equality of their common interest of being church-members, or those which are required of them in the several differences whereby, on any account whatever, they are distinguished one from another amongst themselves; for "love is the bond of perfectness," Col. iii. 14.

Hence, then, it appears what is the union of such a church, and what is the communion to be observed therein, by the appointment of Jesus Christ. The joint consent of all the members of it, in obedience to the command of Christ, from a principle of love, to walk together in the universal celebration of all the ordinances of the worship of God, instituted and appointed to be celebrated in such a church, and to perform all the duties and offices of love which, in reference to one another, in their respective stations and places, are by God required of them, and doing so accordingly, is the union inquired after. See Phil. ii. 1–3, iv. 1–3; 1 Cor. i. 10; 2 Cor. xiii. 11; Rom. xv. 5, 6.

Whereas there are in these churches some rulers, some ruled; some eyes, some hands in this body; some parts visibly comely, some uncomely, upon the account of that variety of gifts and graces which are distributed to them, — in the performance of duties, a regard is to be had to all the particular rules that are given with respect to men in their several places and distributions. Herein doth the union of a particular church consist; herein have the members of it communion among themselves, and with the whole.

4. I shall farther grant and add hereunto, that, over and above the *union* that is between the members of several particular churches, by virtue of their interest in the church catholic, which draws after it a necessity for the occasional exercise of duties of love one towards another; and that communion they have, as members of the general church visible, in the profession of the faith once delivered unto the saints; there is a *communion* also to be observed between these churches, as such,

which is sometimes, or may be, exerted in their assemblies by their delegates, for declaring their sense and determining things of joint concernment unto them. Whether there ought to be an ordinary combination of the officers of these churches, invested with power for the disposal of things and persons that concern one or more of them, in several subordinations, by the institution of Christ; as it is not my judgment that so there is, so it belongs not unto my present undertaking at all to debate.

That which alone remains to be done, is to consider what is our concernment as to the breach of this union, which we profess to be appointed by Jesus Christ; and that both as we are Protestants and as also farther differenced, according to the intimations given at the entrance of this discourse. What hath already been delivered about the nature of schism and the Scripture notion of it might well suffice as to our vindication in this business from any charge that we are or seem obnoxious unto; but because I have no reason to suppose that some men will be so favourable unto us as to take pains for the improvement of principles, though in themselves clearly evinced, on our behalf, the application of them to some present cases, with the removal of objections that lie against my intendment, must be farther added.

Some things there are which, upon what hath been spoken, I shall assume and suppose as granted "in thesi," until I see them otherwise disproved than as yet I have done.

Of these the first is, That the departing or *secession of any man or men* from any particular church, as to that communion which is peculiar to such a church, which he or they have had therewith, is nowhere called schism, nor is so in the nature of the thing itself (as the general signification of the word is restrained by its Scripture use), but is a thing to be judged and receive a title according to the causes and circumstances of it.

Secondly, *One church refusing to hold that communion with another* which ought to be between them is not schism, properly so called.

Thirdly, *The departure of any man or men from the society or communion of any church whatever,* — so it be done without strife, variance, judging, and condemning of others, — because, according the light of their consciences, they cannot in all things in them worship God according to his mind, cannot be rendered evil but from circumstances taken from the persons so doing, or the way and manner whereby and wherein they do it.

Unto these I add, that if any one can show and evince that we have departed from and left the communion of any particular church of Christ, with which we ought to walk according to the order above mentioned, or have disturbed and broken the order and union of Christ's institution, wherein we are or were inwrapped, we put ourselves on the mercy of our judges.

The consideration of what is the charge on any of us on this account was the first thing aimed at in this discourse; and, as it was necessary from the rules of the method wherein I have proceeded, comes now, in the last place, to be put to the issue and trial; which it shall in the next chapter.

Chapter VIII.

Of the church of England — The charge of schism in the name thereof proposed and considered — Several considerations of the church of England — In what sense we were members of it — Of Anabaptism — The subjection due to bishops — Their power examined — Its original in this nation — Of the ministerial power of bishops — Its present continuance — Of the church of England, what it is — Its description — Form peculiar and constitutive — Answer to the charge of schism, on separation from it in its episcopal constitution — How and by what means it was taken away — Things necessary to the constitution of such a church proposed and offered to proof — The second way of constituting a national church considered — Principles agreed on and consented unto between the parties at variance on this account — Judgment of Amyraldus in this case — Inferences from the common principles before consented unto — The case of schism, in reference to a national church in the last sense, debated — Of particular churches, and separation from them — On what accounts justifiable — No necessity of joining to this or that — Separation from some so called, required — Of the church of Corinth — The duty of its members — Austin's judgment of the practice of Elijah — The last objection waived — Inferences upon the whole.

THAT which first presents itself is a plea against us, in the name of the church of England, and those intrusted with the reiglement thereof, as it was settled and established some years since; the sum whereof, if I mistake not, amounts to thus much: —

"You were some time members and children of the church of England, and lived in the communion thereof, professing obedience thereunto, according to its rules and canons. You were in an orderly subjection to the archbishops, bishops, and those acting under them in the hierarchy, who were officers of that church. In that church you were baptized, and joined in the outward worship celebrated therein. But you have now voluntarily, and of your own accord, forsaken and renounced the communion of this church; cast off your subjection to the bishops and rulers; rejected the form of worship appointed in that church, that great bond of its communion; and set up separate churches of your own, according to your pleasures: and so you are properly schismatics."

This I say, if I mistake not, is the sum of the charge against us, on the account of our late attempt for reformation, and reducing of the church of Christ to its primitive institution; which we profess our aim in singleness of heart to have been, and leave the judgment of it unto God.

To acquit ourselves of this imputation, I shall declare, —

1. How far we own ourselves to have been, or to be, members or "children" (as they speak) "of the church of England," as it is called or esteemed.

2. What was the subjection wherein we or any of us stood, or might be supposed to have stood, to the prelates or bishops of that church. And then I shall, —

3. Put the whole to the issue and inquiry, whether we have broken any bond or order which, by the institution and appointment of Jesus Christ, we ought to have preserved entire and unviolated; not doubting but that, on the whole matter in difference, we shall find the charge managed against us to be resolved wholly into the prudence and interest of some men, wherein our consciences are not concerned.

As to the first proposal, the several considerations that the church of England may fall under will make way for the determination of our relation thereunto.

1. There being in this country of England much people of God, many of his elect, called and sanctified by and through the Spirit and blood of Christ, with the "washing of water by the word," so made true living members of the mystical body or catholic church of Christ, holding him as a spiritual head, receiving influences of life and grace from him continually, they may be called, though improperly, the church of England; that is, that part of Christ's catholic church militant which lives in England. In this sense it is the desire of our souls to be found and to abide members of the church of England, to keep with it, whilst we live in this world, the "unity of the Spirit in the bond of peace." Jerusalem which is above is the mother of us all, and one is our Father, which is in heaven; one is our Head, Sovereign, Lord, and Ruler, the dearly-beloved of our souls, the Lord Jesus Christ. If we have grieved, offended, troubled the

least member of this church, so that he may justly take offence at any of our ways, we profess our readiness to lie at his or their feet for reconciliation, according to the mind of Christ. If we bear not love to all the members of the church of England in this sense, without dissimulation (yea, even to them amongst them who, through mistakes and darkness, have on several accounts designed our harm and ruin); if we rejoice not with them and suffer not with them, however they may be differenced in and by their opinions or walkings; if we desire not their good as the good of our own souls, and are not ready to hold any communion with them, wherein their and our light will give and afford unto us peace mutually; if we judge, condemn, despise any of them, as to their persons, spiritual state, and condition, because they walk not with us, let us be esteemed the vilest schismatics that ever lived on the face of the earth. But as to our membership in the church of England on this account, we stand or fall to our own Master.

2. The rulers, governors, teachers, and body of the people of this nation of England, having, by laws, professions, and public protestations, cast off the tyranny, authority, and doctrine of the church of Rome, with its head the pope, and jointly assented unto and publicly professed the doctrine of the gospel, as expressed in their public confession, variously attested and confirmed, declaring their profession by that public confession, preaching, laws, and writings suitable thereunto, may also be called on good account the church of England. In this sense we profess ourselves members of the church of England, and professing and adhering to that doctrine of faith, in the unity of it, which was here established and declared, as was before spoken. As to the attempt of some, who accuse us for everting of fundamentals by our doctrine of election by the free grace of God, of effectual redemption of the elect only, conversion by the irresistible efficacy of grace, and the associate doctrines, which are commonly known, we suppose the more sober part of our adversaries will give them little thanks for their pains therein; if for no other reason, yet at least because they know the cause they have to manage against us is weakened thereby. Indeed, it seems strange to us that we should be charged with schism from the church of England, for endeavouring to reform ourselves as to something relating to the worship of God, by men everting and denying so considerable a portion of the doctrine

of that church, which we sacredly retain entire, as the most urgent of our present adversaries do. In this sense, I say, we still confess ourselves members of the church of England; nor have we made any separation from it, but do daily labour to improve and carry on the light of the gospel which shines therein, and on the account whereof it is renowned in the world.

3. Though I know not how proper that expression of "children of the church" may be under the New Testament, nor can by any means consent unto it, to be the urging of any obedience to any church or churches whatsoever on that account, no such use being made of that consideration by the Holy Ghost, nor any parallel unto it insisted on by him; yet, in a general sense, so far as our receiving our regeneration and new birth, through the grace of God, by the preaching of the word and the saving truths thereof here professed, with the seal of it in our baptism, may be signified by that expression, we own ourselves to have been, and to be, children of the church of England, because we have received all this by the administration of the gospel here in England, as dispensed in several assemblies therein, and are contented that this concession be improved to the utmost.

Here, indeed, we are left by them who renounce the baptism they have received in their infancy, and repeat it again amongst themselves. Yet I suppose that he who, upon that single account, will undertake to prove them schismatical may find himself entangled. Nor is the case with them exactly as it was with the Donatists. They do the same thing with them, but not on the same principles. The Donatists rebaptized those who came to their societies, because they professed themselves to believe that all administration of ordinances not in their assemblies was null, and that they were to be looked on as no such thing. Our Anabaptists do the same thing, but on this plea, that though baptism be, yet infant baptism is not, an institution of Christ, and so is null from the nature of the thing itself, not the way of its administration. But this falls not within the verge of my defence.

In these several considerations we were, and do continue, members of the church of God in England; and as to our failing herein, who is it that convinces us of sin?

The second thing inquired after is, what subjection we stood in, or were supposed to have stood in, to the bishops? Our subjection being regulated by their power, the consideration of this discovers the true state of that.

They had and exercised in this nation a twofold power, and consequently the subjection required of us was twofold:—

1. A power delegated from the supreme magistrate of the nation, conferred on them, and invested in them, by the laws, customs, and usages of this commonwealth; and exercised by them on that account. This not only made them barons of the realm and members of parliament, and gave them many dignities and privileges, but also was the sole fountain and spring of that jurisdiction which they exercised by ways and means such as themselves will not plead to have been purely ecclesiastical and of the institution of Jesus Christ. In this respect we did not cast off our subjection to them, it being our duty to "submit ourselves to every ordinance of man, for the Lord's sake." Only, whenever they commanded things unlawful in themselves or unto us, we always retreated to the old safe rule, "Whether it be right to hearken unto you more than unto God, judge ye." On this foundation, I say, was all the jurisdiction which they exercised among and over the people of this nation built. They had not leave to exercise that which they were invested in on another account, but received formally their authority thereby. The tenure whereby their predecessors held this power before the Reformation, the change of the tenure by the laws of this land, the investiture of the whole original right thereof in another person than formerly by the same means, the legal concession and delegation to them made, the enlarging or contracting of their jurisdiction by the same laws, the civil process of their courts in the exercise of their authority, sufficiently evince from whence they had it. Nor was any thing herein any more of the institution of Jesus Christ than the courts are in Westminster Hall. Sir Edward Coke, who knew the laws of his country, and was skilled in them to a miracle, will satisfy any in the rise and tenor of episcopal jurisdiction: "De jure regis eccles." What there is of primitive institution giving colour and occasion to this kind of jurisdiction, and the exercise of it, shall farther (God assisting) be declared, when I treat of the state of the first churches, and the ways of their degeneracy. Let them, or any for them, in the meantime, evince the jurisdiction they exercised, in respect whereunto our subjection in the first kind was required, to derive its original from the pure institution of Christ in the gospel,

or to be any such thing as it was, in an imagined separation from the human laws whereby it was animated, and more will be asserted than I have had the happiness as yet to see. Now, I say that the subjection to them due on this account we did not cast off; but their whole authority, power, and jurisdiction was removed, taken away, and annulled, by the people of the land assembled in parliament.

"But this," they reply, "is the state of the business in hand: The parliament, as much as in them lay, did so, indeed, as is confessed, and by so doing made the schism; which you by adhering to them, and joining with them in your several places, have made yourselves also guilty of."

But do these men know what they say, or will it ever trouble the conscience of a man in his right wits to be charged with schism on this account? The parliament made alteration of nothing but what they found established by the laws of this nation; pleading that they had power committed to them to alter, abrogate, and annul laws, for the good of the people of the land. If their making alterations in the civil laws and constitutions, in the political administrations of the nation, be schism, we have very little security but that we may be made new schismatics every third year, whilst the constitution of a triennial parliament doth continue. In the removal, then, of all episcopal jurisdiction, founded on the laws and usages of this nation, we are not at all concerned; for the laws enforcing it do not press it as a thing necessary on any other account, but as that which themselves gave rise and life unto. But should this be granted, that the office was appointed by Christ, and the jurisdiction impleaded annexed by him thereunto; yet this, whilst we abide at diocesans, with the several divisions apportioned to them in the nation, will not suffice to constitute a national church, unless some union of those diocesans, or of the churches whereunto they related, into one society and church, by the same appointment, be proved; which, to my present apprehension, will be no easy work for any one to undertake.

2. "Bishops had here a power, as ministers of the gospel, to preach, administer the sacraments, to join in the ordination of ministers, and the like duties of church-officers." To this we say, Let the individuals of them acquit themselves, by the qualifications mentioned in the epistles to Timothy and Titus, with a sedulous exercise of their duty in a due manner, according to

the mind of Christ, to be such indeed, and we will still pay them all the respect, reverence, duty, and obedience, which as such, by virtue of any law or institution of Christ, they can claim. Let them come forth with weapons that are not carnal, evidencing their ministry to the consciences of believers, acting in a spirit and power received from Christ, and who are they that will harm them?

I had once formerly said thus much: "Let the bishops attend the particular flocks over which they are appointed, preaching the word, administering the holy ordinances of the gospel in and to their own flock, there will not be contending about them." It was thought meet to return, by one concerned: "I shall willingly grant herein my suffrage, let them discharge them (and I beseech all who have any way hindered them at length to let and quietly permit them), on condition he will do this as carefully as I. I shall not contend with him concerning the nature of their task. Be it, as he saith, 'the attending to the particular churches over which they are appointed' (the bishop of Oxford over that flock or portion to which he was and is appointed, and so all others in like manner); be it their 'preaching and their administering the holy ordinances of the gospel in and to their own flock,' and whatever else of duty and 'ratione officii' belongs to a rightly-constituted bishop; and let all that have disturbed this course, so duly settled in this church, and in all churches of Christ since the apostles' planting them, discern their error, and return to that peace and unity of the church from whence they have causelessly and inexcusably departed."

Though I was not then speaking of the bishops of England, yet I am contented with the application to them, there being amongst them men of piety and learning, whom I exceedingly honour and reverence. Amongst all the bishops, he of Oxford is, I suppose, peculiarly instanced in, because it may be thought that, living in this place, I may belong to his jurisdiction. But in the condition wherein I now am, by the providence of God, I can plead an exemption on the same foot of account as he can his jurisdiction; so that I am not much concerned in his exercise of it as to my own person. If he have a particular flock at Oxon, which he will attend according to what before I required, he shall have no let or hinderance from me; but seeing he is, as I hear he is, a reverend and learned person, I shall be glad of his neighborhood and acquaintance. But to suppose that the diocese of Oxon, as legally constituted and bounded, is his particular flock or church; that such a church was instituted by Christ, or hath been in being ever since the apostles' times; that, in his presidency in this church, he is to set up courts and exercise a jurisdiction in them, and therewith a power over all the inhabitants of this diocese or shire (excepting the exempt peculiar jurisdiction), although gathered into particular congregations, and united by a participation of the same ordinances; and all this by the will and appointment of Jesus Christ, — is to suppose what will not be granted. I confess, as before, there was once such an order in this place, and that it is now removed by laws, on which foundation alone it stood before; and this is that wherein I am not concerned. Whether we have causelessly and inexcusably departed from the unity of the church is the matter now in inquiry. I am sure, unless the unity can be fixed, our departure will not be proved. A *law* unity I confess; an *evangelical* I am yet in the disquisition of. But I confess it will be to the prejudice of the cause in hand, if it shall be thought that the determination of it depends on the controversy about episcopacy; for if so, it might be righteously expected that the arguments produced in the behalf and defence thereof should be particularly discussed. But the truth is, I shall easily acknowledge all my labour to no purpose, if I have to deal only with men who suppose that if it be granted that bishops, as commonly esteemed in this nation, are of the appointment of Christ, it will thence follow that we have a national church of Christ's appointment; between which, indeed, there is no relation or connection. Should I grant, as I said, diocesan bishops, with churches answerable to their supportment, particled into several congregations, with their inferior officers, yet this would be remote enough from giving subsistence and union to a national church.

What, then, it is which is called the church of England, in respect whereto we are charged with schism, is nextly to be considered.

Now, there are two ways whereby we may come to the discovery of what is intended by the church of England, or there are two ways whereby such a thing doth arise:—

1. "Descendendo;" which is the way of the Prelates.

2. "Ascendendo;" which is the way of the Presbyterians.

For the first, to constitute a national church by *descent*, it must be supposed that all church power is vested in national officers, namely, archbishops, and from them derived to several diocesans by a distribution of power, limited in its exercise, to a certain portion of the nation, and by them communicated by several engines to parochial priests in their several places. A man with half an eye may see that here are many things to be proved.

Thus, their first church is national, which is distributed into several greater portions, termed provinces; those again into others, now called *dioceses*; and those again subdivided into *parochial or particular congregations*. Now, the union of this church consisteth in the due observance of the same worship specifically by all the members of it, and subjection, according to rules of their own appointment (which were called commonly *canons*, by way of distinction), unto the rulers before mentioned, in their several capacities. And this is that which is the peculiar form of this church. That of the *church catholic, absolutely so called*, is its unity with Christ and in itself, by the one Spirit whereby it is animated; that of the *church catholic visibly professing*, the unity of the faith which they do profess, as being by them professed; that of a *particular church*, as such, its observance and performance of the same ordinances of worship numerically, in the confession of the same faith, and subjection to the same rules of love for edification of the whole. Of this *national* [church], as it is called, the unity consists in the subjection of one sort of officers unto another, within a precinct limited, originally, wholly on an account foreign to any church-state whatever. So that it is not called the church of England from its participation of the nature of the catholic church, on the account of its most noble members; nor yet from its participation of the nature of the visible church in the world, on the account of its profession of the truth, — in both which respects we profess our unity with it; nor yet from its participation of the nature of a particular church, which it did not in itself, nor as such, but in some of its particular congregations; but from a peculiar form of its own, as above described, which is to be proved to be of the institution of Jesus Christ.

In this description given of their church-state with whom we have now to do, I have purposely avoided the mention of things odious and exposed to common obloquy, which yet were the very ties and ligaments of their order, because the thing, as it is in itself, being nakedly represented, we may not be prejudiced in judging of the strength and utmost of the charge that lies against any of us on the account of a departure from it.

The communion of this church, they say, we have forsaken, and broken its unity; and therefore are schismatics.

I answer in a word: Laying aside so much of the jurisdiction of it [as was] mentioned before, and the several ways of its administration for which there is no colour or pretence that it should relate to any gospel institution; passing by, also, the consideration of all those things which the men enjoying authority in, or exercising the pretended power of, this church, did use all their authority and power to enjoin and establish, which we judge evil; — let them prove that such a national church as would remain with these things pared off, that is in its best estate imaginable, was ever instituted by Christ, or the apostles in his name, in all the things of absolute necessity to its being and existence, and I will confess myself to be what they please to say of me.

That there was such an order in things relating to the worship of God established by the law of the land, in and over the people thereof; that the worship pleaded for was confirmed by the same law; that the rulers mentioned had power, being by the magistrates assembled, to make rules and canons to become binding to the good people of the commonwealth, when confirmed by the supreme authority of the nation, and not else; that penalties were appointed to the disturbers of this order by the same law, — I grant: but that any thing of all this, as such, — that is, as a part of this whole, or the whole itself, — was instituted by the will and appointment of Jesus Christ, *that* is denied. Let not any one think that because we deny the constitution pleaded about to have had the stamp of the authority of Jesus Christ, that therefore we pulled it down and destroyed it by violence. It was set up before we were born, by them who had power to make laws to bind the people of this nation, and we found men in an orderly legal possession of that power, which, exerting itself several ways, maintained and preserved that constitution, which we had no call to eradicate. Only, whereas they took upon them to act in the name of Christ also, and to interpose their orders and authority in the things of the worship of God, we entreated them that we might pass our pilgrimage quietly in our native country (as Israel would have gone through the land of Edom, without the disturbance of its inhabitants), and worship God according to the light which he had graciously imparted to us; but they would not hearken. But herein also was it our duty to keep the word of Christ's patience. Their removal and the dissolution, of this national church arose, and was carried on, as hath been declared, by other hands, on other accounts.

Now, it is not to any purpose to plead the authority of the church for many of the institutions mentioned; for neither hath any church power, or can have, to institute and appoint the things whereby it is made to be so, — as these things are the very form of the church that we plead about, — nor hath any church any authority but what is answerable to its nature. If itself be of a civil prudential constitution, its authority also is civil, and no more. Denying their church, in that form of it which makes it such, to be of the institution of Christ, it cannot be expected that we should grant that it is, as such, invested with any authority from Christ; so that the dissolution of the unity of this church, as it had its rise on such an account, proceeded from an alteration of the human constitution whereon it was built; and how that was done was before declared. Then let them prove, —

1. That *ordinary officers are before the church,* and *that* in "ecclesia instituta," as well as "instituenda;" which must be the foundation of their work. (We confess extraordinary officers were before the church, nor, considering the way of men's coming to be joined in such societies, was it possible it should be otherwise; but as for ordinary officers, they were an exurgency from a church, and serve to the completion of it, Acts xiv. 23; Tit. i. 5.)

2. That Christ hath appointed any *national officers,* with a plenitude of ordinary power, to be imparted, communicated, and distributed to other recipient subjects, in several degrees, within one nation, and not elsewhere; I mean, such an officer or officers who, in the first instance of their power, should, on their own single account, relate unto a whole nation.

3. That he hath instituted any *national church* as the proper correlatum of such an officer. Concerning which, also, I desire to be informed, whether a catalogue of those he hath so instituted be to be obtained, or their number be left indefinite? whether they have limits and bounds prescribed to them by him, or are left to be commensurate to the civil dominion of any potentate, and so to enjoy or suffer the providential enlargements or straits

that such dominions are continually subject unto? whether we had seven churches here in England during the heptarchy of the Saxons, and one in Wales, or but one in the whole? if seven, how came they to be one? if but one, why those of England, Scotland, and Ireland were not one also, especially since they have been under one civil magistrate? or whether the difference of the civil laws of these nations be not the only cause that there are three churches? and if so, whether from thence any man may not discern whereon the unity of the church of England doth depend?

Briefly; when they have proved metropolitan, diocesan bishops in a firstness of power by the institution of Christ; a national church by the same institution, in the sense pleaded for; a firstness of power in the national officers of that national church to impose a form of worship upon all being within that nation, by the same institution, which should contain the bond of the union of that church; also, that every man who is born, and in his infancy baptized, in that nation, is a member of that national church, by the same institution; and shall have distinguished clearly in and about their administrations, and have told us what they counted to be of ecclesiastical power, and what they grant to be a mere emanation of the civil government of the nation, — we will then treat with them about the business of schism. Until then, if they tell us that we have forsaken the church of England in the sense pleaded for by them, I must answer, "That which is wanting cannot be numbered." It is no crime to depart from nothing. We have not left to be that which we never were. Which may suffice both us and them as to our several respective concernments of conscience and power. It hath been from the darkness of men, and ignorance of the Scriptures, that some have taken advantage to set up a product of the prudence of nations in the name of Jesus Christ; and on that account to require the acceptance of it. When the tabernacle of God is again well fixed amongst men, these shadows will flee away. In the meantime, we owe all these disputes, with innumerable other evils, to the apostasy of the Roman combination; from which we are far, as yet, from being clearly delivered.

I have one thing more to add upon the whole matter, and I shall proceed to what is lastly to be considered.

The church of England, as it is called (that is, the people thereof), separated herself from the church of Rome. To free herself from the imputation of schism in so doing, as she (that is, the learned men of the nation) pleaded the errors and corruptions of that church, under this especial consideration of their being imposed by tyrants; so also by professing her design to do nothing but to reduce religion and the worship of God to its original purity, from which it was fallen. And we all jointly justify both her and all other reformed churches in this plea.

In her design to reduce religion to its primitive purity, she always professed that she did not take her direction from the Scripture only, but also from the councils and examples of the first four or five centuries; to which she laboured to conform her reformation. Let the question now be, Whether there be not corruptions in this church of England, supposing such a national church-state to be instituted? what, I beseech you, shall bind my conscience to acquiesce in what is pleaded from the first four or five centuries, consisting of men that could and did err, more than that did hers which was pleaded from the nine or ten centuries following? Have not I liberty to call for reformation according to the Scripture only? or at least to profess that my conscience cannot be bound to any other? The sum is, — The business of schism from the church of England is a thing built purely and simply on political considerations, so interwoven with them, so influenced from them, as not to be separated. The famous advice of Mæcenas to Augustus, mentioned in Dio Cassius, is the best authority I know against it.

Before we part with this consideration, I must needs prevent one mistake, which perhaps, in the mind of some, may arise upon the preceding discourse; for whereas sundry ordinances of the worship of God are rightly to be administered only in a church, and ministers do evidently relate thereunto, the denying of a national church-state seems to deny that we had either ministers or ordinances here in England. The truth is, it seems so to do, but it doth not; unless you will say, that unless there be a national church-state there is no other, which is too absurd for any one to imagine. It follows, indeed, that there were no national church-officers, that there were no ordinances numerically the same, to be administered in and to the nation at once; but that there was not another church-state in England, and on the account thereof ordinances truly administered by lawful ministers, doth not follow. And now, if by this discourse I only call this business to a review by them who are concerned to assert this national church, I am satisfied. That the church of England is a true church of Christ, they have hitherto maintained against the Romanists, on the account of the doctrine taught in it, and the successive ordination of its officers, through the church of Rome itself, from the primitive times. About the constitution and nature of a national church they have had with them no contention; therein the parties at variance were agreed. The same grounds and principles, improved with a defence of the external worship and ceremonies established on the authority of the church, they managed against the Nonconformists and Separatists at home. But their chief strength against them lay in arguments more forcible, which need not be repeated. The constitution of the church now impleaded deserves, as I said, the review; hitherto it hath been unfurnished of any considerable defensative.

Secondly, There is another way of constituting a national church, which is insisted on by some of our brethren of the presbyterian way. This is, that such a thing should arise from the particular congregations that are in the nation, united by sundry associations and subordinations of assemblies in and by the representatives of those churches; so that though there cannot be an assembly of all the members of those churches in one place for the performance of any worship of God, nor is there any ordinance appointed by Christ to be so celebrated in any assembly of them (which we suppose necessary to the constitution of a particular church), yet there may be an assembly of the representatives of them all, by several elevations, for some end and purpose.

"In this sense," say some, "a church may be called *national*, when all the particular congregations of one nation, living under one civil government, agreeing in doctrine and worship, are governed by their greater and lesser assemblies" (Jus Divinum Minist. Anglic., p. 12). But I would be loath to exclude every man from being a member of the church in England, — that is, from a share in the profession of the faith which is owned and professed by the people of God in England, — who is not a member of a particular congregation. Nor does subjection to one civil government, and agreement in the same doctrine and worship specifically, either jointly or severally, constitute one church, as is known even in the judgment of these brethren. It is the last expression, of "greater and lesser assemblies," that must do it. But as to any such institution of Christ, as a standing ordinance, sufficient to give unity, yea, or denomination to a church, this is the τὸ κρινόμενον. And yet this alone is to be insisted on; for, as was showed before, the other things mentioned contribute nothing to the form nor union of such a church.

It is pleaded that there are prophecies and promises of a national church that should be under the New Testament: as Ps. lxxii. 10–12; Isa. xlix. 23, lx. 10, 16. That it is foretold and promised that many, whole nations, shall be converted to the faith of the gospel, and thereby become the people of God, who before were no people, is granted; but that their way of worship shall be by national churches, governed by lesser and greater assemblies, doth not appear. And when the Jews shall be converted, they shall be a national church as England is; but their way of worship shall be regulated according to the institution of Christ in the gospel. And therefore the publishers of the Life of Dr Gouge have expressed his judgment, found in a paper in his study, that the Jews on their calling shall be gathered together into churches, and not be scattered, as now they are. A nation may be said to be converted, from the professed subjection to the gospel of so many in it as may give demonstration to the whole; but the way of worship for those so converted is peculiarly instituted. It is said, moreover, that [as] the several congregations in one city are called a "church," as in Jerusalem, Acts viii. 1, xii. 1, 5, xv. 4, 22, so also may all the churches in a nation be called a "national church." But this is τὸ ἐν ἀρχῇ· nor is that allowed to be made a medium in another case, which at the same time is "sub judice" in its own. The like, also, may be said of the church of Ephesus, Acts xx. 17; Rev. ii. 1. Nor is it about a mere denomination that we contend, but the union and form of such a church; and if more churches than one were together called a church, it is from their participation of the nature of the general visible church, not of that which is particular, and the seat of ordinances. So where Paul is said to "persecute the church of God," Gal. i. 13, it is spoken of the professors of the faith of Christ in general, and not to be restrained to the churches of Judea, of whom he speaks, verses 22, 23, seeing his rage actually reached to Damascus, a city of another nation, Acts xxii. 5, 6, and his design was πρὸς τὸ γένος. That by the "church," mentioned 1 Cor. xii. 28, x. 32, Eph. iii. 21, is intended the whole visible church of Christ, as made up into one body or church, by a collection of all particular churches in the world by lesser and greater assemblies (a thing that never was in the world, nor ever will be), is denied, and not yet, by any that I know, proved. Not that I am offended at the name of the "church of England;" though I think all professors, as such, are rather to be called so than all the congregations. That all professors of the truth of the gospel, throughout the world, are the visible church of Christ, in the sense before explained, is granted. So may, on the same account, all the professors of that truth in England be called the church of England. But it is the institution of lesser and greater assemblies, comprising the representatives of all the churches in the world, that must give being and union to the visible church in the sense pleaded for, throughout the world, or in this nation, and that bound to this relation by virtue of the same institution that is to be proved.

But of what there is, or seems to be, of divine institution in this order and fabric, what of human prudent creation, what in the matter or manner of it I cannot assent unto, I shall not at present enter into the consideration; but shall only, as to my purpose in hand, take up some principles which lie in common between the men of this persuasion and myself, with some others otherwise minded. Now, of these are the ensuing assertions:—

1. No man can possibly be a member of a national church in this sense, but by virtue of his being a member of some particular church in the nation, which concurs to the making up of the national church; as a man doth not *legally* belong to any county in the nation, unless he belong to some hundred or parish in that county. This is evident from the nature of the thing itself. Nor is it pleaded that we are one national church, because the people of the nation are generally baptized and do profess the true faith; but because the particular congregations in it are ruled, and so consequently the whole, by lesser and greater assemblies. I suppose it will not be, on second thoughts, insisted on that particular congregations, agreeing solemnly in doctrine and worship, under one civil government, do constitute a national church; for if so, its form and unity as such must be given it merely by the civil government.

2. No man can recede from this church, or depart from it, but by departing from some particular church therein. At the same door that a man comes in, he must go out. If I cease to be a member of a national church, it is by the ceasing or abolishing

of that which gave me original right thereunto; which was my relation to the particular church whereof I am.

3. To make men members of any particular church or churches, their own *consent* is required. All men must admit of this who allow it is free for a man to choose where he will fix his habitation.

4. That as yet, at least since possibly we could be personally concerned who are now alive, no such church in this nation hath been formed. It is impossible that a man should be guilty of offending against that which is not. We have not separated from a national church in the presbyterian sense, as never having seen any such thing, unless they will say we have separated from what should be.

5. As to the state of such a church as this, I shall only add to what hath been spoken before the judgment of a very learned and famous man in this case, whom I the rather name, because professedly engaged on the Presbyterians' side. It is Moses Amyraldus, the present professor of divinity at Saumur; whose words are these that follow: — "Scio nonnunquam appellari particularem ecclesiam communionem, ac veluti confœderationem plurium ejusmodi societatum, quas vel ejusdem linguæ usus, vel eadem reipublicæ forma" (the true spring of a national church), "una cum ejusdem disciplinæ regimine consociavit. Sic appellatur ecclesia Gallicana, Anglicana Germanica particularis, ut distinguatur ab universali illa Christianorum societate; quæ omnes Christiani nominis nationes complectitur. At uti supradiximus, ecclesiæ nomen non proprie convenire societati omnium Christianorum, eo modo quo convenit particularibus Christianorum cœtibus; sic consequens est, ut dicamus, eeclesiæ nomen non competere in eam multarum ecclesiarum particularium consociationem eodem plane modo. Vocetur ergo certe ecclesiarum quæ sunt in Gallia communio inter ipsas, et ecclesia, si ecclesia est multarum ecclesiarum confœderatio, non si nomen ecelesiæ ex usu Scripturæ sacræ accipiatur. Paulus enim varias ecclesias particulares quæ erant in Achaia, ecclesias Achaiæ nuncupat, non ecclesiam Achaiæ vel ecclesiam Achaicam," Amyral. Disput. de Ecclesiæ Nom. et Defin. Thes. 28.

These being, if I mistake not, things of mutual acknowledgment (for I have not laid down any principles peculiar to myself and those with whom I consent in the way of the worship of God, which yet we can justly plead in our own defence), this whole business will be brought to a speedy issue. Only, I desire the reader to observe that I am not pleading the right, liberty, and duty of gathering churches in such a state of professors as that of late, and still amongst us, — which is built on other principles and hypotheses than any as yet I have had occasion to mention, — but am only, in general, considering the true notion of schism, and the charge managed against us on that single account, which relates not to gathering of churches, as simply considered. I say, then, —

First, either we have been members by our own *voluntary consent*, according to the mind of Christ, of some particular congregations in such a national church, and that as "de facto" part of such a church, or we have not. If we have not been so (as it is most certain we have not), then we have not as yet broken any bond, or violated any unity, or disturbed any peace or order, of the appointment of Jesus Christ; so that whatever of trouble or division hath followed on our way and walking is to be charged on them who have turned every stone to hinder us [in] our liberty. And I humbly beg of them who, acting on principles of reformation according to the (commonly called) presbyterian platform, do accuse us for separation from the church of England, that they would seriously consider what they intend thereby. Is it that we are departed from the faith of the people of God in England? They will not sustain any such crimination. Is it that we have forsaken the church of England as under its episcopal constitution? Have they not done the same? Have they not rejected their national officers, with all the bonds, ties, and ligaments of the union of that pretended church? Have they not renounced the way of worship established by the law of the land? Do they not disavow all obedience to them who were their legal superiors in that constitution? Do they retain either matter or form, or any thing but the naked name of that church? And will they condemn others in what they practice themselves? As for a church of England in their new sense (which yet in some respects is not new, but old), for what is beyond a voluntary consociation of particular churches, we have not as yet had experience of it.

That we shall be accused of schism for not esteeming ourselves made members of a particular church, against our wills, by buying or hiring a habitation within such a precinct of ground, we expect not, especially considering what is delivered by the chief leaders of them with whom now we are treating, whose words are as followeth:— "We grant that living in parishes is not sufficient to make a man a member of a particular church. A Turk, or pagan, or idolater, may live within the precincts of a parish, and yet be no member of a church. A man must, therefore, in order of nature, be a member of the church visible, and then, living in a parish and making profession of Christianity, may claim admission into the society of Christians within those bounds, and enjoy the privileges and ordinances which are there dispensed," Ans. of Commit., p. 105. This is also pursued by the authors of Jus Divinum Ministerii Anglicani, pp. 9, 10, where, after the repetition of the words first mentioned, they add, that "all that dwell in a parish, and constantly hear the word, are not yet to be admitted to the sacraments;" which excludes them from being "fideles," or church-members, and makes them at best as the catechumeni of old, who were never esteemed members of the church.

If we have been so members by our own voluntary consent, and do not continue so to be, then this congregation wherein we are so members was reformed according to the mind of Christ (for I speak now to them that own reformation, as to their light) or it was not. If it were reformed, and a man were a member of it so reformed by his own voluntary consent, I confess it may be difficult to see how a man can leave such a congregation without their consent in whose power it is to give it him, without giving offence to the church of God. Only, I say, let all by respects be laid aside on the one hand, and on the other all regard to repute and advantage, let love have its perfect work, and no church, knowing the end of its being and constitution to be the edification of believers, will be difficult and tenacious as to the granting a dismission to any member whatever that shall humbly desire it, on the account of applying himself to some other congregation, wherein he supposes and is persuaded that he may be more effectually built up in his most holy faith.

I confess this to be a case of the greatest difficulty that presents itself to my thoughts, in this business: Suppose a man to be a member of a particular church, and that church to be a true church of Christ, and granted so by this person, and yet, upon the account of some defect which is in, or at least he is convinced and persuaded to be in, that church, whose reformation he cannot obtain, he cannot abide in that church to his spiritual advantage and edification; suppose the church, on the other side, cannot be induced to consent to his secession and relinquishment of its ordinary external communion, and that that person is hereby entangled; — what course is to be taken? I profess, for my part, I never knew this case fall out wherein both parties were not blamable; — the person seeking to depart, in making that to be an indispensable cause of departure from a church which is far short of it; and the church, in not condescending to the man's desire, though proceeding from infirmity or temptation. In general, the rule of forbearance and condescension in love, which should salve the difference, is to give place to the rule of obeying God in all things according to our light. And the determining in this case depending on circumstances in great variety, both with reference to the church offending and the person offended, he that can give one certain rule in and upon the whole shall have much praise for his invention. However, I am sure this cannot be rationally objected by them who, esteeming all parishes, as such, to be churches, do yet allow men on such occasions to change their habitations, and consequently their church relations. "Men may be relieved by change of dwelling," Subcom. of Div., p. 52. And when a man's leaving the ordinary external communion of any particular church for his own edification, to join with another whose administration he is persuaded, in some things more or fewer, is carried on more according to the mind of Christ, is, as such, proved to be schism, I shall acknowledge it.

As, then, the not giving a man's self up unto any way, and submitting to any establishment, pretended or pleaded to be of Christ, which he hath not light for, and which he was not by any act of his own formerly engaged in, cannot, with any colour or pretence of reason, be reckoned unto him for schism, though he may, if he persist in his refusal, prejudice his own edification; so no more can a man's peaceable relinquishment of the ordinary communion of one church, in all its relations, to join with another, be so esteemed.

For instance of the first case: Suppose, by the law of this nation, the several parochial churches of the land, according to arbitrary distributions made of them, should be joined in classical associations; and those again, in the like arbitrary disposal, into provincial; and so onward (which cannot be done without such interveniences as will exonerate conscience from the weight of pure institution); — or suppose this not to be done by the law of the land, but by the voluntary consent of the officers of the parochial churches, and others joining with them: the saints of God in this nation who have not formerly been given up unto or disposed of in this order by their own voluntary consent; nor are concerned in it any farther than by their habitation being within some of these different precincts that, by public authority or consent of some amongst them, are combined as above; nor do believe such associations to be the institutions of Christ, whatever they prove to be in the issue, — I say, they are, by their dissent and refusal to subject themselves to this order, not in the least liable to the charge of schism, whatever they are who, neglecting the great duty of love and forbearance, would by any means whatever impose upon them a necessity of so doing; for, besides what they have to plead as to the non-institution of any such ordinary associations, and investiture of them with power and authority in and over the churches, they are not guilty of the disturbance of any order wherein they were stated according to the mind of Christ, nor of the neglect of any duty of love that was incumbent on them.

For the latter: Suppose a man stated in a particular church, wherewith he hath walked for a season; he discovers that some, perhaps, of the principles of its constitution are not according to the mind of Christ, something is wanting or redundant, and imposed in practice on the members of it, which renders the communion of it, by reason of his doubts and scruples, or, it may be, clear convictions, not so useful to him as he might rationally expect it would be, were all things done according to the mind of Christ; that also he hath declared his judgment as he is able, and dissatisfaction; — if no reformation do ensue, this person, I say, is doubtless at liberty to dispose of himself, as to particular church-communion, to his own best advantage.

But now suppose this congregation, whereof a man is supposed to be a member, is not reformed, will not nor cannot reform itself (I desire that it may be minded with whom I have to do, — namely, those who own a necessity of reformation as to the administration of ordinances, in respect to what hath been hitherto observed in most parochial assemblies. Those I have formerly dealt withal are not to be imposed on with this principle of reformation; they acknowledge none to be needful. But they are not concerned in our present inquiry. Their charge lies all in the behalf of the church of England, not of particular assemblies or parishes; which it is not possible that, according to their principle, they should own for churches, or account any separation from any of them to be blameworthy, but only as it respecteth the constitutions of the church national in them to be observed. If any claim arise on that hand as to parochial assemblies, I should take liberty to examine the foundation of the plea, and doubt not but that I may easily frustrate their attempts. But this is not my present business. I deal, as I said, with them who own reformation; and I now suppose the congregation, whereof a man is supposed to be a member on any account whatever, not to be reformed); — In this case, I ask whether it be schism or no for any number of men to reform themselves, by reducing the practice of worship to its original institution, though they be the minor part lying within the parochial precincts, or for any of them to join themselves with others for that end and purpose not living within those precincts? I shall boldly say this schism is commanded by the Holy Ghost, 1 Tim. vi. 5; 2 Tim. iii. 5; Hos. iv. 15. Is this yoke laid upon me by Christ, that, to go along with the multitude where I live, that hate to be reformed, I must forsake my duty and despise the privileges that he hath purchased for me with his own precious blood? Is this a unity of Christ's institution, that I must for ever associate myself with wicked and profane men in the worship of God, to the unspeakable detriment and disadvantage of my own soul?

I suppose nothing can be more *unreasonable* than once to imagine any such thing.

However, not to drive this business any farther, but to put it to its proper issue: When it is proved that this is the will and appointment of Jesus Christ, that every believer who liveth within such a precinct allotted by civil constitutions, wherein the people or inhabitants do, or may usually, meet for the celebration of the worship of God, or which they have light for, or on any account whatever do make profession of, how profane soever that part of them be from whom the whole is denominated, how corrupt soever in their worship, how dead soever as to the power of godliness, must abide with them and join with them in their administrations and worship, and that indispensably, this business may come again under debate. In the meantime, I suppose the people of God are not in any such subjection. I speak not this as laying down this for a principle, that it is the duty of every man to separate from that church wherein evil and wicked men are tolerated (though that opinion must have many other attendancies before it can contract the least affinity with that of the same sound, which was condemned in the Donatists); but this only I say, that where any church is overborne by a multitude of men wicked and profane, so that it cannot reform itself, or will not, according to the mind of Christ, a believer is so far at liberty that he may desert the communion of that society without the least guilt of schism. But this state of things is now little pleaded for.

It is usually objected about the church of Corinth, that there was in it many disorders and enormous miscarriages, divisions, and breaches of love; miscarriages through drink at their meetings, gross sins, the incestuous person tolerated, false doctrine broached, the resurrection denied; — and yet Paul advises no man to separate from it, but all to perform their duty in it.

But how little our present plea and defensative is concerned in this instance, supposed to lie against it, very few considerations will evince: —

First, the church of Corinth was undoubtedly *a true church*, lately instituted according to the mind of Christ, and was not fallen from that privilege by any miscarriage, nor had suffered any thing destructive to its being; which wholly differences between the case proposed, in respect of many particulars, and the instance produced. We confess the abuses and evils mentioned had crept into the church; and do thence grant that many abuses may do so into any of the best of the churches of God. Nor did it ever enter into the heart of any man to think that so soon as any disorders fall out or abuses creep into it, it is instantly the duty of any to fly out of it, like Paul's mariners out of the ship when the storm grew hazardous; it being the duty of all the members of such a church, untainted with the evils and corruptions of it, upon many accounts, to attempt and labour the remedy of those disorders, and rejection of those abuses to the uttermost; which was that which Paul advised the Corinthians all and some[12] unto; in obedience whereunto they were recovered. But yet this I say, had the church of Corinth continued in the condition before described, — that notorious, scandalous sins had gone unpunished, unreproved, drunkenness continued and practised in the assemblies, men abiding by the denial

---

12 All and some, a corruption of an Anglo-Saxon phrase, meaning all together, one and all. — Ed.

of the resurrection, so overturning the whole gospel, and the church refusing to do her duty, and exercise her authority to cast all those disorderly persons, upon their obstinacy, out of her communion, — it had been the duty of every saint of God in that church to have withdrawn from it, to come out from among them, and not to have been partaker of their sins, unless they were willing to partake of their plague also, which on such an apostasy would certainly ensue.

I confess Austin, in his single book against the Donatists, Post Collationem, cap. xx., affirms that Elijah and Elisha communicated with the Israelites in their worship, when they were so corrupted as in their days, and separated not from their sacraments (as he calls them), but only withdrew sometimes for fear of persecution; — a mistake unworthy so great and wise a person as he was. The public worship of those ten tribes, in the days of those prophets, was idolatrous, erected by Jeroboam, confirmed by a law by Omri, and continued by Ahab. That the prophets joined with them in it is not to be imagined. But earnestness of desire for the attaining of any end sometimes leaves no room for the examination of the mediums, offering their service to that purpose.

Let us now see the sum of the whole matter, and what it is that we plead for our discharge as to this crime of schism, allowing the term to pass in its large and usual acceptation, receding, for the sake of the truth's farther ventilation, from the precise propriety of the word annexed to it in the Scripture. The sum is, We have broken no bond of unity, no order instituted or appointed by Jesus Christ, — have causelessly deserted no station that ever we were in, according to his mind; which alone can give countenance to an accusation of this nature. That on pure grounds of conscience we have withdrawn, or do withhold ourselves from partaking in some ways, engaged into upon mere grounds of prudence, we acknowledge.

And thus, from what hath been said, it appears in what a fair capacity, notwithstanding any principle or practice owned by us, we are in to live peaceably, and to exercise all fruits of love towards those who are otherwise minded.

There is not the least necessity on us, may we be permitted to serve God according to our light, for the acquitting ourselves from the charge which hath made such a noise in the world, to charge other men with their failings, great or small, in or about the ways and worship of God. This only is incumbent on us, that we manifest that we have broken no bond, no obligation or tie to communion, which lay upon us by the will and appointment of Jesus Christ, our Lord and Master. What is prudentially to be done in such a nation as this, in such a time as this, as to the worship of God, we will treat with men at farther leisure, and when we are lawfully called thereto.

It may be some will yet say (because it hath been often said), "There is a difference between reforming of churches already gathered and raised, and raising of churches out of mere materials. The first may be allowed, but the latter tends to all manner of confusion."

I have at present not much to say to this objection, because, as I conceive, it concerns not the business we have in hand; nor would I have mentioned it at all, but that it is insisted on by some on every turn, whether suited for the particular cause for which it is produced or no. In brief, then, —

1. I know no other *reformation* of any church, or any thing in a church, but the reducing of it to its primitive institution, and the order allotted to it by Jesus Christ. If any plead for any other reformation of churches, they are, in my judgment, to blame.

And when any society or combination of men (whatever hitherto it hath been esteemed) is not capable of such a reduction and renovation, I suppose I shall not provoke any wise and sober person if I profess I cannot look on such a society as a church of Christ, and thereupon advise those therein who have a due right to the privileges purchased for them by Christ, as to gospel administrations, to take some other peaceable course to make themselves partakers of them.

2. Were I fully to handle the things pointed to in this objection, I must manage principles which, in this discourse, I have not been occasioned to draw forth at all or to improve. Many things of great weight and importance must come under debate and consideration before a clear account can be given of the case stated in this objection; as, —

(1.) The *true* nature of an instituted church under the gospel, as to the matter, form, and all other necessary constitutive causes, is to be investigated and found out.

(2.) The nature and form of such a church is to be *exemplified from the Scripture* and the stories of the first churches, before sensibly infected with the poison of that apostasy which ensued.

(3.) The *extent of the apostasy* under Antichrist, as to the ruining of instituted churches, making them to be Babylon, and their worship fornication, is duly and carefully to be examined. "Hic labor, hoc opus."

Here lie our disorder and division; hence is our darkness and pollution of our garments, which is not an easy thing to free ourselves of: though we may arise, yet we shall not speedily shake ourselves out of the dust.

(4.) By what way and means God begat anew and kept alive his elect in their several generations, when antichristian darkness covered the earth and thick darkness the nations, supposing an intercision of instituted ordinances, so far as to make a nullity in them as to what was of simple and pure institution; what way might be used for the fixing the tabernacle of God again with men, and the setting up of church-worship according to his mind and will. And here the famous case of the United Brethren of Bohemia would come under consideration; who, concluding the whole Papacy to be purely antichristian, could not allow of the ordination of their ministers by any in communion with it, and yet, being persuaded of a necessity of continuing that ordinance in a way of succession, sent some to the Greek and Armenian churches; who, observing their ways, returned with little satisfaction; so that at last, committing themselves and their cause to God, they chose them elders from among themselves, and set them apart by fasting and prayer: which was the foundation of all those churches, which, for piety, zeal, and suffering for Christ, have given place to none in Europe.

(5.) What was the *way of the first Reformation* in this nation, and what *principles* the godly learned men of those days proceeded on; how far what they did may be satisfactory to our consciences at the present, as to our concurrence in them, who from thence have the truth of the gospel derived down to us; whether ordinary officers be before or after the church, and so whether a church-state is preserved in the preservation of officers, by a power foreign to that church whereof they are so, or the office he preserved, and consequently the officers inclusively, in the preservation and constitution of a church; — these, I say, with sundry other things of the like importance, with inferences from them, are to be considered to the bottom before a full resolution can be given to the inquiry couched in this objection, which, as I said, to do is not my present business.

This task, then, is at its issue and close. Some considerations of the manifold miscarriages that have ensued for want of a due and right apprehension of the thing we have now been exercised in the consideration of shall shut it up:—

1. It is not impossible that some may, from what hath been spoken, begin to apprehend that they have been too hasty in judging other men. Indeed, none are more ready to charge highly than those who, when they have so done, are most unable to make good their charge. "Si accusâsse sufficiat, quis erit innocens?" What real schisms in a moral sense have ensued among brethren, by their causeless mutual imputation of schism in things of institution, is known. And when men are in one fault, and are charged with another wherein they are not, it is a ready way to confirm them in that wherein they are. There is more darkness and difficulty in the whole matter of instituted worship than some men are aware of; not that it was so from the beginning, whilst Christianity continued in its naked simplicity, but it is come occasionally upon us by the customs, darkness, and invincible prejudices that have taken hold on the minds of men by a secret diffusion of the poison of that grand apostasy. It were well, then, that men would not be so confident, nor easily persuaded that they presently know how all things ought to be, because they know how they would have some things to be, which suit their temper and interest. Men may easily perhaps see, or think they see, what they do not like, and cry out *schism*! and *separation*! but if they would a little consider what aught to be in this whole matter, according to the mind of God, and what evidences they have of the grounds and principles whereon they condemn others, it might make them yet swift to hear, but slow to speak, and take off from the number of teachers among us. Some are ready to think that all that join not with them are schismatics, and they are so because they go not with them; and other reason they have none, being unable to give any solid foundation of what they profess. What the cause of unity among the people of God hath suffered from this sort of men is not easily to be expressed.

2. In all differences about religion, to drive them to their rise and spring, and to consider them as stated originally, will ease us of much trouble and labour. Perhaps many of them

will not appear so formidable as they are represented. He that sees a great river is not instantly to conclude that all the water in it comes from its first rise and spring; the addition of many brooks, showers, and land-floods, have perhaps swelled it to the condition wherein it is. Every difference in religion is not to be thought to be as big at its rise as it appears to be when it hath passed through many generations, and hath received additions and aggravations from the disputings and contendings of men, on the one hand and the other engaged. What a flood of abominations doth this business of schism seem to be, as rolling down to us through the writings of Cyprian, Austin, and Optatus, of old, the schoolmen, decrees of popish councils, with the contrivances of some among ourselves, concerned to keep up the swelled notion of it! Go to its rise, and you will find it to be, though bad enough, yet quite another thing than what, by the prejudices accruing by the addition of so many generations, it is now generally represented to be.

The great maxim, "To the law and to the testimony," truly improved, would quickly cure all our distempers. In the meantime, let us bless God that though our outward man may possibly be disposed of according to the apprehension that others have of what we do or are, our consciences are concerned only in what he hath appointed. How some men may prevail against us, before whom we must stand or fall according to their corrupt notion of schism, we know not. The rule of our consciences in this, as in all other things, is eternal and unchangeable. Whilst I have an uncontrollable faithful witness that I transgress no limits prescribed to me in the word, that I do not willingly break or dissolve any unity of the institution of Jesus Christ, my mind as to this thing is filled with perfect peace. Blessed be God, that hath reserved the sole sovereignty of our consciences in his hand, and not in the least parcelled it out to any of the sons of men, whose tender mercies being oftentimes cruelty itself, they would perhaps destroy the soul also, when they do so to the body, seeing they stay there, as our Saviour witnesseth, because they can proceed no farther! Here, then, I profess to rest, in this doth my conscience acquiesce: Whilst I have any comfortable persuasion, on grounds infallible, that I hold the head, and that I am by faith a member of the mystical body of Christ; whilst I make profession of all the necessary saving truths of the gospel; whilst I disturb not the peace of that particular church whereof by my own consent I am a member, nor do raise up nor continue in any causeless differences with them, or any of them, with whom I walk in the fellowship and order of the gospel; whilst I labour to exercise faith towards the Lord Jesus Christ, and love towards all the saints, — I do keep the unity which is of the appointment of Christ, And let men say, from principles utterly foreign to the gospel, what they please or can to the contrary, I am no schismatic.

3. Perhaps the discovery which hath been made, how little we are many of us concerned in that which, having mutually charged it on one another, hath been the greatest ball of strife and most effectual engine of difference and distance between us, may be a means to reconcile in love them that truly fear God, though engaged in several ways, as to some particulars. I confess I have not any great hope of much success on this account; for let principles and ways be made as evident as if he that wrote them carried the sun in his hand, yet whilst men are forestalled by prejudices, and have their affections and spirits engaged suitably thereunto, no great alteration in their minds and ways, on the clearest conviction whatever, is to be expected. All our hearts are in the hand of God; and our expectations of what he hath promised are to be proportioned to what he can effect, not to what of outward means we see to be used.

4. To conclude; what vain janglings men are endlessly engaged in, who will lay their own false hypotheses and preconceptions as a ground of farther procedure, is also in part evident by what hath been delivered. Hence, for instance, is that doughty dispute in the world, whether a schismatic doth belong to the church or no? which for the most part is determined in the negative; when it is impossible a man should be so, but by virtue of his being a church-member. A church is that "alienum solum," wherein that evil dwelleth. The most of the inquiries that are made and disputed on, whether this or that sort of men belong to the church or no, are of the same value and import. He belongs to the *church catholic* who is united to Christ by the Spirit, and none other. And he belongs to the *church general visible* who makes profession of the faith of the gospel, and destroys it not by any thing of a just inconsistency with the belief of it. And he belongs to a *particular church* who, having been in due order joined thereunto, hath neither voluntarily deserted it nor been judicially ejected out of it. Thus, one may be a member of the

church catholic who is no member of the general visible church nor of a particular church; as an elect infant, sanctified from the womb, dying before baptism. And one may be a member of the church general visible who is no member of the church catholic nor of a particular church; as a man making profession of the true faith, yet not united to Christ by the Spirit, nor joined to any particular visible church; — or he may be also of the catholic church, and not of a particular, as also of a particular church, and not of the catholic. And a man may be, — every true believer walking orderly ordinarily is, — a member of the church of Christ in every sense insisted on; — of the catholic church, by *a union with Christ, the head*; of the visible general church, by his *profession, of the faith*; and of a particular congregation, by his *voluntarily associating* himself therewith, according to the will and appointment of our Lord Jesus Christ.

A VINDICATION OF THE TREATISE ABOUT THE TRUE NATURE OF SCHISM, ETC.

A review of the true nature of schism, with a vindication of the Congregational churches in England from the imputation thereof, unjustly charged on them by Mr D. Cawdrey, preacher of the word at Billing, in Northamptonshire.

Oxford: 1657.

Δοῦλον Κυρίου οὐ δεῖ μάχεσθαι.
2 Tim. ii. 24

Δεῖ τὸν ἐπίσκοπον ἀνέγκλητον εἶναι, ὡς Θεοῦ οἰκονόμον, μὴ αὐθάδη, μὴ ὀργίλον, μὴ πάροινον, μὴ πλήκτην, μὴ αἰσχροκερδῆ.
Tit. i. 7

PREFATORY NOTE.

THE preceding treatise was too important to pass without a reply. Dr Hammond, engaged at the time in another controversy with Owen, respecting the orthodoxy of Grotius, appended to one of his pamphlets "A Reply to some Passages of the Reviewer," (Owen), "in his late Book on Schism." Giles Firmin, a Nonconformist divine and physician, much respected for his personal worth and attainments, published, in 1658, a work entitled, "Of Schism, Parochial Congregations, and Ordination by Imposition of Hands; wherein Dr Owen's Discovery of the True Nature of Schism is briefly and friendly examined." Dr Owen did not feel it necessary to offer any reply to these reviews of his work. Mr Daniel Cawdrey, however, a Presbyterian minister at Great Billing, in Northamptonshire, in a pamphlet entitled "Independency a Great Schism," assailed both the principles and the character of Dr Owen in no very measured terms. Much would not have been lost to the world if Cawdrey also had been left without an answer; for he does not seem to have managed the discussion to any good purpose. Owen very conclusively repels the charge of inconsistency with which Cawdrey had reproached him, and urges some additional considerations in support of the general argument contained in his first treatise on schism. He earnestly disclaims the sentiment imputed to him, that he held no church except his own to be a true church of Christ, and closes in a strain of calm and dignified rebuke to the petty and offensive spirit in which his opponent had discussed his statements.

In the beginning of the second chapter there will be found, what Owen very rarely gives us, — an allusion to his personal history. So far as it goes, it is a piece of autobiography replete with interest; for it narrates the circumstances in which he was led to embrace Congregational views. In the midst of a keen dispute and the heavy cares of public life, the heart of our author seems to open to us under the remembrances of his youth, and there is some tenderness of feeling in the allusion to his father, whom he describes as "a Nonconformist all his days, and a painful labourer in the vineyard of the Lord."

In all his treatises on schism, Owen adheres with steadiness and decision to his profession as an Independent. He makes, however, in the beginning of the ninth chapter, a statement that deserves some attention: "For my part, so we could once agree in the matter of our churches, I am under some apprehension that it were no impossible thing to reconcile the whole difference as to a Presbyterian church or a single congregation," p. 258. He intimates that he would "offer, ere long, to the consideration of godly men, something that may provoke others of better abilities and more leisure to endeavour to carry on so good a work." A purpose announced in these terms can hardly be restricted to the mere difference in regard to the eldership, of which he has been speaking, but must include the whole difference between Presbytery and Independency. To have reconciled these two systems, or rather the Christians respectively attached to them, would certainly have been "a good work," though many will doubt its practicability. The sentiment shows, at least, the generous and catholic spirit Owen breathed, so superior to the tendency with which weak minds, on such a change as he made, are apt to adopt the extreme position in their new views.

Are those works he published long afterwards, "The Inquiry into Evangelical Churches," and "The True Nature of a Gospel Church," in which Presbyterians think they find a confirmation of their views on some points, a fulfillment of the promise quoted above? Some difficulties in understanding them would be explained if they were. — ED.

To The Reader.

CHRISTIAN READER,

It is now about three weeks since that there was sent unto me a book entitled, "Independency a Great Schism;" as the frontispiece farther promiseth, undertaken to be managed against something written by me in a treatise about the true nature of schism, published about a year ago; with an addition of a charge of inconstancy in opinion upon myself. Of the one and the other the ensuing discourse will give a farther and full account. Coming unto my hands at such a season, wherein, as it is known, I was pressed with more than ordinary occasions of sundry sorts, I thought to have deferred the examination of it until farther leisure might be obtained, supposing that some fair advantage would be administered by it to a farther Christian debate of that discovery of truth and tender of peace which in my treatise I had made. Engaging into a cursory perusal of it, I found the reverend author's design and discourse to be of that tendency and nature as did not require nor would admit of any such delay. His manifold mistakes in apprehending the intention of my treatise and of the severals of it; his open presumption of his own principles as the source and spring of what pretends to be argumentative in his discourse, arbitrarily inferring from them, without the least attempt of proof, whatever tenders its assistance, to cast reproach on them with whom he hath to do; his neglect in providing a defence for himself, by any principles not easily turned upon him, against the same charge which he is pleased to manage against me; his avowed laying the foundation of his whole fabric in the sand of notoriously false suppositions, — quickly delivered me from the thoughts of any necessity to delay the consideration of what he tendered to make good the title of his discourse. The open and manifest injury done not only to myself, — in laying things to my charge which I know not, lading me with reproaches, tending to a rendering of me odious to all the ministers and churches in the world not agreeing with me in some few things concerning gospel administrations, — but also to all other churches and persons of the same judgment with myself, called for a speedy account of true state of the things contended about.

Thou hast therefore here, Christian reader, the product (through the grace of Him who supplieth seed to the sower) of the spare hours of four or five days; in which space of time this ensuing discourse was begun and finished. Expect not, therefore, anything from it but what is necessary for the refutaton of the book whereunto it is opposed; and as to that end and purpose, I leave it to thy strictest judgment. Only, I shall desire thee to take notice that having kept myself to a bare defence, I have resolvedly forborne all re-charge on the presbyterian way, either as to the whole of it (whence, by way of distinction, it is so called), or as to the differences in judgment and practice of them who profess that way among themselves; which at this day, both in this and the neighbour nation, are more and greater than any that our author hath as yet been able to find amongst them whom he doth principally oppose. As the ensuing sheets were almost wrought off at the press, there came to my hand a vindication of that eminent servant of God, Mr John Cotton, from the unjust imputations and charge of the reverend person with whom I have now to do, written by himself not long before his death. The opportunity of publishing that discourse with the ensuing being then lost, I thought meet to let the reader know that a short season will furnish him with it.

Farewell, and love, truth, and peace.
CHRIST CHURCH COLLEGE, OXON,
July 9, 1657.

Chapter I.

The present state of things in the Christian world will, on a slight consideration, yield this account of controversies in religion, that when they are driven to such an issue as, by foreign coincidences, to be rendered the interest of parties at variance, there is not any great success to be obtained by a management of them, though with never so much evidence, and conviction of truth. An answering of the profession that is on us, by a good and lawful means, the paying of that homage and tribute we owe to the truth, the tendering of assistance to the safeguarding of some weaker professors thereof from the sophisms and violence of adversaries, is the most that, in such a posture of things, the most sober writers of controversies can well aim at.

The winning over of men to the truth we seek to maintain, where they have been pre-engaged in an opposition unto it, without the alteration of the outward state of things whence their engagements have insensibly sprung and risen, is not ordinarily to be expected. How far I was from any such thoughts in the composing and publishing my treatise of the nature of schism, I declared in sundry passages in the treatise itself. Though the thing contended about, whatsoever is pretended to the contrary, will not be found amongst the most important heads of our religion, yet knowing how far, on sundry accounts, the stated fixed interest of several sorts of men engageth them to abide by the principles they own in reference thereunto, I was so far from hoping to see speedily any visible fruits of the efficacy of the truth I had managed, that I promised myself a vigorous opposition, until some urgent providence or time, altering the frame of men's spirits, should make way for its acceptance. Freely I left in the hand of Him, whose truth I have good security I had in weakness maintained, to dispose of it, with its issues and events, at his pleasure. I confess, knowing several parties to be concerned in an opposition to it, I was not well able to conjecture from what hand the first assault of it would arise. Probability cast it on them who looked on themselves [as] in the nearest proximity of advantage by the common notion of schism opposed. The truth is, I did apprehend myself not justly chargeable with want of charity, if I thought that opposition would arise from some other principles than mere zeal for a supposed truth; and, therefore, took my aim in conjecturing at the prejudices that men might fear themselves and interests obnoxious unto by a reception and establishment of that notion of schism which I had asserted. Men's contentedness to make use of their quietness in reference to Popery, Socinianism, Arminianism, daily vented amongst us, unless it were in some declamatory expressions against their toleration, which cost no more than they are worth, shaken off by a speedy engagement against my treatise, confirmed such thoughts in me. After, therefore, it had passed in the world for some season, and had found acceptance with many learned and godly persons, reports began to be raised about a design for a refutation of it. That so it should be dealt withal I heard was judged necessary at sundry conventions; what particular hand it was likely the task would fall upon, judging myself not concerned to know, I did not inquire. When I was informed how the disposal of the business did succeed, as I was not at all surprised in reference to the party in general from which it did issue, so I did relieve myself, under my fears and loathing to be engaged in these contests, by these ensuing considerations:— 1. That I was fully persuaded that what I had written was, for the substance of it, the truth of God; and being concerned in it only on truth's account, if it could be demonstrated that the sentence I had asserted was an unlawful pretender thereunto, I should be delivered from paying any farther respect or service to that whereunto none at all was due. 2. That in the treatise itself so threatened, I had laid in provision against all contending about words, expressions, collateral assertions, deductions, positions, all and every thing, though true, that might be separated from the life or substance of the notion or truth pleaded for. 3. That whereas the whole weight of the little pile turned on one single hinge, and that visible and conspicuous, capable of an ocular demonstration as to its confirmation or refutation, I promised myself that any man who should undertake the demolishing of it would be so far from passing that by, and setting himself to the superstruction, that subsists on its single strength and vigour, that indeed finding that one thing necessary for him, he would solely attempt that, and therein rest. This I knew was evident to any considering person that should but view the treatise, that if that foundation were cast down, the whole superstructure would fall with its own weight; but if left standing, a hundred thousand volumes against the rest of the treatise could not in the least prejudice the cause undertaken to be managed in it. Men might, indeed, by such attempts, manifest my weakness and want of skill, in making inferences and deductions from principles of truth wherein I am not concerned, but the truth itself contended for would still abide untouched. 4. Having expressly waived man's day and judgment, I promised myself security from a disturbance by urging against me the authority of any of old or late; supposing that, from the eviction of their several interests, I had emancipated myself from all subjection to their bare judgments in this cause. 5. Whereas I had confined myself to a bare defensative of some, not intending to cast others from the place which, in their own apprehensions, they do enjoy (unless it was the Roman party), I had some expectations that peace-loving, godly men would not be troubled that an apparent immunity from a crime was, without their prejudice or disadvantage, manifested in behalf of their brethren, nor much pain themselves to re-enforce the charge accounted for; so that the bare notion of schism, and the nature of it, abstracted from the consideration of persons, would come under debate. Indeed, I questioned whether, in that friendly composure of affections which, for sundry years, hath been carrying on between sober and godly men of the presbyterian and congregational judgment, any person of real godliness would interest himself to blow the coal of dissension and engage in new exasperations. I confess, I always thought the plea of Cicero for Ligarius against Tubero most unreasonable, — namely, that if he had told (as he calls it) *"an honest and merciful lie"* in his behalf, yet it was not the part of a man to refel it, especially of one who was accused of the same crime; but yet I must needs say, a prompt readiness to follow most questionable accusations against honest defensatives from good men, unjustly accused by others of the same crime, I did not expect. I added this also in my thoughts that the facility of rendering a discourse to the purpose on the business under consideration was obviated by its being led out of the common road, wherein commonplace supplies would be of little use to any that should undertake it; not once suspecting that any man of learning and judgment would make a return unto it out of vulgar discourses about ministers' calling, church-government, or the like. How far these and the like considerations might be a relief unto my thoughts, in my fears of farther controversial engagements, having the pressure of more business upon me than any one man I know of my calling in the whole nation, I leave it to the judgment of them who love truth and peace. But what little confidence I ought, in the present posture of the minds of men, to have placed in any or all of them, the discourse under consideration hath instructed me. That any one thing hath fallen out according to my expectations and conjectures, but only its being a product of the men of the persuasions owned therein, I am yet to seek. The truth is, I cannot blame my adversary, "viis et modis," to make good the opposition he is engaged in. It concerns him and his advisers beyond their interest in the appearing skirts of this controversy. Perhaps, also, an adjudged necessity of endeavouring a disreputation to my person and writings was one ingredient in the undertaking; if so, the whole frame was to be carried on by correspondent mediums. But let the principles and motives to this discourse be what they will, it is now made public, there being a warmer zeal acting therein than in carrying on some other things expected from the same hand.

To what may seem of importance in it, I shall with all possible plainness give a return. Had the reverend author of it thought good to have kept within the bounds by me fixed, and candidly debated the notion proposed, abstracting from the provocations of particular applications, I should most willingly have taken pains for a farther clearing and manifesting of the truth contended about.

But the whole discourse wherewith I have now to do is of another complexion, and the design of it of another tendency, yea, so managed sometimes, that I am ready to question whether it be the product and fruit of his spirit whose name it bears; for though he be an utter stranger to me, yet I have received such a character of him as would raise me to an expectation of any thing from him rather than such a discourse.

The reader will be able to perceive an account of these thoughts in the ensuing view of his treatise.

1. I am, without any provocation intended, and I hope given, *reviled* from one end of it to the other, and called, partly in downright terms, partly by oblique intimations, whose reflections are not to be waived, Satan, atheist, sceptic, Donatist, heretic, schismatic, sectary, Pharisee, etc.; and the closure of the book is merely an attempt to blast my reputation, whereof I shall give a speedy account.

2. The professed design of the whole is to prove "Independency," as he is pleased to call it, — which what it is he declares not, nor (as he manages the business) do I know, — to be a "great *schism*," and that Independents, (by whom it is full well known whom he intends) are "*schismatics*," "sectaries, the "troublers of England," so that it were happy for the nation if they were out of it; or discovering sanguinary thoughts in reference unto them. And these kinds of discourses fill up the book, almost from one end to the other.

3. No Christian care doth seem to have been taken, nor good conscience exercised, from the beginning to the ending, as to imputation of any thing *unto me* or *upon me*, that may serve to help on the design in hand.

Hence, I think, it is repeated near a hundred times, that I deny their ministers to be ministers, and their churches to be churches, — that I deny all the reformed churches in the world but only "our own" (as he calls them) to be true churches; all which is notoriously untrue, contrary to my known judgment, professedly declared on all occasions, contrary to express affirmations in the book he undertakes to confute, and the whole design of the book itself. I cannot easily declare my surprisal on this account. What am I to expect from others, when such reverend men as this author shall, by the power of prejudice, be carried beyond all bounds of moderation and Christian tenderness in offending? I no way doubt but that Satan hath his design in this whole business. He knows how apt we are to fix on such provocations, and to contribute thereupon to the increase of our differences. Can he, according to the course of things in the world, expect any other issue, but that, in the necessary defensative I am put upon, I should not waive such reflections and retortions on him and them with whom I have to do, as present themselves with as fair pleas and pretences unto me as it is possible for me to judge that the charges before mentioned (I mean of schism, heresy, and the like) did unto him? for as to a return of any thing, in its own nature false and untrue as to matter of fact, to meet with that of the like kind wherewith I am entertained, I suppose the devil himself was hopeless to obtain it. Is he not filled with envy to take notice in what love without dissimulation I walk with many of the presbyterian judgment; what Christian intercourse and communion I have with them in England, Scotland, Holland, France; fearing that it may tend to the furtherance of peace and union among the churches of Christ? God assisting, I shall deceive his expectations; and though I be called schismatic and heretic a thousand times, it shall not weaken my love or esteem of or towards any of the godly ministers or people of that way and judgment with whom I am acquainted, or have occasion of converse. And as for this reverend author himself, I shall not fail to pray that none of the things whereby he hath, I fear, administered advantage unto Satan to attempt the exasperations of the spirits of brethren one against another, may ever be laid to his charge. For my own part, I profess in all sincerity that such was my unhappiness, or rather happiness, in the constant converse which, in sundry places, I have with persons of the presbyterian judgment, both of the English and Scottish nation, utterly of another frame of spirit than that which is now showed, that until I saw this treatise, I did not believe that there had remained in any one godly, sober, judicious person in England, such thoughts of heart in reference to our present differences as are visible and legible therein.

"Tantæne animis cœlestibus iræ?"

I hope the reverend author will not be offended if I make bold to tell him that it will be no joy of heart to him one day, that he hath taken pains to cast oil on those flames, which it is every one's duty to labour to extinguish.

But that the whole matter in difference may be the better stated and determined, I shall first pass through with the general concernments of the book itself, and then consider the several chapters of it, as to any particulars in them that may seem to relate to the business in hand. It may possibly not a little conduce towards the removal of those obstructions unto peace and love, laid in our way by this reverend author, and to a clearer stating of the controversy pretended to be ventilated in his discourse, to discover and lay aside those mistakes of his, which, being interwoven with the main discourse from the beginning to the end, seem as principles to animate the whole, and to give it that life of trouble whereof it is partaker. Some of them were, as absolutely considered, remarked before. I shall now renew the mention of them, with respect to that influence which they have into the argumentative part of the treatise under consideration.

1. First, then, it is strenuously supposed all along, *that I deny all or any churches in England to be true churches of Christ*, except only the churches gathered in the congregational way and upon their principles; then, that I deny all the reformed churches beyond the seas to be true churches of Christ. This supposition being laid as the foundation of the whole building, a confutation of my treatise is fixed thereon; a comparison is instituted between the Donatists and myself; arguments are produced to prove their churches to be true churches, and their ministers true ministers; the charge of schism on this bottom is freely given out and asserted; the proof of my schismatical separation from hence deduced; and many terms of reproach are returned as a suitable reply to the provocation of this opinion. How great a portion of a small treatise may easily be taken up with discourses relating to these heads is easy to apprehend. Now, lest all this pains should be found to be useless and causelessly undergone, let us consider how the reverend author proves this to be my judgment. Doth he evince it from any thing delivered in that treatise he undertakes to confute? doth he produce any other testimonies out of what I have spoken, delivered, or written elsewhere, and on other occasions, to make it good? This, I suppose, he thought not of, but took it for granted that either I was of that judgment, or it was fit I should be so, that the difference between us might be as great as he desired to have it appear to be.

Well, to put an end to this controversy, seeing he would not believe what I told the world of my thoughts herein in my book of schism, I now inform him again that all these surmises are fond and untrue. And truly, for his own sake, with that respect which is due to the reputation of religion, I here humbly entreat him not to entertain what is here affirmed with unchristian surmises, which the apostle reckons amongst the works of the flesh, as though I were of another mind, but durst not declare it; as more than once, in some particulars, he insinuates the state of things with me to be. But blessed be the God of my salvation and of all my deliverances, I have yet liberty to declare the whole of my judgment in and about the things of his worship! Blessed be God, it is not as yet in the power of some men to bring in that their conceited happiness into England, which would, in their thoughts, accrue unto it by my removal from my native soil, with all others of my judgment and persuasion! We are yet at peace, and we trust that the Lord will deliver us from the hands of men whose tender mercies are cruel. However, be it known unto them, that if it be the will of the Lord, upon our manifold provocations, to give us up to their disposal, who are pleased to compass us with the ornaments of reproaches before mentioned, that so we might fall as a sacrifice to rage or violence, we shall, through his assistance and presence with us, dare to profess the whole of that truth and those ways of his which he hath been pleased to reveal unto us.

And if, on any other account, this reverend person suppose I may foster opinions and thoughts of mine own and their ways which I dare not own, let him at any time give me a command to wait upon him, and as I will freely and candidly answer to any inquiries he shall be pleased to make, after my judgment and apprehensions of these things, so he shall find that (God assisting) I dare own, and will be ready to maintain, what I shall so deliver to him. It is a sufficient evidence that this reverend author is an utter stranger to me, or he would scarce entertain such surmises of me as he doth. Shall I call in witnesses as to the particular under consideration? One evidence, by way of instance, lies so near at hand that I cannot omit the producing of it. Not above fourteen days before this treatise came to my hands, a learned gentleman, whom I had prevailed withal to answer in the Vespers of our Act, sent me his questions by a doctor of the presbyterian judgment, a friend of his and mine. The first question was, as I remember, to this purpose: "Utrum ministri ecclesiæ Anglicanæ habeant validam ordinationem?" I told the doctor, that since the questions were to pass under my approbation, I must needs confess myself scrupled at the limitation of the subject of the question in that term, "Ecclesia Anglicana," which would be found ambiguous and equivocal in the disputation, and therefore desired that he would rather supply it with "Ecclesiarum Reformatarum," or some other expression of like importance; but as to the thing itself aimed at, — namely, the assertion of the ministry of the godly ministers in England, — I told him, and so now do the reverend author of this treatise, that I shall as willingly engage in the defence of it, with the lawfulness of their churches, as any man whatever. I have only in my treatise questioned the institution of a national church, which this author doth not undertake to maintain, nor hath the least reason so to do, for the asserting of true ministers and churches in England; I mean those of the presbyterian way. What satisfaction now this reverend author shall judge it necessary for him to give me for the public injury which voluntarily he hath done me, in particular for his attempt to expose me to the censure and displeasure of so many godly ministers and churches as I own in England, as a person denying their ministry and church station, I leave it to himself to consider. And by the declaration of this mistake, how great a part of his book is waived, as to my concernments therein, himself full well knows.

2. A second principle of like importance which he is pleased to make use of as a thing granted by me, or at least which he assumes as that which ought so to be, is, that whatever the presbyterian ministers and churches be, I have *separated* from them, as have done all those whom he calls Independents. This is another fountain out of which much bitter water flows. Hence we must needs be thought to condemn their ministry and churches. The Brownists were our fathers, and the Anabaptists are our elder brothers; we make a harlot of our mother, and are schismatics and sectaries from one end of the book to the other: "quod erat demonstrandum." But doth not this reverend author know that this is wholly denied by us? Is it not disproved sufficiently in that very treatise which he undertakes to answer?

He grants, I suppose, that the separation he blames must respect some union of Christ's institution: for any other, we profess ourselves unconcerned in its maintenance or dissolution, as to the business in hand. Now, wherein have we separated from them as to the breach of any such union? For an individual person to change from the constant participation of ordinances in one congregation, to do so in another, barely considered in itself, this reverend author holds to be no separation. However, for my part, who am forced to bear all this wrath and storm, what hath he to lay to my charge? I condemn not their churches in general to be no churches, nor any one that I am acquainted withal in particular; I never disturbed, that I know of, the peace of any one of them, nor separated from them: but having already received my punishment, I expect to hear my crime by the next return.

3. He supposeth throughout that I deny not only the *necessity of a successive ordination*, but, as far as I can understand him, the *lawfulness* of it also. By ordination of ministers, many, upon a mistake, understand only the imposition of hands that is used therein. Ordination of ministers is one thing, and imposition of hands another, differing as whole and part. Ordination in Scripture compriseth the whole authoritative translation of a man from among the number of his brethren into the state of an officer in the church. I suppose he doth not think that this is denied by me, though he tells me, with the same Christian candour and tenderness which he exerciseth in every passage almost of his book, of making myself a minister, and I know not what. I am, I bless the Lord, extremely remote from returning him any of his own coin in satisfaction for this love. For that part of it which consists in the imposition of hands by the presbytery (where it may be obtained according to the mind of Christ), I am also very remote from managing any opposition unto it. I think it necessary by virtue of *precept*, and that [it ought] to be continued in a way of *succession*. It, is, I say, according to the mind of Christ, that he who is to be ordained unto office in any church receive imposition of hands from the elders of that church, if there be any therein; and this is to be done in a way of succession, that so the churches may be perpetuated. That alone which I oppose is the denying of this successive ordination through the authority of Antichrist. Before the blessed and glorious Reformation, begun and carried on by Zuinglius, Luther, Calvin, and others, there were, and had been, two estates of men in the world professing the name of Christ and the gospel, as to the outward profession thereof; — the one of them in glory, splendour, outward beauty, and order, calling themselves *the church*, the *only* church in the world, the *catholic* church, — being in deed and in truth, in that state wherein they so prided themselves, the mother of harlots, the beast, with his false prophet; the other party, poor, despised, persecuted, generally esteemed and called heretics, schismatics, or, as occasion gave advantage for their farther reproach, Waldenses, Albigenses, Lollards, and the like. As to the claim of a successive ordination drawn from the apostles, I made bold to affirm that I could not understand

the validity of that successive ordination, as successive, which was derived down unto us from and by the first party of men in the world.

This reverend author's reply hereunto is like the rest of his discourse. Page 118, he tells me, "This casts dirt in the face of their ministry, as do all their good friends the sectaries;" and that he hath much ado to forbear saying, "The Lord rebuke thee." How he doth forbear it, having so expressed the frame of his heart towards me, others will judge. The Searcher of all hearts knows that I had no design to cast dirt on him, or any other godly man's ministry in England. Might not another answer have been returned without this wrath? This is so, or it is not so, in reference to the ministry of this nation. If it be not so, and they plead not their successive ordination from Rome, there is an end of this difference. If it be so, can Mr C. hardly refrain from calling a man Satan for speaking the truth? It is well if we know of what Spirit we are.

But let us a little farther consider his answer in that place. He asketh first, "Why may not this be a sufficient foundation for their ministry as well as for their baptism?" If it be so, and be so acknowledged, whence is that great provocation that arose from my inquiry after it? For my part, I must tell him that I judge their baptism good and valid, but, to deal clearly with him, not on that foundation. I cannot believe that that idolater, murderer, man of sin, has had, since the days of his open idolatry, persecution, and enmity to Christ, any authority, more or less, from the Lord Jesus committed to him in or over his churches. But he adds, secondly, that "had they received their ordination from the woman flying into the wilderness, the two witnesses, or Waldenses, it had been all one to me and my party; for they had not their ordination from the people (except some extraordinary cases), but from a presbytery, according to the institution of Christ." So, then, ordination by a presbytery is, it seems, opposed by me and my party. But I pray, sir, who told you so? When, wherein, by what means, have I opposed it? I acknowledge myself of no party. I am sorry so grave a minister should suffer himself to be thus transported, that every answer, every reply, must be a reflection, and that without due observation of truth and love. That those first reformers had their ordination from the people is acknowledged; I have formerly evinced it by undeniable testimony: so that the proper succession of a ministry amongst the churches that are their offspring runs up no higher than that rise. Now, the good Lord bless them in their ministry, and the successive ordination they enjoy, to bring forth more fruit in the earth, to the praise of his glorious grace! But upon my disclaiming all thoughts of rejecting the ministry of all those who yet hold their ordination on the account of its successive derivation from Rome, he cries out, "Egregiam veto laudem!" and says, "that yet I secretly derive their pedigree from Rome." Well, then, he doth not so. Why, then, what need these exclamations? We are as to this matter wholly agreed. Nor shall I at present farther pursue his discourse in that place; it is almost totally composed and made up of scornful revilings, reflections, and such other ingredients of the whole.

He frequently and very positively affirms, without the least hesitation, that I have "renounced my own ordination;" and adds hereunto, that "whatever else they pretend, unless they renounce their ordination, nothing will please me;" and that "I condemn all other churches in the world as no churches." But who, I pray, told him these things? Did he inquire so far after my mind in them as, without breach of charity, to be able to make such positive and express assertions concerning them? A good part of his book is taken up in the repetition of such things as these, drawing inferences and conclusions from the suppositions of them, and warming himself by them into a great contempt of myself and "party," as he calls them. I am now necessitated to tell him that all these things are false, and utterly, in part and in whole, untrue, and that he is not able to prove any one of them. And whether this kind of dealing becomes a minister of the gospel, a person professing godliness, I leave it to himself to judge. For my own part, I must confess that as yet I was never so dealt withal by any man, of what party soever, although it hath been my unhappiness to provoke many of them. I do not doubt but that he will be both troubled and ashamed when he shall review these things. That whole chapter which he entitles, "Independentism is Donatism," as to his application of it unto me or any of my persuasion, is of the same importance, as I have sufficiently already evinced. I might instance in sundry other particulars, wherein he ventures, without the least check or supposition, to charge me with what he pleaseth that may serve the turn in hand. So that it may serve to bring in, "He and his party are schismatics, are sectaries, have separated from the church of God, are the cause of all our evils and troubles," with the like terms of reproach and hard censures, lying in a fair subserviency to a design of widening the difference between us, and mutually exasperating the spirits of men professing the gospel of Jesus Christ one against another, nothing almost comes amiss. His sticking upon by-matters, diverting from the main business in hand, answering arguments by reflections, and the like, might also be remarked. One thing wherein he much rejoiceth, and fronts his book with the discovery he hath made of it, — namely, concerning my change of judgment as to the difference under present debate, which is the substance and design of his appendix, — must be particularly considered, and shall be, God assisting, in the next chapter accordingly.

Chapter II.

An answer to the appendix of Mr C.'s charge.

Though, perhaps, impartial men will be willing to give me an acquitment from the charge of altering my judgment in the matters of our present difference, upon the general account of the co-partnership with me of the most inquiring men in this generation, as to things of no less importance; and though I might, against this reverend brother, and others of the same mind and persuasion with him, at present relieve myself sufficiently by a recrimination in reference to their former episcopal engagements, and sundry practices in the worship of God them attending; pleading in the meantime the general issue of changing from error to truth (which that I have done as to any change I have really made, I am ready at any time to maintain to this author): yet it being so much insisted upon by him as it is, and the charge thereof, in the instance given, accompanied with so many evil surmisings and uncharitable reflections, looking like the fruits of another principle than that whereby we ought in the management of our differences to be ruled, I shall give a more particular account of that which hath yielded him this great advantage. The sole instance insisted on by him is a small treatise, published long ago by me, entitled, "The Duty of Pastors and People Distinguished," wherein I profess myself to be of the presbyterian judgment. "Excerpta" out of that treatise, with animadversions and comparisons thereon, make up the appendix, which was judged necessary to be added to the book, to help on with the proof that Independency is a great schism. Had it not been, indeed, needful to cause the person to suffer as well as the thing, some suppose this pains might have been spared. But I am not to prescribe to any what way it is meet for them to proceed in for the compassing of their ends aimed at. The best is, here is no new thing produced, but what the world hath long since taken notice of, and made of it the worst they can. Neither am I troubled that I have a necessity laid upon me to give an account of this whole matter. That little treatise was written by me in the year 1643, and then printed: however, it received the addition of a year in the date affixed to it by the printers; which, for their own advantage, is a thing usual with them. I was then a young man myself, about the age of twenty-six or twenty- seven years. The controversy between Independency and Presbytery was young also, nor, indeed, by me clearly understood, especially as stated on the congregational side. The conceptions delivered in the treatise were not (as appears in the issue) suited to the opinion of the one party nor of the other, but were such as occurred to mine own naked consideration of things, with relation to some differences that were then upheld in the place where I lived. Only, being unacquainted with the congregational way, I professed myself to own the other party, not knowing but that my principles were suited to their judgment and profession, having looked very little farther into those affairs than I was led by an opposition to Episcopacy and ceremonies. Upon a review of what I had there asserted, I found that my principles were far more suited to what is the judgment and practice of the congregational men than those of the presbyterian. Only, whereas I had not received any farther clear information in these ways of the worship of God, which since I have been engaged in, as was said, I professed myself of the presbyterian judgment, in opposition to democratical confusion; and, indeed, so I do still, and so do all the congregational men in England that I am acquainted withal. So that when I compare what then I wrote with my present judgment, I am scarce able to find the least difference between the one and the other; only, a misapplication of names and things by me gives countenance to this charge. Indeed, not long after, I set myself seriously to inquire into the controversies then warmly agitated in these nations. Of the congregational way I was not acquainted with any one person, minister or other; nor had I, to my knowledge, seen any more than one in my life. My acquaintance lay wholly with ministers and people of the presbyterian way. But sundry books being published on either side, I perused and compared them with the Scripture and one another, according as I received ability from God. After a general view of them, as was my manner in other controversies, I fixed on one to take under peculiar consideration and examination, which seemed most methodically and strongly to maintain that which was contrary, as I thought, to my present persuasion. This was Mr Cotton's book of the Keys. The examination and confutation hereof, merely for my own particular satisfaction, with what diligence and sincerity I was able, I engaged in. What progress I made in that undertaking I can manifest unto any by the discourses on that subject and animadversions on that book, yet abiding by me. In the pursuit and management of this work, quite beside and contrary to my expectation, at a time and season wherein I could expect nothing on that account but ruin in this world, without the knowledge or advice of, or conference with, any one person of that judgment, I was prevailed on to receive that and those principles which I had thought to have set myself in an opposition unto. And, indeed, this way of impartial examining all things by the word, comparing causes with causes and things with things, laying aside all prejudicate respects unto persons or present traditions, is a course that I would admonish all to beware of who would avoid the danger of being made Independents. I cannot, indeed, deny but that it was possible I was advantaged in the disquisition of the truth I had in hand from my former embracing of the principles laid down in the treatise insisted on. Now, being by this means settled in the truth, which I am ready to maintain to this reverend and learned author, if he or any other suppose they have any advantage hereby against me as to my reputation, — which alone is sought in such attempts as this, — or if I am blamably liable to the charge of inconstancy and inconsistency with my own principles, which he thought meet to front his book withal, hereupon I shall not labour to divest him of his apprehension, having abundant cause to rejoice in the rich grace of a merciful and tender Father, that, men seeking occasion to speak evil of so poor a worm, tossed up and down in the midst of innumerable temptations, I should be found to fix on that which I know will be found my rejoicing in the day of the Lord Jesus.

    I am necessitated to add somewhat also to a surmise of this reverend man, in reference to my episcopal compliances in former days, and strict observation of their canons. This, indeed, I should not have taken notice of, but that I find others besides this author pleasing themselves with this apprehension, and endeavouring an advantage against the truth I profess thereby.

How little some of my adversaries are like to gain by branding this as a crime is known; and I profess I know not the conscience that is exercised in this matter. But to deliver them once for all from involving themselves in the like unchristian procedure hereafter, let them now know, what they might easily have known before, namely, that this accusation is false, a plain calumny, — a lie. As I was bred up from my infancy under the care of my father, who was a Nonconformist all his days, and a painful labourer in the vineyard of the Lord, so ever since I came to have any distinct knowledge of the things belonging to the worship of God, I have been fixed in judgment against that which I am calumniated withal; which is notoriously known to all that have had any acquaintance with me. What advantage this kind of proceeding is like to bring to his own soul or the cause which he manageth, I leave to himself to judge.

Thus, in general, to take a view of some particular passages in the appendix destined to this good work: The first section tries, with much wit and rhetoric, to improve the pretended alteration of judgment to the blemishing of my reputation, affirming it to be from truth to error; which, as to my particular, so far as it shall appear I am concerned (I am little moved with the bare affirmation of men, especially if induced to it by their interest), I desire him to let me know when and where I may personally wait upon him to be convinced of it. In the meantime, so much for that section. In the second, he declares what my judgment was in that treatise about the distance between pastors and people, and of the extremes that some men on each hand run into; and I now tell him that I am of the same mind still, so that that note hath little availed him. In the third, he relates what I delivered, "That a man not solemnly called to the office of the ministry, by any outward call, might do, as to the preaching of the gospel in a collapsed church-state." Unto this he makes sundry objections, — that my discourse is dark, not clear, and the like; but remembering that his business was not to confute that treatise only, but to prove from it my inconstancy and inconsistency with myself, he says I am changed from what I then delivered. This is denied; I am punctually of the same judgment still. But he proves the contrary by a double argument:— 1. "Because I have renounced my ordination;" 2. "Because I think now, that not only in a complete church-state, but when no such thing can be charged, gifts and consent of the people are enough to make a man a preacher in office;" — both untrue and false in fact. I profess I am astonished to think with what frame of spirit, what neglect of all rules of truth and love, this business is managed. In the fourth section, he chargeth me to have delivered somewhat in that treatise about the personal indwelling of the Holy Ghost in believers; and my words to that purpose are quoted at large. What then? am I changed in this also? No; but "that is an error, in the judgment of all that be orthodox." But that is not the business in hand, but the alteration of my judgment; wherefore he makes a kind of exposition upon my words in that treatise, to show that I was not then of the mind that I have now delivered myself to be of in my book of schism. But I could easily answer the weakness of his exceptions and pretended expositions of my former assertions, and evidence my consistency in judgment with myself in this business ever since. But this, he saith, is an error which he gathered out of my book of schism; and somebody hath sent him word from Oxford that I preached the same doctrine at St Mary's. I wish his informer had never more deceived him. It is most true I have done so, and since printed at large what then I delivered, with sundry additions thereunto; and if this reverend author shall think good to examine what I have published on that account (not in the way in this treatise proceeded in, which in due time will be abhorred of himself and all good men, but with candour, and a spirit of Christian ingenuity and meekness), I shall acknowledge myself obliged to him. And, in the meantime, I desire him to be cautious of large expressions concerning all the orthodox, to oppose that opinion, seeing evidences of the contrary lie at hand in great plenty; and let him learn from hence how little his insulting in his book on this account is to be valued. Sect. 5, he shows that I then proved "the name of priests not to be proper, or to be ascribed to the ministers of the gospel; but that now" (as is supposed in scorn) "I call the ministers of their particular congregations parochial priests." Untrue! In the description of the prelatical church, I showed what they esteemed and called "parish ministers" amongst them. I never called the presbyterian ministers of particular congregations "parochial priests." Love, truth, and peace; these things ought not thus to be. Sect. 6, he labours to find some difference in the tendency of several expressions in that treatise; which is not at all to the purpose in hand, nor true, as will appear to any that shall read the treatise itself. In sect. 7–11, he takes here and there a sentence out of the treatise and examines it, interlacing his discourse with untrue reflections, surmises, and prognostications, and in particular, pp. 238, 239. But what doth all this avail him in reference to his design in hand? Not only before, but even since his exceptions to the things then delivered, I am of the same mind that I was, without the least alteration; and in the reviewing of what I had then asserted, I find nothing strange to me but the sad discovery of what frame of spirit the charge proceeded from. Sect. doth the whole work; there I acknowledge myself to be of the presbyterian judgment, and not of the independent or congregational! Had this reverend author thought meet to have confined his charge to this one quotation, he had prevented much evil that spreads itself over the rest of his discourse, and yet have attained the utmost of what he can hope for from the whole; and hereof I have already given an account. But he will yet proceed, and, sect. 13, inform his reader that in that treatise I aver that two things are required in a teacher, as to formal ministerial teaching, — 1. Gifts from God; 2. Authority from the church. Well! what then? I am of the same mind still. But now "I cry down ordination by presbytery." "What! and is not this a great alteration and sign of inconstancy?" Truly, sir, there is more need of humiliation in yourself than triumphing against me, for the assertion is most untrue, and your charge altogether groundless; which I desire you would be satisfied in, and not be led any more, by evil surmises, to wrong me and your own soul. He adds, sect. 14, two cautions, which in that treatise I give to private Christians in the exercise of their gifts; and closeth the last of them with a juvenile epiphonema, divinely spoken, and like a true Presbyterian. And yet there is not one word in either of these cautions that I do not still own and allow; which confirms the unhappiness of the charge. Of all that is substantial in any thing that follows, I affirm the same as to all that which is gone before. Only, as to the liberty to be allowed unto them which meet in private, who cannot in conscience join in the celebration of public ordinances as they are performed amongst us, I confess myself to be otherwise minded at present than the words there quoted by this author do express. But this is nothing to the difference between Presbytery and Independency. And he that can glory that in fourteen years he hath not altered or improved in his conception of some things of no greater importance than that mentioned shall not have me for his rival. And this is the sum of Mr C.'s appendix; the discourse whereof being carried on with such a temper of spirit as it is, and suited to the advantage aimed at by so many evil surmises, false suggestions, and uncharitable reflections, I am persuaded the taking of that pains will one day be no joy of heart unto him.

Chapter III.

A review of the charger's preface.

His first chapter consists, for the most part, in a repetition of my words, or so much of the discourse of my first chapter as he could wrest, by cutting off one and another parcel of it from its coherence in the whole, with the interposure of glosses of his own, to serve him to make biting reflections upon them with whom he hath to deal. How unbecoming such a course of procedure is for a person of his worth, gravity, and profession, perhaps his δεύτεραι φροντίδες have by this time convinced him. If men have a mind to perpetuate controversies unto an endless, fruitless reciprocation of words and cavils; if to provoke to easy and facile retortions, if to heighten and aggravate differences beyond any hope of reconciliation, — they may do well to deal after this manner with the writings of one another. Mr C. knows how easy it were to make his own words dress him up in all those ornaments wherein he labours to make me appear in the world, by such glosses, inversions, additions, and interpositions, as he is pleased to make use of; but "meliora speramus." Such particulars as seem to be of any importance to our business in hand may be remarked as we pass through it. Page 1, he tells us the Donatists had two principles, — "1. That they were the only church of Christ, in a corner of Africa; and left no church in the world but their own. 2. That none were truly baptized, or entered members of the church of Christ, but by some minister of their party." These principles, he says, are again improved by men of another party, whom, though yet he name not, it is evident whom he intends; and, p. 3, he requires my judgment of those principles.

Because I would not willingly be wanting in any thing that may tend to his satisfaction, though I have some reason to conjecture at my unhappiness in respect of the event, I shall with all integrity give him my thoughts of the principles expressed above.

Then, if they were considered in reference to the Donatists, who owned them, I say they were wicked, corrupt, erroneous principles, tending to the disturbance of the communion of saints, and everting all the rules of love that our Lord Jesus Christ hath given to his disciples and servants to observe. If he intend my judgment of them in reference to the churches of England which he calls Independent, I am sorry that he should think he hath any reason to make this inquiry. I know not that man in the world who is less concerned in obtaining countenance to those principles than I am. Let them who are so ready, on all occasions or provocations, to cast abroad the solemn forms of reproach, "schismatics," "sectaries," "heretics," and the like, search their own hearts as to a conformity of spirit unto these principles. It is not what men say, but what men do, that they shall be judged by. As the Donatists were not the first who in story were charged with schism, no more was their schism confined to Africa. The agreement of multitudes in any [evil] principles makes it in itself not one whit better, and in effect worse. For my part, I acknowledge the churches in England, Scotland, and France, Helvetia, the Netherlands, Germany, Greece, Muscovia, etc., as far as I know of them, to be true churches. Such, for aught I know, may be in Italy or Spain; and what pretence or colour this reverend person hath to fix a contrary persuasion upon me, with so many odious imputations and reflections of being "one of the restorers of all lost churches," and the like, I profess I know not. These things will not be peace in the latter end. "Shall the sword devour for ever?" I dare not suppose that he will ask, Why then do I separate from them? He hath read my book of schism, wherein I have undeniably proved that I separated from none of them; and I am loath to say, though I fear before the close of my discourse I shall be compelled to it, that this reverend author hath answered a matter before he understood it, and confuted a book whose main and chief design he did not once apprehend. The rest of this chapter is composed of reflections upon me from my own words, wrested at his pleasure, and added to according to the purpose in hand, and the taking for granted unto that end that they are in the right, we in the wrong; that their churches are true churches, and yet not esteemed so by me; that we have separated from those churches; with such like easy suppositions. He is troubled that I thought the mutual chargings of each other with schism between the Presbyterians and Independents was as to its heat abated, and ready to vanish; wherein he hath invincibly compelled me to acknowledge my mistake: and I assure him I am heartily sorry that I was mistaken; it will not be somebody's joy one day that I was so. He seems to be offended with my notion of schism, because, if it be true, it will carry it almost out of the world, and bless the churches with everlasting peace. He tells me that a learned doctor said "my book was one great schism." I hope that is but one doctor's opinion, because, being nonsense, it is not fit it should be entertained by many. In the process of his discourse he culls out sundry passages, delivered by me in reference to the great divisions and differences that are in the world among men professing the name of Christ, and applies them to the difference between the Presbyterians and Independents, with many notable lashes in his way, when they were very little in my thoughts; nor are the things spoken by me in any tolerable measure applicable to them. I suppose no rational man will expect that I should follow our reverend author in such ways and paths as these; it were easy, in so doing, to enter into an endless maze of words to little purpose, and I have no mind to deal with him as he hath done by me. I like not the copy so well as to write by it. So his first chapter is discussed and forgiven.

Chapter IV.

Of the nature of schism.

The second chapter of my book, whose examination this author undertakes in the second of his, containing the foundation of many inferences that ensue, and in particular of that description of schism which he intends to oppose, it might have been expected that he should not have culled out passages at his pleasure to descant upon, but either have transcribed the whole, or at least under one view have laid down clearly what I proposed to confirmation, that the state of the controversy being rightly formed, all might understand what we say and whereof we do affirm. But he thought better of another way of procedure, which I am now bound to allow him in; the reason whereof he knows, and other men may conjecture.

The first words he fixes on are the first of the chapter, "The thing whereof we treat being a disorder in the instituted worship of God." Whereunto he replies, "It is an ill sign or omen, to stumble at the threshold in going out. These words are ambiguous, and may have a double sense; either that schism is to be found in matter of instituted worship only, or only in the differences made in the time of celebrating instituted worship; and neither of these is yet true or yet proved, and so a mere begging of the thing in question: for," saith he, "schism may be in and about other matter besides instituted worship."

What measure I am to expect for the future from this entrance or beginning is not hard to conjecture. The truth is, the reverend author understood me not at all in what I affirmed. I say not that schism in the church is either about instituted worship or only in the time of worship, but that the thing I treat of is a disorder in the instituted worship of God; and so it is, if the being and constitution of any church be a part of God's worship. But when men are given to disputing, they think it incumbent on them to question every word and expression that may possibly give them an advantage. But we must, now we are engaged, take all in good part as it comes.

Having, nextly, granted my request of standing to the sole determination of Scripture in the controversy about the nature of schism, he insists on the Scripture use and notion of the word, according to what I had proposed: only, in the metaphorical sense of the word, as applied unto civil and political bodies, he endeavours to make it appear that it doth not only denote the difference and division that falls among them in judgment, but their secession also into parties; which though he proves not from any of the instances produced, yet that he may not trouble himself any farther in the like kind of needless labour, I do here inform him, that if he suppose that I deny that to be a schism where there is a separation, anal that *because there is a separation*, as though schism were in its whole nature exclusive of all separation, and lost its being when separation ensued, he hath taken my mind as rightly as he has done the whole design of my book, and my sense in his first animadversions on this chapter. But yet, because this is not proved, I shall desire him not to make use of it for the future, as though it were so. The first place urged is that of John vii. 43, "There was a schism among the people." It is not pretended that here was any separation. Acts xiv. 4, "The multitude of the city was divided," — that is, in their judgment about the apostles and their doctrine; but not only so, for οἱ μὲν ἦσαν is spoken of them, which expresses their separation into parties. What weight this new criticism is like to find with others, I know not: for my part, I know the words enforce not the thing aimed at, and the utmost that seems to be intended by that expression is the siding of the multitude, some with one, some with another, whilst they were all in a public commotion; nor doth the context require any more. The same is the case, Acts xxiii. 7, where the Pharisees and Sadducees were divided about Paul, whilst abiding in the place where the sanhedrim sat, being divided into parties long before. And in the testimony cited in my margin for the use of the word in other authors, the author makes even that διεμερίσθησαν εἰς τὰ μέρη to stand in opposition only to ὡμονόησαν, — nor was it any more. There was not among the people of Rome such a separation as to break up the corporation or to divide the government, as is known from the story. The place of his own producing, Acts xix. 9, proves, indeed, that then and there there was a separation; but, as the author confesses in the margin, the word there used to express it hath no relation to σχίσμα. Applied to ecclesiastical things, the reverend author confesses with me that the word is only used in 1 Cor. xi. 18, 19; and, therefore, that from thence the proper use and importance of it is to be learned. Having laid down the use of the word, to denote difference of mind and judgment, with troubles ensuing thereupon, amongst men met in some one assembly, about the compassing of a common end and design, I proceed to the particular accommodation of it to church-rents and schism, in that solitary instance given of it in the church of Corinth. What says our author hereunto? Says he, p. 26, "This is a forestalling the reader's judgment by a mere begging of the thing in question. As it hath in part been proved from the Scripture itself, where it is used for separation into parties in the political use of the word, why it may not so be used in the ecclesiastical sense, I see no reason." But if this be the way of begging the question, I confess I know not what course to take to prove what I intend. Such words are used sometimes in warm disputes causelessly; it were well they were placed where there is some pretence for them. Certainly they will not serve every turn. Before I asserted the use of the word, I instanced in all the places where it is used, and evinced the sense of it from them. If this be begging, it is not that lazy trade of begging which some use, but such as a man had as good professedly work as follow. How well he hath disproved this sense of the word from Scripture we have seen. I am not concerned in his seeing no reason why it may not be used in the ecclesiastical sense, according to his conception; my inquiry was how it was used, not how it might be used in this reverend author's judgment. And this is the substance of all that is offered to overthrow that principle, which, if it abide and stand, he must needs confess all his following pains to be to no purpose, "He sees no reason but it may be as he says!"

After the declaration of some such suspicions of his as we are now wonted unto, and which we cannot deny him the liberty of expressing, though I profess he does it unto my injury, he says, "This is the way, on the one hand, to free all church-separation from schism; and, on the other, to make all particular churches more or less inschismatical." Well, the first is denied; what is offered for the confirmation of the second? Saith he, "What one congregation almost is there in the world where there are not differences of judgment, whence ensue many troubles, about the compassing of one common end and design? I doubt whether his own be free therefrom." If any testimony may remove his scruple, I assure him, through the grace of God, hitherto it hath been so, and I hope it is so with multitudes of other churches; those with whom it is otherwise, it will appear at last to be more or less blamable on the account of schism.

Omitting my farther explication of what I had proposed, he passes unto p. 27 [102] of my book, and thence transcribes these words: "They had differences among themselves about unnecessary things. On these they engaged in disputes and sidings even in their solemn assemblies. Probably much vain jangling, alienation of affections, exasperation of spirit, with a neglect of due offices of love, ensued hereupon." Whereunto he subjoins, "That the apostle charges this upon them is true, but was that all? were there not divisions into parties as well as in judgments? We shall consider that ere long." But I am sorry he hath waived this proper place for the consideration of this important assertion. The truth is, "hic pes figendus," if he remove not this position, he labours in vain for the future. I desire also to know what he intends by "divisions into parties." If he intend that some were of one party, some of another, in these divisions and differences, it is granted; there can be no difference in judgment amongst men, but they must on that account be divided into parties. But if he intend thereby that they divided into several churches, assemblies, or congregations, any of them setting up new churches on a new account, or separating from the public assemblies of the church whereof they were, and that their so doing is reproved by the apostle under the name of schism, then I tell him that this is that indeed whose proof is incumbent on him. Fail he herein, the whole foundation of my discourse continues firm and unshaken. The truth is, I cannot meet with any one attempt to prove this, which alone was to be proved, if he intended that I should be any farther concerned in his discourse than only to find myself reviled and abused.

Passing over what I produce to give light and evidence unto my assertion, he proceeds to the consideration of the observations and inferences I make upon it, p. 29 [103] and onward.

The first he insists upon is, "That the thing mentioned is entirely in one church, amongst the members of one particular society. No mention is there in the least of one church divided against another, or separated from another."

1. To this he replies, — "That the church of Corinth was a collective church, made up of many congregations, and that I myself confess they had solemn assemblies, not one assembly only; that I beg the question, by taking it for one single congregation." But I suppose one particular congregation may have more than one solemn assembly, even as many as are the times wherein they solemnly assemble.

2. I supposed I had proved that it was "only one congregation," that used to assemble in one place, that the apostle charged this crime upon; and that this reverend author was pleased to overlook what was produced to that purpose, I am not to be blamed.

3. Here is another discovery that this reverend person never yet clearly understood the design of my treatise nor the principles I proceed upon. Doth he think it is any thing to my present business whether the church of Corinth were such a church as Presbyterians suppose it to be, or such a one as the Indedendents affirm it? Whilst all acknowledge it to be one church, be that particular church of what kind it will, if the schism rebuked by the apostle consisted in division in it, and not in separation from it, as such, I have evinced all that I intended by the observation under consideration. Yet this he again pursues, and tells me, that "there were more particular churches in and about Corinth, as that at Cenchrea; and that their differences were not confined to the verge of one church (for there were differences abroad out of the church) and says, that at unawares I confess that they disputed from house to house, and in the public assemblies." But I will assure the reverend author I was aware of what I said. Is it possible he should suppose that by the "verge of one church" I intended the meeting-place, and the assembly therein? Was it at all incumbent on me to prove that they did not manage their differences in private as well as in public? Is it likely any such thing should be? Did I deny that they sided and made parties about their divisions and differences? Is it any thing to me, or to any thing I affirm, how, where, and when, they managed their disputes and debated their controversies? It is true, there is mention of a church at Cenchrea, but is there any mention that that church made any separation from the church of Corinth, or that the differences mentioned were between the

members of these several churches? Is it any thing to my present design though there were twenty particular congregations in Corinth, supposing that, on any consideration, they were one church? I assure you, sir, I am more troubled with your not understanding the business and design I manage, than I am with all your reviling terms you have laden me withal.

Once for all, unless you prove that there was a separation from that church of Corinth (be it of what constitution it may by any be supposed), as such, into another church, and that this is reproved by the apostle under the name of schism, you speak not one word to invalidate the principle by me laid down. And for what he adds, "That for what I say, ' There was no one church divided against another, or separated from another,' it is assumed, but not proved, unless by a negative, which is invalid," he wrests my words. I say not there was *no such thing*, but that there was *no mention of any such thing*; for though it be as clear as the noonday that indeed there was no such thing, it sufficeth my purpose that there was no mention of any such thing, and therefore no such thing reproved under the name of schism. With this one observation I might well dismiss the whole ensuing treatise, seeing of how little use it is like to prove as to the business in hand, when the author of it indeed apprehends not the principle which he pretends to oppose. I shall once more tell him, that he abide not in his mistake, that if he intend to evert the principle here by me insisted on, it must be by a demonstration that the schism charged on the Corinthians by Paul consisted in the separation from, and relinquishment of, that church whereof they were members, and congregating into another not before erected or established; for this is that which the reformed churches are charged to do by the Romanists in respect of their churches, and accused of schism thereupon. But the differences which he thinks good to manage and maintain with and against the Independents do so possess the thoughts of this reverend author, that whatever occurs to him is immediately measured by the regard which it seems to bear, or may possibly bear, thereunto, though that consideration were least of all regarded in its proposal.

The next observation upon the former thesis that he takes into his examination, so far as he is pleased to transcribe it, is this: "Here is no mention of any particular man or number of men separating from the assembly of the whole church, or subducting of themselves from its power; only, they had groundless, causeless differences amongst themselves."[13] Hereunto our author variously replies, and says, first, "Was this all? were not separations made, if not from that church, yet in that church, as well as divisions? Let the Scripture determine. 1 Cor. i. 12, iii. 4, 'I am a disciple of Paul,' said one, 'And I a disciple of Apollos,' said another. In our language, 'I am a member of such a minister's congregation,' says one; 'Such a man for my money;' and so a third. And hereupon they most probably separated themselves into such and such congregations; and is not separation the ordinary issue of such envyings?"

I doubt not but that our reverend author supposeth that he hath here spoken to the purpose and matter in hand; and so, perhaps, may some others think also. I must crave leave to enter my dissent upon the account of the ensuing reasons; for, — 1. It is not separation *in* the church, by men's divisions and differences, whilst they continue members of the same church, that I deny to be here charged under the name of schism, but such a separation *from* the church as was before described. 2. The disputes amongst them about Paul and Apollos, the instruments of their conversion, cannot possibly be supposed to relate unto ministers of distinct congregations among them. Paul and Apollos were not so, and could not be figures of them that were; so that those expressions do not at all answer those which he is pleased to make parallel unto them. 3. Grant all this, yet this proves nothing to the cause in hand. Men may cry up, some the minister of one congregation, some of another, and yet neither of them separate from the one or other, or the congregations themselves fall into any separation. Wherefore, 4. He says, "Probably they separated into such and such congregations." But this is most improbable; for — (1.) There is no mention at all of those many congregations that are supposed; but rather the contrary, as I have declared, is expressly asserted. (2.) There is no such thing mentioned or intimated; nor, (3.) Are they in the least rebuked for any such thing, though the forementioned differences, which are a less evil, are reproved again and again

---

13 If the reader turn to p. 103, he will find slight differences between the sentence as originally given and as it stands here. It is given, however, in both instances, according to the original editions of the treatises; and the difference, therefore, does not arise from inaccuracy in the subsequent printing of them. — Ed.

under the name of schism. So that this most improbable improbability, or rather vain conjecture, is a very mean refuge and retreat from the evidence of express Scripture; which in this place is alone inquired after. Doth, indeed, the reverend author think, will he pretend so to do, that the holy apostle should so expressly, weightily, and earnestly reprove their dissensions in the church whereof they were members, and yet not speak one word or give the least intimation of their separation from the church, had there indeed been any such thing? I dare leave this to the conscience of the most partially addicted person under heaven to the author's cause, who hath any conscience at all; nor dare I dwell longer on the confutation of this fiction, though it be, upon the matter, the whole of what I am to contend withal. But he farther informs us that "there was a separation to parties in the church of Corinth, at least as to one ordinance of the Lord's supper, as appears chap. xi. 18, 20–22; and this was part of their schism, verse 16. And not long after they separated into other churches, slighting and undervaluing the first ministers and churches as nothing, or less pure than their own; which we see practised sufficiently at this day." *Ans.* Were not this the head and seat of the first part of the controversy insisted on, I should not be able to prevail with myself to cast away precious time in the consideration of such things as these, being tendered as suitable to the business in hand. It is acknowledged that there were differences amongst them, and disorders in the administration of the Lord's supper; that therein they used "respect of persons," — as the place quoted in the margin by our author, James ii. 1–4, manifests that they were ready to do in other places. The disorder the apostle blames in the administration of the ordinance was, "when they came together in the church," 1 Cor. xi. 18, when they "came together in one place," verse 20, there they "tarried not one for another," as they ought, verse 33, but coming unprepared, some having eaten before, some being hungry, verse 21, all things were managed with great confusion amongst them, verse 22. And if this prove not that the schism they were charged withal consisted in a separation from that church with which they came together in one place, we are hopeless of any farther evidence to be tendered to that purpose. That there were disorders amongst them in the celebration of the Lord's supper is certain; that they separated into several congregations on that account, or one from another, or any from all, is not, in the least intimation, signified; but the plain contrary shines in the whole state of things, as there represented. Had that been done, and had so to do been such an evil as is pleaded (as causelessly to do it is no small evil), it had not passed unreproved from him who was resolved, in the things of God, not to "spare" them. 2. That they afterward fell into the separation aimed at to be asserted our reverend author affirms, that so he may make way for a reflection on the things of his present disquietment. But as we are not as yet concerning ourselves in what they did afterward, so when we are, we shall expect somewhat more than bare affirmations for the proof of it, being more than ordinarily confident that he is not able, from the Scripture, nor any other story of credit, to give the least countenance to what he here affirms. But now, as if the matter were well discharged, when there hath not one word been spoken that in the least reaches the case in hand, he saith, — 3. "By way of supposition that there was but one single congregation at Corinth, yet," saith he, "the apostle dehorts the brethren from schism, and writes to more than the church of Corinth, chap. i. 2." *Ans.* I have told him before, that though I am full well resolved that there was but one single congregation at Corinth in those days, yet I am not at all convinced, as to the proposition under confirmation, to assert any such thing, but will suppose the church to be of what kind my author pleaseth, whilst he will acknowledge it to be the particular church of Corinth. I confess the apostle dehorts the brethren from schism, even others as well as those at Corinth, — so far as the church of God, in all places and ages, is concerned in his instructions and dehortations, — when they fall under the case stated, parallel with that which is the ground of his dealing with them at Corinth. But what that schism was from which he dehorts them, he declares only in the instance of the church of Corinth; and thence is the measure of it to be taken in reference to all dehorted from it. Unto the third observation added by me he makes no return, but only lays down some exceptions to the exemplification given of the whole matter, in another schism that fell out in that church about forty years after the composure of this, which was the occasion of that excellent epistle unto them from the church of Rome, called the epistle of Clement, dissuading them from persisting in that strife and contention, and pressing them to unity and agreement among themselves. Some things our reverend author offers as to this instance, but so as that I cannot but suppose that he consulted not the epistle on this particular occasion; and therefore now I desire him that he would do so, and I am persuaded he will not a second time give countenance to any such apprehension of the then state of the church, as though there were any separation made from it by any of the members thereof doing or suffering the injury there complained of, about which those differences and contentions arose. I shall not need to go over again the severals of that epistle. One word mentioned by myself, namely, μετηγάγετε, he insists on, and informs us that it implies a separation into other assemblies; which, he says, I waived to understand. I confess I did so in this place; and so would he also, if he had once consulted it. The speech of the church of Rome is there to the church of Corinth, in reference to the elders whom they had deposed. The whole sentence is, Ὁρῶμεν γὰρ ὅτι ἐνίους ὑμεῖς μετηγάγετε καλῶς πολιτευομένους ἐκ τῆς ἀμέμπτως αὐτοῖς τετιμημένης λειτουργίας· and the words immediately going before are, Μακάριοι οἱ προοδοιπορήσαντες πρεσβύτεροι οἵτινες ἔγκαρπον καὶ τελείαν ἔσχον τὴν ἀνάλυσιν, οὐ γὰρ εὐλαβοῦνται μή τις αὐτοὺς μεταστήσῃ ἀπὸ τοῦ ἱδρυμένου αὐτοῖς τόπου· then follows that ὁρῶμεν γὰρ. Our author, I suppose, understands Greek, and so I shall spare my pains of transcribing Mr Young's Latin translation, or adding one in English of mine own; and if he be pleased to read these words, I think we shall have no more of his μετηγάγετε.

If a fair opportunity call me forth to the farther management of this controversy, I shall not doubt but from that epistle and some other pieces of undoubted antiquity, as the epistles of the churches of Vienne and Lyons, of Smyrna, with some public records of those days, as yet preserved (worthy all of them to be written in letters of gold), to evince that state of the churches of Christ in those days, as will give abundant light to the principles I proceed upon in this whole business.

And thus have I briefly vindicated what was proposed as the precise Scripture notion of schism; against which, indeed, not any one objection hath been raised that speaks directly to the thing in hand. Our reverend author being full of warm affections against the Independents, and exercised greatly in disputing the common principles which either they hold or are supposed so to do, measures every thing that is spoken by his apprehension of those differences wherein, as he thinks, their concernment doth lie. Had it not been for some such prejudice (for I am unwilling to ascribe it to more blamable principles), it would have been almost impossible that he should have once imagined that he had made the least attempt towards the eversion of what I had asserted, much less that he had made good the title of his book, though he scarce forgets it, or any thing concerning it but its *proof*, in any one whole leaf of his treatise. It remains, then, that the nature and notion of schism, as revealed and described in the Scripture, was rightly fixed in my former discourse; and I must assure this reverend author that I am not affrighted from the embracing and maintaining of it with those scare-crows of "new light," "singularity," and the like, which he is pleased frequently to set up to that purpose. The discourse that ensues in our author concerning a parity of reason, to prove that if that be schism, then much more is separation so, shall afterward, if need be, be considered, when I proceed to show what yet farther may be granted without the least prejudice of truth, though none can necessitate me to recede from the precise notion of the name and thing delivered in the Scripture. I confess I cannot but marvel that any man undertaking the examination of that treatise, and expressing so much indignation at the thoughts of my discourse that lieth in this business, should so slightly pass over that whereon he knew I laid the great weight of the whole. Hath he so much as endeavoured to prove that that place to the Corinthians is not the only place wherein there is, in the Scripture, any mention of schism in an ecclesiastical sense, or that the church of Corinth was not a particular church? Is any thing of importance offered to impair the assertion, that the evil reproved was within the verge of that church, and without separation from it? And do I need any more to make good to the utmost that which I have asserted? But of these things afterward.

In all that follows to the end of this chapter, I meet with nothing of importance that deserves farther notice. That which is spoken is for the most part built upon mistakes; as, that when I speak of a member or the members of one particular Church, I intend only one single congregation, exclusively to any other acceptation of that expression, in reference to the apprehension of others; that I deny the reformed churches to be true churches, because I deny the church of Rome to be so, and deny the institution of a national church, which yet our author pleads not for. He would have it for granted that because schism consists in a difference among church-members, therefore he that raises such a difference, whether he be a member of that church wherein the difference is raised, or of any other, or no (suppose he be a Mohammedan or a Jew), is a schismatic; pleads for the old definition of schism, as suitable to the Scripture, after the whole foundation of it is taken away; wrests many of my expressions, — as that in particular, in not making the matter of schism to be things relating to the worship of God, — to needless discourses about doctrine and discipline, not apprehending what I intended by that expression, of "the worship of God;" and I suppose it not advisable to follow him in such extravagancies. The usual aggravations of schism he thought good to re-enforce; whether he hoped that I would dispute with him about them I cannot tell. I shall now assure him that I will not, though, if I may have his good leave to say so, I lay much more weight on those insisted on by myself, wherein I am encouraged by his approbation of them.

Chapter V.

The third chapter of my treatise, consisting in the preventing and removing such objections as the precedent discourse might seem liable and obnoxious unto, is proposed to examination by our reverend author in the third chapter of his book, and the objections mentioned undertaken to be managed by him; with what success, some few considerations will evince.

The first objection by me proposed was taken from the common apprehension of the nature of schism, and the issue of stating it as by me laid down, — namely, hence it would follow that the "separation of any man or men from a true church, or of one church from others, is not schism." But now waiving, for the present, the more large consideration of the name and thing, — which yet in the process of my discourse I do condescend upon, according to the principle laid down, — I say that, in the precise signification of the word, and description of the thing as given by the Holy Ghost, this is true. No such separation is in the Scripture so called, or so accounted: whether it may not in a large sense be esteemed as such, I do not dispute; yea, I afterward grant it so far as to make that concession the bottom and foundation of my whole plea for the vindication of the reformed churches from that crime. Our reverend author re-enforces the objection by sundry instances: as, — 1. "That he hath disproved that sense or precise signification of the word in Scripture;" how well, let the reader judge. 2. "That supposing that to be the only sense mentioned in that case of the Corinthians, yet may another sense be intimated in Scripture, and deduced by regular and rational consequence." Perhaps this will not be so easy an undertaking, this being the only place where the name is mentioned or thing spoken of in an ecclesiastical sense; but when any proof is tendered of what is here affirmed, we shall attend unto it. It is said, indeed, that "if separation in judgment in a church be a schism, much more to separate from a church." But our question is about the precise notion of the word in Scripture, and consequences from thence, not about consequents from the nature of things; concerning which, if our author had been pleased to have stayed a while, he would have found me granting as much as he could well desire. 3. 1 John ii. 19 is sacrificed, ἀμετρίᾳ τῆς ἀνθολκῆς, and interpreted of schism; where (to make one venture in imitation of our author) all orthodox interpreters and writers of controversies expound it of apostasy, neither will the context or arguing of the apostle admit of another exposition. Men's wresting of Scripture to give countenance to inveterate errors is one of their worst concomitants. So, then, that separation from churches is oftentimes evil is readily granted. Of what nature that evil is, with what are the aggravations of it, a judgment is to be made from the pleas and pretences that its circumstances afford. So far as it proceeds from such dissensions as before were mentioned, so far it proceeds from schism; but in its own nature, absolutely considered, it is not so.

To render my former assertions the more unquestionably evident, I consider the several accounts given of men's blamable departures from any church or churches mentioned in Scripture, and manifest that none of them come under the head of schism. "Apostasy, irregularity of walking, and professed sensuality," are the heads whereinto all blamable departures from the churches in the Scripture are referred.

That there are other accounts of this crime our author doth not assert; he only says, that "all or some of the places" I produce as "instances of a blamable separation from a church do mind the nature of schism as precedaneous to the separation." Whatever the matter is, I do not find him speaking so faintly and with so much caution through his whole discourse as in this place: "All or some do it; they mind the nature of schism; they mind it as precedaneous to the separation." So the sum of what he aims at in contesting about the exposition of those places of Scripture is this: "Some of them do mind" (I know not how) "the nature of schism, which he never once named as precedaneous to separation; therefore, the precise notion of schism in the Scripture doth not denote differences and divisions in a church only." "Quod erat demonstrandum." That I should spend time in debating a consideration so remote from the state of the controversy in hand, I am sure will not be expected by such as understand it.

Page 77 [p. 122] of my treatise I affirm, "That for a man to withdraw or withhold himself from the communion external and visible of any church or churches, on the pretension or plea, be it true or otherwise, that the worship, doctrine, or: discipline instituted by Christ is corrupted among them, with which corruption he dares not defile himself, it is nowhere in the Scripture called schism; nor is that case particularly exemplified or expressly supposed, whereby a judgment may be made of the fact at large, but we are left upon the whole matter to the guidance of such general rules and principles as are given us for that end and purpose." Such is my meanness of apprehension, that I could not understand but that either this assertion must be subscribed unto as of irrefragable verity, or else that instances to the contrary must have been given out of the Scripture; for on that hinge alone doth this present controversy (and that by consent) turn itself. But our reverend author thinks good to take another course (for which his reasons may easily be conjectured), and excepts against the assertion itself in general, first, as "ambiguous and fallacious," and then also intimates that he will scan the words in particular. "Mihi jussa capessere [fas est]." 1. He says that, "I tell not whether a man may separate where there is corruption in some one of these only, or in all of them; nor, 2. How far some or all of these must be corrupted before we separate." *Ans.* This is no small vanity under the sun, that men will not only measure themselves by themselves, but others also by their own measure. Our author is still with his finger in the sore, and therefore supposes that others must needs take the same course. Is there any thing in my assertion whether a man may separate from any church or no? any thing upon what corruption he may lawfully so do? any thing of stating the difference betwixt the Presbyterians and Independents? do I at all fix it on this foot of account when I come so to do? I humbly beg of this author, that if I have so obscurely and intricately delivered myself and meaning that he cannot come to the understanding of my design nor import of my expressions, he would favour me with a command to explain myself before he engage into a public refutation of what he doth not so clearly apprehend. Alas! I do not in this place in the least intend to justify any separation, nor to show what pleas are sufficient to justify a separation, nor what corruption in the church separated from is necessary thereunto, nor at all regard the controversy his eye is always on; but only declare what is not comprised in the precise Scripture notion of schism, as also how a judgment is to be made of that which is so by me excluded, whether it be good or evil. Would he have been pleased to have spoken to the business in hand, or any thing to the present purpose, it must not have been by an inquiry into the grounds and reasons of separation, how far it may be justified by the plea mentioned, or how far not; when that plea is to be allowed, and when rejected; but this only was incumbent on him to prove, — namely, that such a separation upon that plea, or the like, is called schism in the Scripture, and as such a thing condemned. What my concernment is in the ensuing observations, that "the Judaical church was as corrupt as ours, — that if a bare plea, true or false, will serve to justify men, all separatists may be justified," he himself will easily perceive. But, however, I cannot but tell him by the way, that he who will dogmatize in this controversy from the Judaical church, and the course of proceedings amongst them, to the direction and limitation of duty as to the churches of the gospel, — considering the vast and important differences between the constitutions of the one and the other, with the infallible obligation to certain principles, on the account of the typical institution in that primitive church, when there neither was nor could be any more in the world, — must expect to bring other arguments to compass his design than the analogy pretended. [As] for the justification of separatists of the reason, if it will ensue upon the examination for separation, and the circumstances of the separating, whereunto I refer them, let it follow, and let who will complain.

But to fill up the measure of the mistake he is engaged in, he tells us, p. 75, that "this is the pinch of the question, whether a man or a company of men may separate from a true church, upon a plea of corruption in it, true or false, and set up another church as to ordinances, renouncing that church to be a true church. This," saith he, "is plainly our case at present with the doctor and his associates." Truly, I do not know that ever I was necessitated to a more sad and fruitless employment in this kind of labour and travail. Is that the question in present agitation? is any thing, word, tittle, or iota spoken to it? Is it my present, business to state the difference between the Presbyterians and Independents? Do I anywhere do it upon this account? Do

I not everywhere positively deny that there is any such separation made? Nay, can common honesty allow such a state of a question, if that were the business in hand, to be put upon me? Are their ordinances and churches so denied by me as is pretended? What I have often said must again be repeated: the reverend author hath his eye so fixed on the difference between the Presbyterians and the Independents, that he is at every turn led out of the way, into such mistakes as it was not possible he should otherwise be overtaken withal. This is, perhaps, "mentis gratissimus error;" but I hope it would be no death to him to be delivered from it. When I laid down the principles which it was his good will to oppose, I had many things under consideration as to the settling of conscience in respect of manifold oppositions, and, to tell him the truth, least valued that which he is pleased to manage and to look upon as my sole intendment. If it be not possible to deliver him from this strong imagination, that carries the images and species of Independency always before his eyes, we shall scarce speak "ad idem" in this whole discourse. I desire, then, that he would take notice, that as the state of the controversy he proposes doth no more relate to that which peculiarly is pretended to lie under his consideration than any other thing whatever that he might have mentioned; so when the peculiar difference between him and the Independents comes to be managed, scarce any one term of his state will be allowed.

Exceptions are, in the next place, attempted to be put in to my assertion, that there is no example in the Scripture of any one church's departure from the union which they ought to hold with others, unless it be in some of their departures from the common faith, which is not schism; much with the same success as formerly. Let him produce one instance, and "en herbam."[14] I grant the Roman church, on a supposition that it is a church (which yet I utterly deny), to be a *schismatical* church, upon the account of the *intestine divisions* of all sorts; on what other accounts other men urge them with the same guilt, I suppose he knows by this that I am not concerned. Having finished this exploit, because I had said "*if* I were unwilling I did not understand how I might be compelled to carry on the notion of schism any farther," he tells me, "though I be unwilling, he doubts not but to be able to compel me." But who told him I was

---

14 "I am cast to the ground, I own myself conquered." — Ed.

unwilling so to do? Do I not immediately, without any compulsion, very freely fall upon the work? Did I say I was unwilling? Certainly it ought not to be thus. Of his abilities in other things I do not doubt; in this discourse he is pleased to exercise more of something else.

There is but one passage more that needs to be remarked, and so this chapter also is dismissed. He puts in a caveat, that I limit not schism to the worship of God, upon these words of mine: "The consideration of what sort of union in reference to the worship of God" (where he inserts in the repetition, "mark that!"), "as instituted by Jesus Christ, is the foundation of what I have farther to offer;" whereto he subjoins, "The design of this is, that he may have a fair retreat when he is charged with breach of union in other respects, and so with schism, to escape by this evasion. This breach of union is not in reference to the worship of God in one assembly met to that end." I wish we had once an end of these mistakes and false, uncharitable surmises. By the "worship of God" I intend the whole compass of institutions, and their tendency thereunto; and I know that I speak properly enough. In so doing I have no such design as I am charged withal, nor do I need it. I walk not in fear of this author's forces, that I should be providing beforehand to secure my retreat. I have passed the bounds of the precise notion of schism before insisted on, and yet doubt not but, God assisting, to make good my ground. If he judge I cannot, let him command my *personal attendance* on him at any time, to be driven from it by him. Let him by any means prove against me, at any time, a breach of any union instituted by Jesus Christ, and I will promise him that with all speed I will retreat from that state or thing whereby I have so done. I must profess to this reverend author that I like not the cause he manages one whit the better for the way whereby he manageth it. We had need watch and pray that we be not led into temptation, seeing we are in some measure not ignorant of the vices of Satan.

Now, that he may see this door of escape shut up, that so he may not need to trouble himself any more in taking care lest I escape that way, when he intends to fall upon me with those blows, which as yet I have not felt, I shall shut it fast myself, beyond all possibility of my opening it again. I here, then, declare unto him, that whenever he shall prove that I have broken any union of the institution of Jesus Christ, of what sort soever, I will not, in excuse of myself, insist on the plea mentioned, but will submit to the discipline which shall be thought meet by him to be exercised towards any one offending in that kind. Yet truly, on this engagement, I would willingly contract with him, that in his next reply he should not deal with me as he hath done in this, neither as to my person nor as to the differences between us.

Chapter VI.

Having declared and vindicated the Scripture proper notion of schism, and thence discovered the nature of it, with all its aggravations, with the mistakes that men have run into who have suited their apprehensions concerning it unto what was their interests to have it thought to be, and opened a way thereby for the furtherance of peace among professors of the gospel of Jesus Christ; for the farther security of the consciences of men unjustly accused and charged with the guilt of this evil, I proceeded to the consideration of it in the usual common acceptation of the word and thing, that so I might obviate whatever, with any tolerable pretence, is insisted on, as deduced by a parity of reason from what is delivered in the Scripture, in reference to the charge managed by some or other against all sorts of Protestants. Hereupon I grant that it may be looked on in general as διαίρεσις ἑνότητος, "a breach of union," so that it be granted also that that union be a union of the institution of Jesus Christ. To find out, then, the nature of schism under the consideration of the condescension made, and to discover wherein the guilt of it doth consist, it is necessary that we find out what that union is, and wherein it doth consist, whereof it is the breach and interruption, or is supposed so to be, over and above the breach above mentioned and described. Now, this union being the union of the church, the several acceptations of the "church" in Scripture are to be investigated, that the union inquired after may be made known. The "church" in Scripture being taken either for the church catholic, or the whole number of elect believers in the world (for we lay aside the consideration of that part of this great family of God which is already in heaven from this distinction), or else for the general visible body of those who profess the gospel of Christ, or for a particular society joining together in the celebration of the ordinances of the New Testament instituted by Christ, to be so celebrated by them, the union of it, with the breach of that union in these several respects, with the application of the whole to the business under consideration, was to be inquired after; which also was performed.

I began with the consideration of the catholic invisible church of Christ, and the union thereof. Having declared the rise of this distinction, and the necessity of it from the nature of the things themselves, as to the matter of this church, or the church of Christ as here militant on earth, I affirm and evince it to be *all and only elect believers*. The union of this church consists in the inhabitation of the same Spirit in all the members of it, uniting them to the head, Christ Jesus, and therein to one another. The breach of this union I manifested to consist in the loss of that Spirit, With all the peculiar consequences and effects of him in the hearts of them in whom he dwells. This I manifest, according to our principles, to be impossible, and upon a supposition of it, how remote it would be from schism, under any notion or acceptation of the word; so closing that discourse with a charge on the Romanists of their distance from an interest in this church of Jesus Christ.

Our reverend author professes that he hath but little to say to these things. Some exceptions he puts in unto some expressions used in the explication of my sense in this particular. That which he chiefly insists upon, is the accommodation of that promise, Matt. xvi. 18, "Upon this rock I will build my church," to the church in this sense; which he concludes to belong to the visible church of professors. Now, as I am not at all concerned, as to the truth of what I am in confirmation of, to which of these it be applied, so I am far from being alone in that application of it to the catholic church which I insist upon. All our divines that from hence prove the perseverance of all individual believers, — as all do that I have met withal who write on that subject, — are of the same mind with me. Moreover, the church is built on this rock in its individuals, or I know not how it is so built. The building on Christ doth not denote a mere relation of a general body to his truth, that it shall always have an existence, but the union of the individuals with him, in their being built on him, to whom the promise is made. I acknowledge it for as unquestionable a truth as any we believe, that Christ hath had, and ever shall have, to the end of the world; a visible number of those that profess his name and subjection to his kingdom, because of the necessary consequence of profession upon believing; but that that truth is intended in this promise, any farther but in respect of this consequence, I am not convinced. And I would be loath to say that this promise is not made to every particular believer, and only unto them, being willing to vindicate to the saints of God all those grounds of consolation which he is so willing they should be made partakers of.

As to the union of this church and the breach of it, our reverend author hath a little to say. Because there may be "some decays in true grace in the members of this church," he affirms, "that in a sort there may be said to be a breach in this union; and so, consequently, a schism in this body." He seemed formerly to be afraid lest all schism should be thrust out of the world; if he can retrieve it on the account of any true believer's failing in grace, or falling for a season, I suppose he needs not fear the loss of it whilst this world continues. But it is fit wise and learned men should take the liberty of calling things by what names they please, so they will be pleased withal not to impose their conceptions and use of terms on them who are not able to understand the reasons of them. It is true, there may be a schism among the members of this church, but not as members of this church, nor with reference to the union thereof. It is granted that schism is the breach of *union*, but not of *every union*, much less not a breach of that, which if it were a breach of, it were not schism. However, by the way, I am bold to tell this reverend author that this doctrine of his concerning schism in the catholic invisible church, by the failing in grace in any of the members of it for a season, is a new notion; which as he cannot justify to us, because it is false, so I wonder how he will justify it to himself, because it is "new." And what hath been obtained by the author against my principles in this chapter I cannot perceive. The nature of the church in the state considered is not opposed; the union asserted not disproved; the breach of that union is denied, as I suppose, no less by him than myself. That the instances that some saints, as members of this church, may sometimes fail in grace, more or less, for some season, and that the members of this church, though not as members of this church, yet on other considerations, may be guilty of schism, concern not the business under debate, himself I hope is satisfied.

Chapter VII.

Our progress, in the next place, is to the consideration of the *catholic church visible*. Who are the members of this church, whereof it is constituted, what is required to make them so, on what account men visibly professing the gospel may be esteemed justly divested of the privilege of being members of this church, with sundry respects of the church in that sense, are in my treatise discussed. The union of this church, that is proper and peculiar unto it as such, I declared to be the profession of the saving doctrines of the gospel, not everted by any of the miscarriages, errors, or oppositions to it, that are there recounted. The breach of this Union I manifest to consist in apostasy from the profession of the faith, and so to be no schism, upon whomsoever the guilt of it doth fall; pleading the immunity of the Protestants, as such, from the guilt of the breach of this union, and charging it upon the Romanists, in all the ways whereby it may be broken, an issue is put to that discourse.

What course our reverend author takes in the examination of this chapter, and the severals of it, wherein the strength of the controversy doth lie, is now to be considered. Doth he deny this church to be a collection of all that are duly called Christians in respect of their profession? to be that great multitude who, throughout the world, profess the doctrine of the gospel and subjection to Jesus Christ? Doth he deny the union of this church, or that whereby that great multitude are incorporated into one body as visible and professing, to be the profession of the saving doctrines of the gospel, and of subjection to Jesus Christ according to them? Doth he deny the dissolution of this union, as to the interest of any member by it in the body, to be by apostasy from the profession of the gospel? Doth he charge that apostasy upon those whom he calls Independents, as such? or if he should, could he tolerably defend his charge? Doth he prove that the breach of this union is, under that formality, properly schism? Nothing less, as far as I can gather. Might not, then, the trouble of this chapter have been spared? Or shall I be necessitated to defend every expression in my book, though nothing at all to the main business under debate, or else Independency must go for "a great schism?" I confess this is a somewhat hard law, and such as I cannot proceed in obedience unto, without acknowledging his ability to compel me to go on farther than I am willing; yet I do it with this engagement, that I will so look to myself, that he shall never have that power over me any more, nor will I, upon any compulsion of useless, needless cavils and exceptions, do so again. So that in his reply he now knows how to order his affairs, so as to be freed from the trouble of a rejoinder.

His first attempt in this chapter is upon a short discourse of mine in my process, which I profess not to be needful to the purpose in hand, relating to some later disputes about the *nature* of this church; wherein some had affirmed it to be a *genus* to particular churches, which are so many distinct *species* of it; and others, that it was a *totum* made up of particular churches as its parts; — both which in some sense I denied; partly, out of a desire to keep off all debates about the things of God from being inwrapped and agitated in and under philosophical notions and feigned terms of art, which hath exceedingly multiplied controversies in the world and rendered them endless, and doth more or less straiten or oppose every truth that is so dealt withal; partly, because I evidently saw men deducing false consequents from the supposition of such notions of this church. For the first way, our reverend author lets it pass, only with a remark upon my dissenting from Mr Hooker of New England, which he could not but note by the way, although he approves what I affirm. A worthy note! as though all the brethren of the presbyterian way were agreed among themselves in all things of the like importance, or that I were in my judgment inthralled to any man or men, so that it should deserve a note when I dissent from them. Truly, I bless God I am utterly unacquainted with any such frame of spirit or bondage of mind as must be supposed to be in them whose dissent from other men is a matter of such observation. One is my Master, to whom alone my heart and judgment are in subjection. For the latter, I do not say absolutely that particular churches are not the parts of the catholic visible [church] in any sense, but that they are not so parts of it as such, so that it should be constituted and made up by them and of them, for the order and purpose of an instituted church, for the celebration of the worship of God and institutions of Christ, according to the gospel; which when our author proves that it is, I shall acknowledge myself obliged to him. He says, indeed, that "it was once possible that all the members of the catholic church should meet together to hear one sermon," etc. But he is to prove that they were bound to do so as that catholic church, and not that it was possible for all the members of it under any other notion or consideration so to convene. But he says they are bound to do so still, but that the multitude makes it impossible. "Credat Apella," that Christ hath bound his church to that which himself makes impossible! Neither are they so bound. They are bound, by his own acknowledgment, to be members of particular churches; and in that capacity are they bound so to convene, those churches being, by the will of God, appointed for the seat of ordinances. And so what he adds in the next place, of particular churches being bound, according to the institution of Christ, to assemble for the celebration of ordinances, is absolutely destructive of the former figment. But he would know a reason why forty or more, that are not members of one particular church, but only of the catholic, meeting together, may not join together in all ordinances, as well as they may meet to hear the word preached, and often do. To which I answer, that it is because Jesus Christ hath appointed particular churches, and there is more required to them than the occasional meeting of some, any, or all if possible, of the members of the catholic church, as such, will afford.

His reflections upon myself added in that place are now grown so common that they deserve not any notice. In his ensuing discourse, if I may take leave to speak freely to our reverend author, he wrangles about terms and expressions, adding to and altering those by me used in this business at his pleasure, to make a talk to no purpose. The sum of what he pretends to oppose is, — That this *universal church*, or the universality of professors considered as such, neither formally as members of the church catholic mystically elect, nor as members of any particular church, have, as such, any church-form of the institution of Christ, by virtue whereof they should make up one instituted church, for the end and purpose of the celebration of the ordinances of the gospel therein. If he suppose he can prove the contrary, let him cease from cavilling at words and by-expressions, — which is a facile task for any man to engage in, and no way useful, but to make controversies endless, — and answer my reasons against it, which here he passeth over, and produce his testimonies and arguments for that purpose. This trivial ventilation of particular passages cut off from their influence into the whole is not worth a nut-shell, but is a business fit for them who have nothing else to employ themselves about.

Coming to consider the *union* that I assign to this church, after whose breach an inquiry is to be made, — which is the main and only thing of his concernment as to the aim he hath proposed to himself, — he passeth it over very slightly, taking no notice at all of my whole discourse from p. 116 to p. 133 [pp. 138–145] of my treatise, wherein I disprove the pretensions of other things to be the union or bond of union to this church. He fixes a very little while on what I assign to be that union. This, I say, is "profession of the faith of the gospel, and subjection to Jesus Christ according to it." To which he adds, that they are bound to more than this, namely, "to the exercise of the same specifical ordinances, as also to love one another, to subjection to the same discipline, and, where it is possible, to the exercise of the same numerical worship." All this was expressly affirmed by me before; it is all virtually contained in their "profession," so far as the things mentioned are revealed in the gospel. Only, as to the celebrating of the same numerical ordinances, I cannot grant that they are obliged hereunto, as formally considered members of that church; nor shall, until our reverend author shall think meet to prove that particular congregations are not the institutions of Jesus Christ. But hereupon he affirms that that is a strange assertion used by me, p. 117 [p. 139], namely, "That if there be not an institution for the joining in the same numerical ordinances, the union of this church is not really a church union." This is no more but what was declared before, nor more than what I urged the testimony of a learned Presbyterian for; no more but this, that the universality of Christians throughout the world are not, under such an institution as that, to assemble together for the celebration of the same numerical ordinances, the pretence of any such institution being supplied by Christ's acknowledged institution of particular churches for that purpose.

What I have offered in my treatise as evidence that Protestants are not guilty of the breach of this union, and that where any are, their crime, is not schism but apostasy, either as to profession or conversation, I leave to the judgment of all candid, sober, and ingenuous readers. For such as love strife, and debates, and disputes, whereof the world is full, I would crave of them, that if they must choose me for their adversary, they would allow me to answer in person, "vivâ voce," to prevent this tedious trouble of writing; which, for the most part, is fruitless and needless. Some exceptions our author lays in against the properties of the profession by me required as necessary to the preservation of this union. As to the first, of "professing all necessary saving truths of the gospel," he excepts that the apostles were ignorant of many necessary truths of the gospel for a season, and some had never heard of the Holy Ghost, Acts xix. 2, and yet they kept the union of the catholic church. And yet our author, before he closeth this chapter, will charge the breach of this union on some whose errors cannot well be apprehended to lie in the denial of any necessary truth of the gospel that is indispensably necessary to salvation! As to his instance of the apostles, he knows it is one thing not to know clearly and distinctly for some season some truths "in hypothesi," and another to deny them, being sufficiently; and clearly revealed "in thesi." And for those in the Acts, it is probable they were ignorant of the dispensations of the Holy Ghost, with his marvellous effects under the gospel, rather than of the person of the Holy Ghost; for even in respect of the former, it is absolutely said that "the Holy Ghost was not yet, because that Jesus was not yet glorified." I shall not pursue his other exceptions, being sorry that his judgment leads him to make them; that which alone bears any aspect to the business in hand, he insists on, p. 99, in these words: "I have intimated, and partly proved, that there may be a breach of union with respect to the catholic church upon other considerations" (namely, besides the renunciation of the profession of the gospel); "as, first, There is a bond that obliges every member of this church to join together in exercising the same ordinances of worship. When, then, any man shall refuse to join with others, or refuse others to join with him, here is a breach of love and union among the members of the catholic church, and in the particular churches, as parts of the catholic."

The reader must pardon me for producing and insisting on these things, seeing I do it with this profession, that I can fix on nothing else so much to the purpose in hand; and yet how little these are so cannot but be evident, upon a slight view, to the meanest capacities: for, — 1. He tells us that "there may be a breach of union with respect to the catholic church upon other considerations;" not that there may be a breach of the union of the catholic church. 2. That there is a bond binding men to the exercise of ordinances; so there is, binding man to all holiness; — and yet he denies the vilest profane persons to break that bond or this union. 3. That there may be a breach of union among the members of the church; but who knows it not that knows all members of particular churches are also members of this church general? Our inquiry is after the union of the catholic church visible, what it is, how broken, and what the crime or evil is whereby it is broken; also, what obligations lie on the members of that church, as they stand under any other formal considerations. What is the evil they are any of them guilty of in not answering these obligations, we were not at all inquiring; nor doth it in this place concern us so to do. And in what he afterward tells us of some proceedings contrary to the practice of the universal church, he intends, I suppose, all the churches in the world wherein the members of the universal church have walked or do so: for the universal church, as such, hath no practice as to celebration of ordinances; and if he suppose it hath, let him tell us what it is, and *when that practice was*. His appeal to the primitive believers and their small number will not avail him: for although they should be granted to be the then catholic visible church (against which he knows what exceptions may be laid from the believers amongst the Jews, such as Cornelius, to whom Christ had not as yet been preached as the Messiah come and exhibited), yet as such they joined not in the celebration of ordinances, but (as yet they were) as a particular congregation; yea, though all the apostles were amongst them, — the foundation of all the churches that afterward were called.

He concludes this chapter with an exception to my assertion, that "if the catholic church be a political body, it must have a visible political head," which nothing but the pope claims to be. Of this he says, — "1. There is no necessity; for," saith he, "he confesses the commonwealth of the Jews was a political body, and God, who is invisible, was their political head. 2. Jesus Christ is a visible head, yea, sometimes more, 'visus,' seen of men whilst on earth; though now for a time, in majesty (as some great princes do), he hath withdrawn himself from the sight of men on earth, yet is he seen of angels and saints in heaven." *Ans.* 1. I confess God was the king and ruler of the Jews; but yet, that they might be a visible political body, the invisible God appointed to them, under him, a visible head; as the pope blasphemously pretends to be appointed under Jesus Christ. 2. Jesus Christ is in his human nature still visible; as to his person, wherein he is the head of his church, he ever was, and is still, invisible. His present absence, is not upon the account of majesty, seeing in his majesty he is still present with us; and as to his bodily absence, he gives other accounts than that here insinuated. Now, it sufficeth not to constitute a visible political body, that the head of it in any respect may be seen, unless as their head he is seen. Christ is visible, as this church is visible; — he in his laws, in his word; that in its profession, in its obedience. But I marvel that our reverend author, thus concluding for Christ to be the political head of this church, as a church, should at the same time contend for such subjects of this head as he doth, p. 96, — namely, persons "contradicting their profession of the knowledge of God by a course of wickedness, manifesting principles of profaneness, wherewith the belief of the truth they profess hath an absolute inconsistency," as I expressly describe the persons whose membership in this church, and relation thereby to Christ their head, he pleads for. Are, indeed, these persons any better than Mohammedans as to church privileges? They are, indeed, in some places, as to providential advantages of hearing the word preached; but woe unto them on that account! it shall be more tolerable for Mohammedans in the day of Christ than for them. Shall their baptism avail them? Though it were valid in its administration, — that is, was celebrated in obedience to the command of Christ, — is it not null to them? Is not their circumcision uncircumcision? Shall such persons give their children any right to church privileges? Let them, if you please, be so subject to Christ as rebels and traitors are subject to their earthly princes. They ought, indeed, to be so, but are they so? Do they own their authority? are they obedient to them? do they enjoy any privilege of laws? or doth the apostle anywhere call such persons as live in a course of wickedness, manifesting principles utterly inconsistent with the profession of the gospel,

"Brethren?" God forbid we should once imagine these things so to be! And so much for that chapter.

Chapter VIII.

Of Independentism and Donatism.

The title of our author's book is, "Independency a Great Schism;" of this chapter, that it may be the better known what kind of schism it is, "Independentism is Donatism." Men may give what title they please to their books and chapters, though perhaps few books make good their titles. I am sure this doth not as yet, "nisi accusâsse sufficiat." Attempts of proof we have not as yet met withal; what this chapter will furnish us withal we shall now consider. He, indeed, that shall weigh the title, "Independentism is Donatism," and then, casting his eye upon the first lines of the chapter itself, find that the reverend author says he cannot but "acknowledge what I plead for the vindication of Protestants from the charge of schism, in their separation from Rome, as the catholic church, to be rational, solid, and judicious," will perhaps be at a loss in conjecturing how I am like to be dealt withal in the following discourse. A little patience will let him see that our author lays more weight upon the title than the preface of this chapter, and that, with all my fine trappings, I am enrolled in the black book of the Donatists; but, "Quod fors feret, feramus æquo animo;" or as another saith, "Debemus optare optima, cogitare difficillima, ferre quæcunque erunt." As the case is fallen out, we must deal with it as we can. First, he saith, "he is not satisfied that he not only denies the church of Rome (so called) to be a particular church, p. 119 [p. 154], but also affirms it to be no church at all." That he is not satisfied with what I affirm of that synagogue of Satan, where he hath his throne, I cannot help it, though I am sorry for it.

I am not, also, without some trouble that I cannot understand what he means by placing my words so as to intimate that I say not only that the church of Rome is no particular church, but also that it is no church at all; as though it might, in his judgment or mine, be *any church*, if it be not a *particular church*: for I verily suppose neither he nor I judge it to be that catholic church whereto it pretends. But yet, as I have no great reason to expect that this reverend author should be satisfied in any thing that I affirm, so I hope that it is not impossible but that, without any great difficulty, he may be reconciled to himself, affirming the very same thing that I do, p. 113 [p. 137]. It is of Rome in that sense wherein it claims itself to be a church that I speak: and in that sense he says it is no church of Christ's institution; and so, for my part, I account it no church at all. But he adds, that he is "far more unsatisfied that I undertake the cause of the Donatists, and labour to exempt them from schism, though I allow them guilty of other crimes." But do I indeed undertake the cause of the Donatists? do I plead for them? Will he manifest it by saying more against them in no more words than I have done? Do I labour to exempt them from schism? Are these the ways of peace, love, and truth, that the reverend author walks in? Do I not condemn all their practices and pretensions from the beginning to the end? Can I not speak of their cause in reference to the catholic church and its union, but it must be affirmed that I plead for them? But yet, as if righteousness and truth had been observed in this crimination, he undertakes, as of a thing granted, to give my grounds of doing what he affirms me to have done. "The first is," as he says, "his singular notion of schism, limiting it only to differences in a particular assembly. Secondly, his jealousy of the charge of schism to be objected to himself and party, if separating from the true churches of Christ be truly called schism." *Ans.* What may I expect from others, when so grave and reverend a person as this author is reported to be shall thus deal with me? Sir, I have no singular notion of schism, but embrace that which Paul hath long since declared; nor can you manifest any difference in my notion from what he hath delivered. Nor is that notion of schism at all under consideration in reference to what I affirm of the Donatists (who, in truth, were concerned in it, the most of them to the utmost), but the union of the church catholic and the breach thereof. Neither am I jealous or fearful of the charge of schism from any person living on the earth, and least of all from men proceeding in church affairs upon the principles you proceed on. Had you not been pleased to have supposed what you please, without the least ground, or colour, or reason, perhaps you would have as little satisfied yourself in the charge you have undertaken to manage against me, as you have done many good men, as the case now stands, even of your own judgment in other things.

Having made this entrance, he proceeds in the same way, and, p. 164, lays the foundation of the title of his book and this chapter, of his charge of Donatism, in these words: "This lies in full force against him and his party, who have broken the union of our churches, and separated themselves from all the protestant churches in the world not of their own constitution, and that as no true churches of Christ." This, I say, is the foundation of his whole ensuing discourse, all the ground that he hath to stand upon in the defence of the invidious title of this chapter; and what fruit he expects from this kind of proceeding I know not. The day will manifest of what sort this work is. Although he may have some mistaken apprehensions to countenance his conscience in the first part of his assertion, as that it may be forgiven to inveterate prejudice, though it be false, — namely, that I and my party (that is the phraseology this author, in his love to unity, delights in) have broken the union of their churches (which we have no more done than they have broken the union of ours, for we began our reformation with them on even terms, and were as early at work as they), — yet what colour, what excuse can be invented to alleviate the guilt of the latter part of it, that we have separated from all the reformed churches, as no churches? And yet he repeats this again, p. 106, with especial reflection on myself. "I wonder not," saith he, "that the doctor hath unchurched Rome, for he hath done as much to England and all foreign protestant churches, and makes none to be members of the church but such as are, by covenant and consent, joined to some of their congregations." Now, truly, though all righteous laws of men in the world will afford recompense and satisfaction for calumniating accusations and slanders of much less importance than this here publicly owned by our reverend author, yet, seeing the gospel of the blessed God requires to forgive and pass by greater injuries, I shall labour, in the strength of his grace, to bring my heart unto conformity to his will therein; notwithstanding which, because by his providence I am in that place and condition that others also that fear his name may be some way concerned in this unjust imputation, I must declare that this is open unrighteousness, wherein neither love nor truth hath been observed. How little I am concerned in his following parallel of Independentism and Donatism, — wherein he proceeds with the same truth and candour, — or in all that follows thereupon, is easy for any one to judge. He proceeds to scan my answers to the Romanists, as in reference to their charge of schism upon us, and says, "I do it suitably to my own principles;" and truly if I had not, I think I had been much to blame. I refer the reader to the answers given in my book; and if he like them not, notwithstanding this author's exceptions, I wish he may fix on those that please him better; in them there given my conscience doth acquiesce.

But he comes, in the next place, to *arguments*; wherein if he prove more happy than he hath done in *accusations*, he will have great cause to rejoice. By a double argument, as he says, he will prove that there may be schism besides that in a particular church. His first is this: "Schism is a breach of union; but there may be a breach of union in the catholic visible church." His second this: "Where there are differences raised in matter of faith professed, wherein the union of the catholic church consists, there may be a breach of union; but there may be differences in the catholic, or among the members of the catholic church in matter of faith professed: *ergo*." Having thus laid down his arguments, he falls to conjecture what I will answer, and how I will evade. But it will quickly appear that he is no less unhappy in arguing and conjecturing than he is and was in accusing. For, to consider his first argument, if he will undertake to make it good as to its form, I will, by the same way of arguing, engage myself to prove what he would be unwilling to find in a regular conclusion. But as to the matter of it, — First, Is schism every breach of union? or is every breach of union schism? Schism, in the ecclesiastical notion, is granted to be, in the present dispute, *the breach of the union of a church*, which it hath by the institution of Christ, and this not of *any* union of Christ's institution, but of one certain kind of union; for, as was proved, there is a union whose breach can neither, in the language of the Scripture, nor in reason, nor common sense, be called or accounted schism, nor ever was by any man in the world, nor can be, without destroying the particular nature of schism, and allowing only the general notion of any separation, good or bad, in what kind soever. So that, secondly, It is granted not only that there may be a *breach of union in the catholic church*, but also that there may be a *breach of the union of the catholic church* by a denial or relinquishment of the profession wherein it consists; but that this breach of union is schism, because schism is a breach of union, is as true as that every man who hath two eyes is every thing that hath two eyes. For his second, it is of the same importance with the first. There may be differences in the catholic church, and breaches of union among the members of it, which are far enough from the breach of the union of that church as such. Two professors may fall out and differ, and yet, I think, continue both of them professors still. Paul and Barnabas did so; Chrysostom and Epiphanius did so; Cyril and Theodoret did so. That which I denied was, that the breach of the union of the catholic church as such is schism. He proves the contrary, by affirming there may be differences among the members of the catholic church, that do not break the union of it as such. "But," he says, "though there be apostasy or heresy, yet there may be schism also;" but not in respect of the breach of the same union, which only he was to prove. Besides evil surmises, reproaches, false criminations, and undue suggestions, I find nothing wherein my discourse is concerned to the end of this chapter. Page 109, upon the passage of mine, "We are thus come off from this part of schism, for the relinquishment of the catholic church, which we have not done, and so to do is not schism, but a sin of other nature and importance," he adds, that "the ground I go upon why separation from a true church" (he must mean the catholic church, or he speaks nothing at all to the business in hand) "is no schism is that aforementioned, that a schism in the Scripture notion is only a division of judgment in a particular assembly." But who so blind as they that will not see? The ground I proceeded on evidently, openly, solely, was taken from the nature of the catholic church, its union, and the breach of that union; and if "obiter" I once mention that notion, I do it upon my confidence of its truth, which I here again tender myself in a readiness to make good to this reverend author, if at any time he will be pleased to command my personal attendance upon him to that purpose. To repeat more of the like mistakes and surmises, with the wranglings that ensue on such false suppositions, to the end of this chapter, is certainly needless. For my part, in and about this whole business of separation from the catholic church, I had not the least respect to Presbyterians or Independents, as such, nor to the differences between them; which alone our author, out of his zeal to the truth and peace, attends unto.

If he will fasten the guilt of schism on any on the account of separation from the catholic church, let him prove that that church is not made up of the universality of professors of the gospel throughout the world, under the limitations expressed; that the union of it as such doth not consist in the profession of the truth; and that the breach of that union, whereby a man ceases to be a member of that church, is schism. Otherwise, to tell me that I am a "sectary," a "schismatic," to fill up his pages with vain surmises and supposals, to talk of a difference and schism among the members of the catholic church, or the like impertinences, will never farther his discourse among men, either rational, solid, or judicious. All that ensues, to the end of this chapter, is about the ordination of ministers; wherein, however, he hath been pleased to deal with me in much bitterness of spirit, with many clamours and false accusations. I am glad to find him, p. 120, renouncing ordination from the authority of the church of Rome as such, for I am assured that by so doing he can claim it no way from, by, or through Rome; for nothing came to us from thence but what came in and by the authority of that church.

Chapter IX.

We are now gathering towards what seems of most immediate concernment as to this reverend author's undertaking, — namely, to treat of the nature of a particular church, its union, and the breach of that union. The description I give of such a church is this: "It is a society of men called by the word to the obedience of the faith in Christ, and joint performance of the worship of God in the same individual ordinances, according to the order by Christ prescribed." This I profess to be a general description of its nature, waiving all contests about accurate definitions, which usually tend very little to the discovery or establishment of truth. After some canvassing of this description, our author tells us that he grants it to be the definition of a particular church, which is more than I intended it for; only he adds, that according to this description, their churches are as true as ours; which, I presume, by this time he knows was not the thing in question. His ensuing discourse of the will of Christ that men should join not all in the same individual congregation, but in this or that, is by me wholly assented unto, and the matter of it contended for by me as I am able. What he is pleased to add about explicit covenanting, and the like, I am not at all, for the present, concerned in. I purposely waived all expressions concerning it, one way or other, that I might not involve the business in hand with any unnecessary contests; it is possible somewhat hereafter may be spoken to that subject, in a tendency unto the reconciliation of the parties at variance. His argument, in the close of the section, for a presbyterian church, from Acts xx. 17, "because there is mention of more elders than one in that church, and therefore it was not one single congregation," I do not understand. I think no one single congregation is wholly completed according to the mind of Christ unless there be more elders than one in it. There should be "*elders in every church;*" and, for my part, so we could once agree practically in the matter of our churches, I am under some apprehension that it were no impossible thing to reconcile the whole difference as to a presbyterian church or a single congregation. And though I be reproved anew for my pains, I may offer, ere long, to the candid consideration of godly men, something that may provoke others of better abilities and more leisure to endeavour the carrying on of so good a work. Proceeding to the consideration of the unity of this church, he takes notice of three things laid down by me, previously to what I was farther to assert; all which he grants to be true, but yet will not let them pass without his animadversions.

The first two are, that, — "1. A man may be a member of the catholic invisible church, and, 2. Of the visible catholic church, and yet not be joined to a particular church." These, as I said, he owns to be true, but asks how I can "reconcile this with what I said before, — namely, that the members of the catholic visible church are initiated into the profession of the faith by baptism." But where lies the difference? Why, saith he, "baptism, according to his principles, is an ordinance of worship only to be enjoyed in a particular church, whilst he will grant (what yet he doth deny, but will be forced to grant) that a minister is a minister to more than his own church, even to the catholic church, and may administer baptism out of a particular church, as Philip did to the eunuch." *Ans.* How well this author is acquainted with my principles hath been already manifested; as to his present mistake I shall not complain, seeing that some occasion may be administered unto it from an expression of mine, at least as it is printed, of which I shall speak afterward. For the present, he may be pleased to take notice that I am so far from confining baptism subjectively to a particular congregation, that I do not believe that any member of a particular church was ever regularly baptized. Baptism precedes admission into church membership, as to a particular church; the subjects of it are professing believers and their seed; as such they have right unto it, whether they be joined to any particular church or no. Suitable to this judgment hath been my constant and uninterrupted practice. I desire also to know who told him that I deny a minister to be *a minister to more than his own church*, or averred that he may perform ministerial duty only in and towards the members of his own congregation; for so much as men are appointed the objects of the dispensation of the word, I grant a man, in the dispensations of it, to act ministerially towards not only the members of the catholic church, but the visible members of the world also, in contradistinction thereunto.

The third thing laid down by me, whereunto also he assents, is, "That every believer is obliged to join himself to some one of those churches, that therein he may abide in 'doctrine and fellowship, and in breaking of bread, and in prayers:'" but my reasons whereby I prove this he says he likes not so well; and truly I can not help it. I have little hope he should like any thing well which is done by me. Let him be pleased to furnish me with better, and I shall make use of them; but yet when he shall attempt so to do, it is odds but that one or other will find as many flaws in them as he pretends to do in mine. But this, he saith, he shall make use of, and that he shall make advantage of, and I know not what; as if he were playing a prize upon a stage. The third reason is that which he likes worst of all, and I like the business the better that what he understands least that he likes worst; it is, "That Christ hath given no direction for any duty of worship merely and purely of sovereign institution, but only to them and by them who are so joined." Hereupon he asks:— 1. "Is baptism a part of worship?" *Ans.* Yes, and to be so performed *by them*, — that is, a minister *in* or *of them*. I fear my expression in this place led him to his whole mistake in this matter. 2. "Prayer and reading of the word in private families, are they no duty of worship?" *Ans.* Not merely and purely of sovereign institution. 3. "Is preaching to convert heathens a duty of worship?" Not, as described, in all cases. When it is, it is to be performed by a minister; and so he knows my answer to his next invidious inquiry, relating to my own person.

Against my fourth reason, taken from the apostle's care to leave none out of this order who were converted, where it was possible, he gives in the instance of the eunuch, and others converted where there were not enough to engage in such societies, — that is, in them with whom it was impossible. My fifth is from Christ's providing of officers for these churches. This also, he saith, is "weak as the rest: for, first, Christ provided officers at first for the catholic church, — that is, the apostles; secondly, All ordinary officers are set first in the catholic church, and every minister is first a minister to the catholic church; and if," saith he, "he deny this, he knows where to find a learned antagonist." *Ans.* But see what it is to have a mind to dispute. Will he deny that Christ appointed officers for particular churches? or if he should have a mind to do it, will his arguments evince any such thing? Christ appointed apostles, catholic officers; therefore, he did not appoint officers for particular churches though he commanded that "elders should be ordained in every, church"! Pastors and teachers are set first in the catholic church; therefore, Christ hath not ordained officers for particular churches! But this is the way with our author. If any word offer itself, whence it is possible to draw out the mention of any thing that is, or hath at any time been, in difference between Presbyterians and Independents, that presently is run away withal. For my part, I had not the least thought of the controversy which, to no purpose at all, he would here lead me to. But yet I must tell him that my judgment is, that ordinary officers are firstly to be ordained in particular churches; and as I know where to find a "learned antagonist" as to that particular, so I do in respect of every thing that I affirm or deny in the business of religion; and yet I bless the Lord I am not in the least disquieted or shaken in my adherence to the truth I profess.

My last reason, he saith, is "fallacious and inconsequent;" and that because he hath put an inference upon it never intended in it. Now, the position that these reasons were produced to confirm being true, and so acknowledged by himself, because it is a truth that indeed I lay some more than ordinary weight, upon, it being of great use in the days wherein we live, I would humbly entreat this reverend author to send me his reasons whereby it may be confirmed; and I shall promise him, if they be found of more validity than those which, according to my best skill, I have already used, he shall obtain many thanks and much respect for his favour.

What he remarks upon or adds to my next discourse, about instituted worship in general, I shall not need to insist on; only, by the way, I cannot but take notice of that which he calls "a chief piece of Independency;" and that is, "that those who are joined in church fellowship are so confined that they cannot, or may not, worship God in the same ordinances in other churches." How this comes to be "a chief piece of Independency," I know not. It is contrary to the known practice of all the churches of England that I am acquainted with which he calls Independents. For my part, I know but one man of that mind, and he is no child in these things.

For the ensuing discourse, about the intercision of ordinances, it being a matter of great importance, and inquired into by me merely in reference to the Roman apostasy, it needs a more serious disquisition than any thing at present administered by our author will give occasion unto; possibly, in convenient time, I may offer somewhat farther towards the investigation of the mind of God therein. Every thing in this present contest is so warped to the petty differences between Presbyterians and Independents, that no fair progress nor opportunity for it can be afforded. If, it may be, in my next debate of it, I shall waive all mention of those meaner differences, and as, I remember, I have not insisted on them in what I have already proposed to this purpose, so possibly the next time I may utterly escape. For the present, I do not doubt but the Spirit of God in the Scripture is furnished with sufficient authority to erect new churches, and set up the celebration of all ordinances, on supposition that there was an intercision of them. To declare the way of his exerting his authority to this purpose, with the obviating of all objections to the contrary, is not a matter to be tossed up and down in this scrambling chase; and I am not a little unhappy that this reverend person was in the dark as to my design and aim all along, which hath entangled this dispute with so many impertinences. But, however, I shall answer a question which he is pleased to put to me in particular. He asks me, then, "Whether I do not think in my conscience that there were no true churches in England until the Brownists our fathers, the Anabaptists our elder brothers, and ourselves, arose and gathered new churches?" With thanks for the civility of the inquiry in the manner of its expression, I answer, No; I have no such thoughts. And his pretence of my insinuation of any such thing is most vain, as also is his insultation thereupon. Truly, if men will, in all things, take liberty to speak what they please, they have no reason but to think that they may, at one time or other, hear that which will displease.

Having investigated the nature of a particular church, I proceed, in my treatise of schism, to inquire after the union of it, wherein it doth consist, and what is the breach thereof. The sum is, "The joint consent of the members to walk together in celebration of the same numerical ordinances, according to the mind of Jesus Christ, is that wherein the union of such a church doth consist." This is variously excepted against; and I know not what disputes about an implicit and explicit covenant, of specificating forms, of the practice of New and Old England, of admission of church-members, of the right of the members of the catholic church to all ordinances, of the miscarriage of the Independents, of church matriculations, and such like things, not once considered by me in my proposal of the matter in hand, are fallen upon. By the way, he falls upon my judgment about the inhabitation of the Spirit, calls it an error, and says so it hath been reputed by all that are orthodox; raising terrible suspicions and intimations of judgments on our way from God by my falling into that error; when yet I say no more than the Scripture saith in express terms forty times; for which I refer him to what I have written on that subject, wherein I have also the concurrence of Polanus, Bucanus, Dorchetus, with sundry others, Lutherans and Calvinists. It may be, when he hath seriously weighed what I have offered to the clearing of that glorious truth of the gospel, he may entertain more gentle thoughts both concerning it and me.

The rest of the chapter I have passed through once and again, and cannot fix on any thing worthy of farther debate. A difference is attempted to be found in my description of the union of a particular church, in this and another place. Because in one place I require the consent of the members to walk together, in another mention only their so doing, — when the mention of that only was necessary in that place, not speaking of it absolutely, but as it is the difference of such a church from the church catholic, — some impropriety of expression is pretended to be discovered ("id populus curat scilicet"); which yet is a pure mistake of his, not considering unto what especial end and purpose the words are used. He repeats sundry things as in opposition to me, that are things laid down by myself and granted! Doth he attempt to prove that the union of a church is not rightly stated? He confesseth the form of such a church consists in *the observance and performance of the same ordinances of worship numerically*. I ask, is it not the command of Christ that believers should so do? Is not their obedience to that command their consent so to do? Are not particular churches instituted of Christ? Is it not the duty of every believer to join himself to some one of them? Was not this acknowledged above? Can any one do so without his consenting to do so? Is this consent any thing but his voluntary submission to the ordinances of worship therein? As an express consent and subjection to Christ in general is required to constitute a man a member of the church catholic visible; so if the Lord Jesus hath appointed any particular church for the celebration of his ordinances, is not their consent who are to walk in them necessary thereunto? But the topic of an explicit covenant presenting itself with an advantage to take up some leaves could not be waived, though nothing at all to the purpose in hand. After this, my confession, made in as much condescension unto compliance as I could well imagine, of the use of greater assemblies, is examined and excepted against, as "being in my esteem," he saith, "though it be not so indeed, a matter of prudence only." But I know full well that he knows not what esteem or disesteem I have of sundry things of no less importance. The consideration of my "postulata," proposed in a preparation to what was to be insisted on in the next chapter, as influenced from the foregoing dissertations, alone remains, and indeed alone deserves our notice.

My first is this: "The departing of any man or men from any particular church, as to the communion peculiar to such a church, is nowhere called schism, nor is so in the nature of the thing itself; but is a thing to be judged and receive a title according to the circumstances of it." To this he adjoins, "This is not the question. A simple secession of a man or men, upon some just occasion, is not called schism; but to make causeless differences in a church, and then separating from it as no church, denying communion with it, hath the nature and name of schism in all men's judgments but his own." *Ans.* What question doth our reverend author mean? I fear he is still fancying of the difference between Presbyterians and Independents, and squaring all things by that imagination. Whether it be a question stated to his mind or no I cannot tell; but it is an assertion expressive of mine own, which he may do well to disprove if he can. Who told him that raising causeless differences in a church, and then separating from it, is not in my judgment schism? May I possibly retain hopes of making myself understood by this reverend author? I suppose though that a pertinacious abiding in a mistake is neither schism nor heresy; and so this may be passed over.

My second is: "One church refusing to hold that communion with another which ought to be between them is not schism, properly so called." The reply hereunto is twofold:—

1. "That one church may raise differences in and with another church, and so cause schism." 2. "That the Independents deny any communion of churches but what is prudential; and so, that communion cannot be broken." To the first I have spoken sufficiently before; the latter is but a harping on the same string. I am not speaking of Independent churches, nor upon the principles of Independents, much less on them which are imposed on them. Let the reverend author suppose or aver what communion of churches he pleaseth, my petition holds in reference to it; nor can he disprove it. However, for my part, I am not acquainted with those Independents who allow no communion of churches but what is prudential; and yet it is thought that I know as many as this reverend author doth.

Upon the last proposal we are wholly agreed, so that I shall not need to repeat it; only he gives me a sad farewell at the close of the chapter, which must be taken notice of. "Is not," saith he, "the design of this book to prove, if he could, and condemn us as no churches? Let the world be judge." And I say; let all the saints of God judge; and Jesus Christ will judge whether I have not outrageous injury done me in this imputation. "But," saith he, "unless this be proved, he can never justify his separation." Sir, when your and our brethren told the bishops they thanked God they were none of them, and defied the prelatical church, did they make a separation or no? were they guilty of schism? I suppose you will not say so, nor do I; yet have I done any such thing in reference to you or your churches? I have no more separated from you than you have done from me; and as for the distance which is between us upon our disagreement about the way of reformation, let all the churches of God judge on which side it hath been managed with more breach of love, — on yours or mine. Let me assure you, sir, through the mercy of God in Jesus Christ, I can freely forgive unto you all your reproaches, revilings, hard censurings, and endeavours to expose me to public obloquy, and yet hope that I may have, before we die, a place in your heart and prayers.

Chapter X.

Independency no schism.

We are come now to the chapter that must do the work intended, or else "operam et oleum perdidimus." "Independentism a Great Schism," is the title of it. What this Independentism is he doth neither here declare, nor in any other part of his book; nor do I know what it is that he intends by it. I hear, indeed, from him that it is a "schism," a "sect;" but of what peculiar import, or wherein it consists, he hath not declared. I suppose he would have it taken for separation from true churches; but neither doth the notion of the name, though individiously broached, and disavowed by them to whom it is ascribed, import any such thing, nor is the thing itself owned by them with whom he pretends to have to do. I find, indeed, that he tells us that all sectaries are Independents, — Anabaptists, Seekers, Ranters, Quakers. Doth he expect that I should undertake their defence? What if it should appear that I have done more against them than our reverend author, and many of his brethren joined with him? He may, perhaps, be willing to load myself and those which he is pleased to call my "associates," my "party," I know not what, with their evils and miscarriages; but is this done as becomes a Christian, a minister, a brother? What security hath he that, had he been the only judge and disposer of things in religion in this nation, if I and my associates had been sent to plant churches among the Indians, he should have prevented eruption of the errors and abominations which we have been exercised withal in this generation, unless he had sent for Duke d'Alva's instruments to work his ends by? and, indeed, there is scarce any sect in the nation but had they their desires, they would take that course. This may be done by any that are uppermost, if they please. But how shall we know what it is he intends by Independentism? All, it may be, that are not Presbyterians are Independents. Among these some professedly separate both from them and us (for there are none that separate from them but withal they separate from us, that I know of), because, as they say, neither theirs nor ours are true churches. We grant them to be true churches, but withal deny that we separate from them. Is it possible at once to defend both these sects of men? Is it possible at once with the same arguments to charge them? The whole discourse, then, of our reverend author being uniform, it can concern but one of these sects of Independents; which it is, any man may judge that takes the least view of his treatise. He deals with them that unchurch their churches, unminister their ministers, disannul their ordinances, leaving them churchless, officerless, and in the like sad condition. Is this Independentism a schism? Though that it is properly so called he cannot prove, yet I hope he did not expect that I should plead for it. What I shall do in this case, I profess, well I know not. I here deny that I unminister their ministers, unchurch their churches. Hath this author any more to say to me or those of my persuasion? Doth not this whole discourse proceed upon a supposition that it is otherwise with them with whom he hath to do? Only, I must tell him by the way, that if he suppose by this concession that I justify and own their way, wherein they differ from the congregational ministers in England, to be of Christ's institution, or that I grant all things to be done regularly among them and according to the mind of Christ, therein I must profess he is mistaken. In brief, by Independentism he intends a separation from true churches, with condemning them to be no churches, and their ministers no ministers, and their ordinances none or antichristian. Whatever becomes of the nature of schism, I disavow the appearing as an advocate in the behalf of this Independentism. If by Independentism he understand the peaceable proceeding of any of the people of God in this nation, in the several parts of it, to join themselves, by their free consent, to walk together in the observation and celebration of all the ordinances of Christ appointed to be observed and celebrated in particular churches, so to reform themselves from the disorders wherein they were entangled, — being not able in some things to join in that way of reformation which many godly ministers, commonly called Presbyterians, have engaged in and seek to promote, without judging and condemning them as to the whole of their station or ordinances; — if this, I say, be intended by Independentism, when the reverend author shall undertake to prove it schism, having not in this book spoken one word or tittle to it, his discourse will be attended unto. This whole chapter, then, being spent against them who deny them to be true churches and defend separation, I marvel what can be said unto it by me, or how I come to be concerned in it, who grant them true churches and deny separation.

But our reverend author, knowing that if this bottom be taken from under him, he hath no foundation for any thing he asserts, thought it not sufficient to charge me over and over with what is here denied, but at length attempts to make it good from mine own words; which if he do effect and make good, I confess he changes the whole nature and state of the dispute in hand. Let us see, then, how he answers this undertaking.

From those words of mine, "The reformation of any church, or any thing in it, is the reducing of it to its primitive institution," approving the assertion as true, he labours to evince that I deny their churches to be true churches. How so, I pray? "Why, we erect new churches out of no churches; and it had been happy for England if we had all gone to do this work among the Indians." What will prove England's happiness or unhappiness the day will manifest; this is but man's day and judgment; He is coming who will not judge by the seeing of the eye, nor by the hearing of the ear. In the meantime we bless God, and think all England hath cause to bless God, whatever become of us, that he and our brethren of the same mind with him in the things of God have their liberty to preach the gospel and carry on the work of reformation in their native soil, and are not sent into the ends of the earth, as many of ours have been. But how doth our gathering of churches deny them to be true churches? Doth our granting them to be true churches also grant that all the saints in England are members of their churches? It is notoriously known that it is and was otherwise, and that when they and we began to reform, thousands of the people of God in these nations had no reason to suppose themselves to belong to one particular church rather than another. They lived in one parish, heard in another, removed up and down for their advantage, and were in bondage on that account all their days.

But he says, "In some words following I discover my very heart." I cannot but by the way tell him, that it is a sufficient evidence of his unacquaintedness with me, that he thinks there is need of searching and raking my words to discover my very heart in any thing that belongs (though in never so remote a distance) to the worship of God. All that know me, know how open and free I am in these things, how ready on all occasions to declare my whole heart; it is neither fear nor favour can influence me unto another frame. But what are the words that make this noble discovery? They are these that follow: "When any society or combination of men (whatever hitherto it hath been esteemed) is not capable of such a reduction and revocation" (that is, to its primitive institution), "I suppose I shall never provoke any wise or sober person if I profess I cannot look on such a society as a church of Christ." His reply hereunto is the hinge upon which his whole discourse turneth, and must therefore be considered. Thus then he: "Is not this, reader, at once to unchurch all the churches of England since the Reformation? for it is known during the reign of the prelates they were not capable of that reduction; and what capacity our churches are now in for that reduction, partly by want of power and assistance from the magistrate, without which some dare not set upon a reformation, for fear of a premunire, partly by our divisions amongst ourselves, fomented by he knows whom, he cannot but see as well as we lament." And hereupon he proceeds with sundry complaints of my dealing with them. And now, Christian reader, what shall we say to these things? A naked supposition, of no strength nor weight, that will not hold in any thing or case, — namely, that a thing is not to be judged capable of that which by some external force it is withheld from, — is the sole bottom of all this charge! The churches of England were capable of that reduction to their primitive institution under the prelates, though in some things hindered by them from an actual reducement; so they are now, in sundry places where the work is not so much as attempted. The sluggard's field is capable of being weeded. The present pretended want of capacity from the non-assistance of the magistrate, whilst perfect liberty for reformation is given, and the work in its several degrees encouraged, will be found to be a sad plea for some when things come to be tried out by the rule of the gospel. And for our divisions, I confess I begin to discover somewhat more by whom they are fomented than I did four days ago. For the matter itself, I desire our reverend author to take notice that I judge every church capable of a reduction to its primitive institution; which, all outward hinderances being removed, and all assistances granted that are necessary for reformation according to the gospel, may be reduced into the form and order appointed unto a particular church by Jesus Christ. And where any society is not so capable, let them call themselves what they please, I shall advise those therein who have personally a due right to the privileges purchased for them by Jesus Christ, in the way of their administration by him appointed, to take some other peaceable course to make themselves partakers of them; and for giving this advice, I neither dread the anger nor indignation of any man living in the world. And so I suppose by this time the author knows what has become of his "quod erat demonstrandum;" and here, in room of it, I desire him to accept of this return.

Those who, in the judgment of charity, were and continue members of the church catholic invisible, by virtue of their union with Christ, the head thereof; and members of the general visible church, by their due profession of the saving truths of the gospel, and subjection to Christ Jesus, their King and Saviour, according to them; and do walk in love and concord in the particular churches whereof, by their own consent and choice, they are members, not judging and condemning other particular churches of Christ, where they are not members, as they are such, as to their station and privileges, being ready for all instituted communion with them as revealed; are not, according to any gospel rule, nor by any principles acknowledged amongst Christians, to be judged or condemned as guilty of schism; — but such are all they for whom, under any consideration whatever, I have pleaded as to their immunity from this charge in my treatise of schism: therefore, they are not to be judged so guilty. If you please, you may add, "Quod erat demonstratum."

I shall not digress to a recharge upon this reverend author, and those of the same profession with him, as to their mistakes and miscarriages in the work of reformation, nor discuss their ways and principles, wherein I am not satisfied as to their procedure. I yet hope for better things than to be necessitated to carry on the defensative of the way wherein I walk by opposing theirs. It is true, that he who stands upon mere defence is thought to stand upon none at all; but I wait for better things from men than their hearts will yet allow them to think of. I hope the reverend author thinks that as I have reasons wherewith I am satisfied as to my own way, so I have those that are of the same weight with me against him. But whatever he may surmise, I have no mind to foment the divisions that are amongst us; hence I willingly bear all his imputations without retortion. I know in part how the case is in the world. The greatest chargers have not always the most of truth; witness Papists, Lutherans, Prelatists, Anabaptists. I hope I can say in sincerity I am for peace, though others make themselves ready for war.

But we must proceed a little farther, though, as to the cause by me undertaken to be managed, causelessly. The discourse of our author from the place fixed on, wherein he faintly endeavours to make good the foundation of this chapter, which I have already considered, consists of two parts:— 1. His animadversions on some principles which I lay down, as necessary to be stated aright and determined, that the question about *gathering churches* may be clearly and satisfactorily debated. Some of them, he says, have been handled by others; which if it be a rule of silence to him and me, it might have prevented this tedious debate. Whatever his thoughts may be of my pamphlet, I do not fear to affirm of his treatise that I have found nothing in it, from the beginning to the ending, but what hath lien neglected on booksellers' stalls for above these seven years. For the rest of those principles which he excepts against as he thinks meet, I leave their consideration to that farther inquiry which, the Lord assisting, I have destined them unto. The way of gathering churches upon a supposition of their antecedency to officers, he says, is very pretty; and he loads it with the difficulty of men's coming to be baptized in such a case. But as I can tell him of that which is neither true nor pretty in the practice of some whom he knows, or hath reason so to do, so I can assure him that we are not concerned in his objection about baptism; and with them who may possibly be so, it is a ridiculous thing to think it an objection. And for that part of my inquiry, whether the church be before ordinary officers, or they before it, as light as he is pleased to make of it, it will be found to lie very near the bottom of all our differences, and the right stating of it to conduce to the composure and determination of them. His charges and reflections, which he casts about in his passage, are not now to be farther mentioned; we have had them over and over, — indeed we have had little else. If strong, vehement, passionate affirmations, complaints, charges, false imputations, and the like, will amount to a demonstration in this business, he hath demonstrated *Independentism* to be a *great schism.*

He shuts up his discourse as he began it, reciting my words adding, interposing, perverting, commenting, inquiring; he makes them speak what he pleases, and compasses the ends of his delight upon them. What contentment he hath received in his so doing know not, nor shall I express what thoughts I have of such a course of procedure. This only I shall say, it is a facile way of writing treatises and proving whatever men have a mind unto.

My last task is, to look back to the beginning of this last chapter, and to gather up in our passage what may seem to respect the business in hand; and so the whole matter will be dismissed. The plea insisted on for immunity from the charge of schism, with reference to the episcopal government of the church of England, and the constitution which, under it, it is pretended to have had, he passes over; though, on sundry accounts, his concernments lie as deeply in it as in any thing pleaded in that treatise. The things he is pleased to take notice of, as far as they tend in the least to the issue of the debate between us, shall be reviewed. Considering the several senses wherein that expression, "The church of England," may be taken, I manifest in my treatise in which of them, and how far, we acknowledge ourselves to have been, and to continue, *members of the church of England.* The first is as it comprises the *elect believers* in England. What the unity of the church in this sense is was before evinced. Our desire to be found members of this church, with our endeavour to keep the unity of it in the bond of peace, was declared. I am grieved to repeat our reverend author's exceptions to this declaration. Says he, "Unless he think there are no members of this church in England but those that are of his formed particular churches, I fear he will be found to break the union that ought to be between them." And why so, I pray? The union of the members of the church in this sense consists in their joint union to and with Christ, their head, by one Spirit. What hath the reverend author to charge upon me with reference thereunto? Let him speak out to the utmost. Yea, I have some reason to think that he will scarce spare where he can strike. God forbid that I should think all the members of the catholic church in England to be comprised, either jointly or severally, in their churches or ours, seeing it cannot be avoided;

but you will keep up those notes of division. I doubt not but there be many thousands of them who walk neither with you nor us. He adds, that "by gathering saints of the first magnitude, we do what lies in us to make the invisible church visible." It is confessed we do so; yea, we know that that church which is invisible in some respects, and under one formal consideration, is visible as to its profession which it makes unto salvation. This, with all that lies in us, we draw them out unto. What he adds about the churches being elect, and the uncomely parts of it, which they may be for a season who are elect believers (because it must be spoken), are useless cavils. For the scornful rejection of what I affirm concerning our love to all the members of this church, and readiness to tender them satisfaction in case of offence, with his insinuation of my want of modesty and truth in asserting these thoughts, because he will one day know that the words he so despises were spoken in sincerity, and with reverence of the great God, and out of love to all his saints, I shall not farther vindicate them. Such hay and stubble must needs burn.

My next profession of our relation to the church of England [was] in respect of that denomination given to the body of professors in this nation cleaving to the doctrine of the gospel, here preached and established by law as the public profession of this nation. But he tells me, — 1. "That many independent churches of this nation are grossly apostatized from that doctrine, and so are heretical." 2. "That the worship was professed, and protested, and established, as well as the doctrine, and that we are all departed from it, and so are schismatical; for we hold communion with them," he says, "in the same doctrine, but not in the same worship." *Ans.* 1. His first exception ariseth from the advantage he makes use of from his large use of the word "Independent;" which will serve him, in his sense, for what end he pleaseth. In the sense before declared his charge is denied. Let him prove it by instance, if he be able. Surely God hath not given orthodox men leave to speak what they please, without due regard to love and truth. 2. As to the worship established in this nation by law (he means the way of worship, for the substantials of it we are all agreed in), I suppose he will not say a relinquishment of the practice of it is schism. If he do, I know what use some men will make of his affirmation, though I know not how he will free himself from being schismatical. For his renewed charge of schism, I cannot, I confess, be moved at it, proceeding from him who neither doth nor will know what it is. His next endeavour is, to make use of another concession of mine, concerning our receiving of our regeneration and new birth by the preaching of the word in England, saying, "Could they make use of our preaching," etc. But the truth is, when the most of us, by the free grace of God, received our new birth through the preaching of the word, neither they nor we, as to the practice of our ways, were in England; so that their concernment, as such, in the concession is very small: and we hope, since, in respect of others, our own ministry hath not been altogether fruitless, though we make no comparison with them.

In rendering of the next passage, which is concerning Anabaptists and Anabaptism, I shall not contend with him; he hath not in the least impaired the truth of what I assert in reference to them and their way. I cannot but take notice of that passage, which, for the substance of it, hath so often occurred, and that is this, "Doth not himself labour in this book to prove that the administration of ordinances in our assemblies is null, our ordination null and antichristian?" for the proof of which suggestion he refers his reader to p. 197 [p. 172] of my book. I confess, seeing this particular quotation, I was somewhat surprised, and began to fear that some expression of mine (though contrary to my professed judgment) might have given countenance to this mistake, and so be pleaded as a justification of all the uncharitableness, and something else, wherewith his book is replenished; but turning to the place, I was quickly delivered from my trouble, though I must ingenuously confess I was cast into another, which I shall not now mention.

Page 167, we arrive at that which alone almost I expected would have been insisted on, and, quite contrary thereto, it is utterly waived, — namely, the whole business of a national church; upon which account, indeed, all the pretence of the charge this reverend author is pleased to manage doth arise. Take that out of the way, and certainly *they* and *we* are upon even terms; and if we will be judged by them who were last in possession of the reiglement of that church, upon supposition that there is such a church still, they are no more interested in it than we, yea, are as guilty of schism from it as we. But that being set aside, and *particular churches* only remaining, it will be very difficult for him to raise the least pretence of his great charge. But let us consider what he thinks meet to fasten on in that discourse of mine about a national Church. The first thing is, my inquiry whether the denial of the institution of a national church (which he pleads not for) doth not deny, in consequence, that we had either ordinances or ministry amongst us? to which I say, that though it seems so to do, yet indeed it doth not, because there was then another church-state, even that of particular churches, amongst us. With many kind reflections of "my renouncing my ministry, and rejecting of my jejune and empty vindication of their ministry" (which yet is the very same that himself fixes on), he asks me "how I can in my conscience believe that there were any true ministers in this church in the time of its being national?" and so proceeds to infer from hence my denying of all ministry and ordinances among them. Truly, though I were more to be despised than I am (if that be possible), yet it were not common prudence for any man to take so much pains to make me his enemy whether I will or no. He cannot but know that I deny utterly that ever we had indeed, whatever men thought, a national church; for I grant no such thing as a national church, in the present sense contended about. That in England, under the rule of the prelates, when they looked on the church as national, there were true churches and true ministers, though in much disorder, as to the way of entering into the ministry and dispensing of ordinances, I grant freely: which is all this reverend author, if I understand him, pleads for; and this, he says, I was unwilling to acknowledge, lest I should thereby condemn myself as a schismatic. Truly, in the many sad differences and divisions that are in the world amongst Christians, I have not been without sad and jealous thoughts of heart, lest, by any doctrine or practice of mine, I should occasionally contribute any thing unto them; if it hath been otherwise with this author, I envy not his frame of spirit. But I must freely say, that having together with them weighed the reasons for them, I have been very little moved with the clamorous accusations and insinuations of this author. In the meantime, if it be possible to give him satisfaction, I here let him know that I assent unto that sum of all he hath to say as to the church of England, — namely, "That the true and faithful ministers, with the people in their several congregations, administering the true ordinances of Jesus Christ, whereof baptism is one, was and is the true church-state of England;" from which I am not separated. Nor do I think that some addition of human prudence, or imprudence, can disannul the ordinances of Jesus Christ, upon the disavower made of any other national church-state, and the assertion of this, to answer all intents and purposes. I suppose now that the reverend author knows that it is incumbent on him to prove that we have been members of some of these particular churches in due order, according to the mind of Christ, to all intents and purposes of church membership, and that we have, in our individual persons, raised causeless differences in those particular churches whereof we were members respectively, and so separated from them with the condemnation of them; or else, according to his own principles, he fails in his brotherly conclusion, ἰδοὺ Ῥόδος, ἰδοὺ πήδημα. I suppose the reader is weary of pursuing things so little to our purpose. If he will hear any farther that Independents are schismatics; that the setting up of their way hath opened a door to all evils and confusions; that they have separated from all churches, and condemn all churches in the world but their own; that they have hindered reformation and the setting up of the presbyterian church; that being members of our churches, as they are members of the nation, because they are born in it, yet they have deserted them; that they gather churches, which they pretend to be "spick and span new," they have separated from us; that they countenance Quakers and all other sectaries; that they will reform a national church whether men will or no, though they say that they only desire to reform themselves, and plead for liberty to that end; — if any man, I say, have a mind to read or hear of this any more, let him read the rest of this chapter, or else converse with some persons whom I can direct him to, who talk at this wholesome rate all the day long.

What seems to be my particular concernment I shall a little farther attend unto. Some words (for that is the manner of managing this controversy) are culled out from pp. 259, 260 [p. 198], to be made the matter of farther contest. Thus they lie in my treatise: "As the not giving a man's self up unto any way, and submitting to any establishment, pretended or pleaded to be of Christ, which he hath not light for, and which he was not by any act of his own formerly engaged in, cannot, with any colour or pretence of reason, be reckoned to him for schism, though he may, if he persist in his refusal, prejudice his own edification; so no more can a man's peaceable relinquishment of the ordinary communion of one church, in all its relations, be so esteemed." These words have as yet, unto me, a very harmless aspect; — but our reverend author is sharp-sighted, and sees I know not what monsters in them; for, first, saith he, "Here he seems to me to be a very sceptic in his way of Independency." Why so, I pray? "This will gratify all sects, Quakers and all, with a toleration." How, I pray? It is schism, not toleration, we are treating about. "But this leaves them to judge, as well as others, of what is and what is not according to the mind of Christ." Why, pray, sir, who is appointed to judge finally for them? "Why, then, should they be denied their liberty?" But is that the thing under consideration? Had you concluded that their not submitting to what they have not light for its institution is not properly schism, you should have seen how far I had been concerned in the inference; (but excursions unto Quakers, etc., are one topic of such discourses.) But now he asks me one question, it seems, to try whether I am a sceptic or no. "Whether," saith he, "does he believe his own way to be the only true way of Christ (for he hath instituted but one way), having run from and renounced all other ways in this nation?" I promise you this is a hard question, and not easily answered. If I *deny* it, he will say I am a sceptic, and other things also will be brought in. If I *affirm* it, it may be he will say that I condemn their churches for no churches, and the like. It is good to be wary when a man hath to deal with wise men. How if I should say that our way and their way is, for the substance of them, one way, and so I cannot say that my way is the only true way exclusively to theirs? I suppose this may do pretty well. But I fear this will scarce give satisfaction, and yet I know not well how I can go any farther. Yet this I will add: I do indeed believe that wherein their way and our way differ, our way is according to the mind of Christ, and not theirs; and this I am ready at any time (God assisting) personally to maintain to him. And as for my running from ways of religion, I dare again tell him these reproaches and calumnies become him not at all. But he proceeds. "If so," saith he, "is not every man bound to come into it, and not upon every conceived new light to relinquish it?" Truly, I think Mr C. himself is bound to come into it, and yet I do not think that his not so doing makes him a schismatic; and as for relinquishment, I assert no more than what he himself concludes to be lawful.

And thus, Christian reader, I have given thee a brief account of all things of any importance that I could meet withal in this treatise, and of many which are of very little. If thou shalt be pleased to compare my treatise of schism with the refutation of it, thou wilt quickly see how short this is of that which it, pretends to; how untouched my principles do abide; and how the most material parts of my discourse are utterly passed by, without any notice taken of them. The truth is, in the way chosen by this reverend author to proceed in, men may multiply writings to the world's end without driving any controversy to an issue. Descanting and harping on words, making exceptions to particular passages, and the like, is an easy and facile, and, to some men, a pleasant labour. What small reason our author had to give his book the title it bears, unless it were to discover his design, I hope doth by this time appear. Much of the proof of it lies in the repeated asseverations of it," It is so, and it is so." If he shall be pleased to send me word of one argument tending that way that is not founded in an evident mistake, I will promise him, if I live, a reconsideration of it.

In the meantime, I humbly beg of this reverend author that he would review; in the presence of the Lord, the frame of spirit wherein he wrote this charge; as also, that he would take into his thoughts all the reproaches and all that obloquy he hath endeavoured to load me causelessly and falsely withal. As for myself, my name, reputation, and esteem with the churches of God, to whom he hath endeavoured to render me odious, I commit the whole concernment of them to Him whose presence, through grace, I have hitherto enjoyed, and whose promise I lean upon, that he will "never leave me nor forsake me." I shall not complain of my usage (but what am I?) — of the usage of many precious saints and holy churches of Jesus Christ, into Him that lives and sees, any farther than by begging that it may not be laid to his charge. And if so mean a person as I am can in any way be serviceable to him, or to any of the churches that he pleads for, in reference to the gospel of Christ, I hope my life will not be dear to me that it may effect it; and I shall not cease to pray that both he and those who promoted this work in his hand may at length consider the many calls of God that are evident upon them, to lay aside these unseemly animosities, and to endeavour a coalition in love with all those who in sincerity call upon the name of the Lord Jesus Christ, their Lord and ours.

For the distances themselves that are between us, wherein we are not as yet agreed; what is the just state of them, the truth and warrantableness of the principles whereupon we proceed, with the necessity of our practice in conformity thereunto; in what we judge our brethren to come short of, or wherein to go beyond the mind of Jesus Christ; with a farther ventilation of this business of schism, — I have some good grounds of expectation that possibly, ere long, we may see a fair discussion of these things, in a pursuit of truth and peace.

AN ANSWER TO A LATE TREATISE ABOUT THE NATURE OF SCHISM.

Oxford: 1658.

Δεῖ τὸν ἐπίσκοπον ἀνέγλητον εἶναι, ὡς Θεοῦ οἰκονόμον, μὴ αὐθάδη, μὴ ὀργίλον, μὴ πάροινον, μὴ πλήκτην, μὴ αἰσχροκερδῆ.
Tit. i. 7

PREFATORY NOTE.

THE two foregoing treatises had appeared in 1657, and in the year following our author had to reply to another work by his opponent Cawdrey, "Independency further Proved to be a Schism." The latter had been previously engaged in a controversy on the subject of church government with Mr John Cotton, an eminent Congregationalist of New England, to whose work on "The Keys of the Kingdom of Heaven," Cawdrey had replied in his "Vindiciæ Clavium," and in another work, "The Inconsistency of the Independent Way with Scripture and Itself." A manuscript by Cotton in defence of his book had been committed to Owen, who cherished a respect for his memory, as it was the perusal of his work, "The Keys of the Kingdom of Heaven," which led our author to reconsider and modify his views respecting the nature and polity of the church. To meet the last assault of Cawdrey he gave the manuscript of Cotton to the press, and accompanied it with a lengthy preface in vindication of himself from the charges of his opponent. The disproof of the alleged contradictions with which he was reproached is complete, but it cannot be said that there is much of novelty or importance in the statements contained in this treatise. After a lapse of twenty-two years, Dr Owen had again to vindicate his denomination from the same charge of schism, in very different circumstances, and against a more adroit and accomplished adversary. Accordingly, with the different works of Owen on the subject of schism, we have connected his pamphlet on the same subject in reply to Stillingfleet, though the interval just specified ensued before he broke a lance in controversy with the learned Dean of St Paul's. — ED.

To The Reader.

CHRISTIAN READER,

I HAVE not much to say unto thee concerning the ensuing treatise, — it will speak for itself with all impartial men; much less shall I insist on commendation of its author, who also being dead ἔτι λαλεῖται, and will be so, I am persuaded whilst Christ hath a church upon the earth. The treatise itself was written sundry years ago, immediately upon the publishing of Mr Cawdrey's accusation against him. I shall not need to give an account whence it hath been that it saw the light no sooner; it may suffice that, in mine own behalf and that of others, I do acknowledge that, in the doing of sundry things seeming of more importance, this ought not to have been omitted. The judgment of the author approving of this vindication of himself as necessary, considering the place he held in the church of God, should have been a rule unto us for the performance of that duty, which is owing to his worth and piety in doing and suffering for the truth of God. It is now about seven months ago since it came into my hands; and since I engaged myself unto the publication of it, my not immediate proceeding therein being sharply rebuked by a fresh charge upon myself from that hand under which this worthy person so far suffered as to be necessitated to the ensuing defensative, I have here discharged that engagement. The author of the charge against him, in his epistle to that against me, tells his reader that "it is thought that it was intended by another (and now promised by myself) to be published, to cast a slur upon him." So are our intentions judged, so our ways, by thoughts and reports! Why a vindication of Mr Cotton should cast a slur upon Mr Cawdrey, I know not. Is he concerned in spirit or reputation in the acquitment of a holy, reverend person, now at rest with Christ, from imputations of inconstancy and self-contradiction? Is there not room enough in the world to bear the good names of Mr Cotton and

Mr Cawdrey, but that if one be vindicated the other must be slurred? He shall find now, by experience, what assistance he found from Him who loved him to bear his charge and to repel it, without any such reflection on his accuser as might savour of an intention to slur him. "Mala mens, malus animus." The measure that men fear from others they have commonly meted out unto them beforehand. He wishes those "that intend to rake in the ashes of the dead to consider whether they shall deserve any thanks for their labour." How *the covering of the dead* with their own comely garments comes to be *a raking into their ashes*, I know not. His name is alive, though he be dead. It was that, not his person, that was attempted to be wounded by the charge against him. To pour forth that balm for its healing, now he is dead, which himself provided whilst he was alive, without adding or diminishing one syllable, is no raking into his ashes; and I hope the δεύτεραι θροντίδες of the reverend author will not allow him to be offended that this friendly office is performed to a dead brother, to publish this his defence of his own innocency, written in obedience to a prime dictate of the law of nature, against the wrong which was not done him in secret.

But the intendment of this prefatory discourse being my own concernment in reference to a late tract of Mr Cawdrey's, bearing on its title and superscription a vindication from my "unjust clamours and false aspersions," I shall not detain the reader with any farther discourse of that which he will find fully debated in the ensuing treatise itself, but immediately address myself to that which is my present peculiar design. By what ways and means the difference betwixt us is come to that issue wherein now it stands stated in the expressions before mentioned, I shall not need to repeat. Who first let out those waters of strife, who hath filled their streams with bitterness, clamour, and false aspersions, is left to the judgment of all that fear the Lord, who shall have occasion at any time to reflect upon those discourses. However, it is come to pass, I must acknowledge, that the state of the controversy between us is now degenerated into such a useless strife of words as that I dare publicly own engagements into studies of so much more importance unto the interest of truth, piety, and literature, as that I cannot, with peace in my own retirement, be much farther conversant therein. Only, whereas I am not in the least convinced that Mr Cawdrey hath given satisfaction to my former expostulations about the injuries done me in his other treatise, and hath evidently added to the number and weight of them in this, I could not but lay hold of this opportunity, given by my discharging a former promise, once more to remind him of some miscarriages, exceedingly unbecoming his profession and calling, which I shall do in a brief review of his epistle and treatise: upon the consideration whereof, without charging him or his way with schism in great letters on the title-page of this book, I doubt not but it will appear that the guilt of the crime he falsely, unjustly, and uncharitably chargeth upon others, may be laid more equitably at his own door; and that the shortness of the covering used by him and others to hide themselves from the inquisition made after them for schism, upon their own principles, will not be supplied by such outcries as those he is pleased to use after them who are least of all men concerned in the matter under contest, there being no solid medium whereby they may be impleaded. And in this discourse I shall, as I suppose, put an end to my engagement in this controversy. I know no man whose patience will enable him to abide always in the consideration of things to so little purpose. Were it not that men bear themselves on high by resting on the partial adherence of many to their dictates, it were impossible they should reap any contentment in their retirements from such a management of controversies as this: "Independency is a great schism, it hath made all the divisions amongst us." "Brownists, Anabaptists, and all sectaries, are Independents." "They deny our ministers and churches; they separate from us; all errors come from among them." "This I have been told," and, "That I have heard;" — [which] is the sum of this treatise. Who they are of whom he speaks; how they came into such a possession of all church-state in England, that all that are not with them are schismatics; how, "de jure" or "de facto," they came to be so instated; what claim they can make to their present stations without schism, on their own principles; whether, granting the church of England, as constituted when they and we began that which we call Reformation, to have been a true instituted church, they have any power of rule in it but what hath been got by violence; what that is purely theirs hath any pretence of establishment from the Scripture, antiquity, and the laws of this land; — I say, with these and the like things, which are incumbent on him to clear up before his charges with us will be of any value, our author troubleth not himself. But to proceed to the particulars by him insisted on.

1. He tells the reader in his epistle that his unwillingness to this rejoinder was heightened by the necessity he found of *discovering some personal weaknesses and forgetfulnesses in me, upon my denial of some things which were known to be true if he should proceed therein.* For what he intimates of the unpleasantness that it is to him to discover things of that importance in me, when he professeth his design to be to impair my authority so far that the cause I own may receive no countenance thereby, I leave it to Him who will one day reveal the secrets of all hearts, which at present are open and naked unto Him. But how, I pray, are the things by me denied known to be true? Seeing it was unpleasant and distasteful to him to insist upon them, men might expect that his evidence of them was not only open, clear, undeniable, and manifest as to its truth, but cogent as to their publication. The whole insisted on is, "If there be any truth in reports," "hic nigræ succus loliginis, hæc est ærugo mera." Is this a bottom for a minister of the gospel to proceed upon to such charges as those insinuated? Is not the course of nature set on fire at this day by reports? Is any thing more contrary to the royal law of charity than to take up reports as the ground of charges and accusations? Is there any thing more unbecoming a man, — laying aside all considerations of Christianity, — than to suffer his judgment to be tainted, much more his words and public expressions in charging and accusing others to be regulated, by reports? And whereas we are commanded to speak evil of no man, may we not on this ground speak evil of all men, and justify ourselves by saying, "It is so, if reports be true?" The prophet tells us that a combination for his defaming and reproach was managed among his adversaries: Jer. xx. 10, "I heard the defaming of many, fear on every side. Report, say they, and we will report it." If they can have any to go before them in the transgression of that law, which He who knows how the tongues of men are "set on fire of hell" gave out to lay a restraint upon them, "Thou shalt not raise a false report," Exod. xxiii. 1, they will second it, and spread it abroad to the utmost, for his disadvantage and trouble. Whether this procedure of our reverend author come not up to the practice of their design, I leave to his own conscience to judge. Should men suffer their spirits to be heightened by provocations of this nature, unto a recharge from

the same offensive dunghill of reports, what monsters should we speedily be transformed into! But this being far from being the only place wherein appeal is made to reports and hear-says by our author, I shall have occasion, in the consideration of the severals of them, to reassume this discourse. For what he adds about the space of time wherein my former reply was drawn up, because I know not whether he had heard any report insinuated to the contrary to what I affirmed, I shall not trouble him with giving evidence thereunto, but only add, that here he hath the product of half that time, which I now interpose upon the review of my transcribed papers; only, whereas it is said that Mr Cawdrey is an ancient man, I cannot but wonder he should be so easy of belief. Aristotle, Rhetor. lib. ii. cap. 18, tells us, Οἱ πρεσβύτεροι, ἄπιστοι δι' ἐμπειρίαν, and not apt to believe, whence on all occasions of discourse προστιθέασιν ἀεὶ τὸ ἴσως καὶ τάχα? but he believes all that comes to hand with an easy faith, which he hath totally in his own power to dispose of at pleasure. That I was in passion when I wrote my review is his judgment; but this is but man's day; we are in expectation of that wherein "the world shall be judged in righteousness." It is too possible that my spirit was not in that frame, in all things, wherein it ought to have been; but that the reverend author knows not. I have nothing to say to this but that of the philosopher, Ἐάν τίς σοι ἀπαγγείλη ὅτι ὁ δεῖνα σε κακῶς λέγει, μὴ ἀπολογοῦ πρὸς τὰ λεχθέντα, ἀλλ' ἀποκρίνου ὅτι ἀγνόει, τὰ γὰρ ἄλλα προσιόντα μοι κακὰ ἐπεὶ οὐκ ἂν ταῦτα μόνα ἔλεγεν, Epic., cap. 48. Much, I confess, was not spoken by me (which he afterward insisteth on) to the argumentative part of his book; which as in an answer I was not to look for, so to find had been a difficult task. As he hath nothing to say unto the differences among themselves, both in judgment and practice, so how little there is in his recrimination of the differences among us, — as, that one and the same man differeth from himself, which charge he casts upon Mr Cotton and myself, — will speedily be manifested to all impartial men. For the treatise itself, whose consideration I now proceed unto, that I may reduce what I have to say unto it into the bounds intended, in confining my defensative unto this preface to the treatise of another, I shall refer it unto certain heads, that will be comprehensive of the whole, and give the reader a clear and distinct view thereof.

I shall begin with that which is least handled in the two books of this reverend author, though the sum of what was pleaded by me in my treatise of schism. For the discovery of the true nature of schism, and the vindication of them who were falsely charged with the crime thereof, I laid down two principles as the foundation of all that I asserted in the whole cause insisted on, which may briefly be reduced to these two syllogisms:—

1. If in all and every place of the New Testament where there is mention made of schism, name or thing, in an ecclesiastical sense, there is nothing intended by it but a *division* in a particular church, then that is the proper Scripture notion of schism in the ecclesiastical sense; but in all and every place, etc.: *ergo*. The proposition being clear and evident in its own light, the assumption was confirmed in my treatise by an induction of the several instances that might any way seem to belong unto it.

2. My second principle was raised upon a concession of the general nature of schism, restrained with one necessary limitation, and amounts unto this argument:— If schism in an ecclesiastical sense be the breach of a union of Christ's institution, then they who are not guilty of the breach of a union of Christ's institution are not guilty of schism; but so is schism: *ergo*.

The proposition also of this syllogism, with its inference, being unquestionable, for the confirmation of the assumption, I considered the nature of all church-union as instituted by Christ, and pleaded the innocency of those whose defence, in several degrees, I had undertaken, by their freedom from the breach of any church-union. Not finding the reverend author, in his first answer, to speak clearly and distinctly to either of those principles, but to proceed in a course of perpetual diversion from the thing in question, with reflections, charges, etc., — all rather, I hope, out of an unacquaintedness with the true nature of argumentation than any perverseness of spirit, in cavilling at what he found he could not answer, — I earnestly desired him, in my review, that we might have a fair and friendly meeting, Personally to debate those principles which he had undertaken to oppose, and so to prevent trouble to ourselves and others, in writing and reading things remote from the merit of the cause under agitation. What returns I have had hitherto the reader is now acquainted withal from his rejoinder, the particulars whereof shall be farther inquired into afterward.

The other parts of his two books consist in his charges upon me about my judgment in sundry particulars, not relating in the least, that I can as yet understand, unto the controversy in hand. As to his excursions about Brownists, Anabaptists, Seekers, rending the peace of their churches, separating from them, the errors of the Separatists, and the like, I cannot apprehend myself concerned to take notice of them; to the other things an answer shall be returned and a defence made, so far as I can judge it necessary. It may be our anchor seeks a relief from the charge of schism that lies upon him and his party (as they are called) from others, by managing the same charge against them who, he thinks, will not return it upon them; but for my part, I shall assure him that were he not, in my judgment, more acquitted upon my principles than upon his own, I should be necessitated to stand upon even terms with him herein. But to have advantages from want of charity, as the Donatists had against the Catholics, is no argument of a good cause.

In the first chapter there occurs not any thing of real difference, as to the cause under agitation, that should require a review, being spent wholly in things ἔξω τοῦ παράγματος, and therefore I shall briefly animadvert on what seems of most concernment therein, on the manner of his procedure. His former discourse, and this also, consisting much of my words perverted by adding in the close something that might wrest them to his own purpose, he tells me, in the beginning of his third chapter, that "this is to turn my testimony against myself which is," as he saith, "an allowed way of the clearest victory," which it seemeth he aimeth at; but nothing can be more remote from being defended with that pretence than this way of proceeding. It is not of urging a testimony from me against me that I complained, but the perverting of my words, by either heading or closing of them with his own, quite to other purposes than those of their own intendment; — a way whereby any man may make other men's words to speak what he pleaseth; as Mr Biddle, by his leading questions, and knitting of scriptures to his expressions in them, makes an appearance of constraining the word of God to speak out all his Socinian blasphemies.

In this course he still continues, and his very entrance gives us a pledge of what we are to expect in the process of his management of the present business. Whereas I had said, that, "considering the various interests of parties at difference, there is no great success to be promised by the management of controversies, though with never so much evidence and conviction of truth;" to the repetition of my words he subjoins the instance of "sectaries, not restrained by the clearest demonstration of truth;" not weighing how facile a task it is to supply "Presbyterians" in their room; which in his account is, it seems, to turn his testimony against himself, and, as he somewhere phraseth it, "to turn the point of his sword into his own bowels." But "nobis non tam licet esse disertis;" neither do we here either learn or teach any such way of disputation.

His following leaves are spent, for the most part, in slighting the notion of schism by me insisted on, and in reporting my arguments for it, pp. 8, 9, 12, in such a way and manner as argues that he either never understood them or is willing to pervert them. The true nature and importance of them I have before laid down, and shall not now again repeat; though I shall add, that his frequent repetition of his disproving that principle, which it appears that he never yet contended withal in its full strength, brings but little advantage to his cause with persons whose interest doth not compel them to take up things on trust. How well he clears himself from the charge of reviling and using opprobrious, reproachful terms, although he profess himself to have been astonished at the charge, may be seen in his justification of himself therein, pp. 16–19, with his re-enforcing every particular expression instanced in; and yet he tells me, for inferring that he discovered sanguinary thoughts in reference unto them whose removal from their native soil into the wilderness he affirms England's happiness would have consisted in, that he hath "much ado to forbear once more to say, 'The Lord rebuke thee.'" For my part, I have received such a satisfactory taste of his spirit and way, that as I shall not from henceforth desire him to keep in any thing that he can hardly forbear to let out, but rather to use his utmost liberty, so I must assure him that I am very little concerned, or not at all, in what he shall be pleased to say or to forbear for the time to come; himself hath freed me from that concernment.

The first particular of value insisted on, is his charge upon me for *the denial of all the churches of England to be true churches of Christ, except the churches gathered in a congregational way*. Having frequently, and without hesitation, charged this opinion upon me in his first answer, knowing it to be very false, I expostulated with him about it in my review. Instead of accepting the satisfaction tendered in my express denial of any such thought or persuasion, or tendering any satisfaction as to the wrong done me, he seeks to justify himself in his charge, and so persisteth therein. The reasons he gives for his so doing are not unworthy a little to be remarked.

The first is this: He "supposed me to be an Independent," and therefore made that charge; the consequent of which supposition is much too weak to justify this reverend author in his accusation. Doth he suppose that he may without offence lay what he pleases to the charge of an Independent? But he saith, secondly, that he "took the word Independent generally, as comprehending Brownists, and Anabaptists, and other sectaries." But herein also he doth but delude his own conscience, seeing he personally speaks to me and to my design in that book of schism which he undertook to confute; which also removes his third intimation, that he "formerly intended any kind of Independence," etc. The rest that follow are of the same nature, and, however compounded, will not make a salve to heal the wound made in his reputation by his own weapon. For the learned author called "vox populi," which he is pleased here to urge, I first question whether he be willing to be produced to maintain this charge; and if he shall appear, I must needs tell him (what he here questions whether it be so or no) that he is a very liar. For any principles in my treatise whence a denial of their ministers and churches may be regularly deduced, let him produce them if he can; and if not, acknowledge that there had been a more Christian and ingenuous way of coming off an engagement into that charge than that by him chosen to be insisted on. "Animos et iram ex crimine sumunt." And again we have "vox populi" cited on the like occasion, p. 34, about my refusal to answer whether I were a minister or not; which as the thing itself, of such a refusal of mine, on any occasion in the world (because it must be spoken), is "purum putum mendacium," so it is no truer that that was "vox populi" at Oxford, which is pretended. That which is "vox populi" must be public; "publicum" was once "populicum." Now, set aside the whispers of, it may be, two or three ardelios,[15] notorious triflers, whose lavish impertinency will deliver any man from the danger of being

---

15 Ardelio, a busy-body, a meddler; a term borrowed from Phædrus, lib ii. Fab. 5. — Ed.

slandered by their tongues, and there will be little ground left for the report that is fathered on "vox populi." And I tell him here once again, — which is a sufficient answer, indeed, to his whole first chapter, — that I do not deny presbyterian churches to be true churches of Jesus Christ, nor the ministers of them to be true ministers, nor do maintain a nullity in their ordination, as to what is the proper use and end of salvation[16] (taking it in the sense wherein by them it is taken), though I think it neither administered by them in due order, nor to have in itself that force and efficacy, singly considered, which by many of them is ascribed unto it. Thus much of my judgment I have publicly declared long ago; and I thought I might have expected, from persons professing Christianity, that they would not voluntarily engage themselves into an opposition against me, and, waiving my judgment, which I had constantly published and preached, have gathered up reports from private and table discourses, most of them false and untrue, all of them uncertain, the occasions and coherences of those discourses from whence they have been raised and taken being utterly lost, or at present by him wholly omitted. His following excursions, about a successive ordination from Rome, wherein he runs cross to the most eminent lights of all the reformed churches, and their declared judgments, with practice, in re-ordaining those who come unto them with that Roman stamp upon them, I shall not farther interest myself in, nor think myself concerned so to do, until I see a satisfactory answer given unto Beza and others on this very point. And yet I must here again profess that I cannot understand that distinction, of deriving ordination from the church of Rome, but not from the Roman church. Let him but seriously peruse these ensuing words of Beza, and tell me whether he have any ground of a particular quarrel against me upon this account:—

"Sed præterea quænam ista est, quæso, ordinaria vocatio, quam eos habuisse dicis, quos Deus paucis quibusdam exceptis, excitavit? Certe papistica. Nam hæc tua verba sunt; hodie si episcopi Gallicanarum ecclesiarum se et suas ecclesias a tyrannide episcopi Romani vindicare velint, et eas ab omni idololatria et superstitione repurgare, non habent opus alia vocatione ab ea quam habent. Quid ergo? Papisticas ordinationes, — in quibus neque morum examen præcessit, neque leges ullæ servatæ sunt

---

16 Vid. Gerard. loc. Com. de Minist. Ecclesiast. Sect. 11, 12.

inviolabiliter ex divino jure in electionibus et ordinationibus præscriptæ, in quibus puri etiam omnes canones impudentissime violati sunt: quæ nihil aliud sunt, quam fœdissima Romani prostibuli nundinatio, quâvis meretricum mercede, quam Deus templo suo inferri prohibuit, inquinatior: quibus denique alii non ad prædicandum sed pervertendum evangelium: alii non ad docendum, sed ad rursus sacrificandum, et ad abominandum βδέλυγμα sunt ordinati, — usque adeo firmas tecum esse censebimus, ut quoties tali cuipiam pseudoepiscopo Deus concesserit, ad verum Christianismum transire, omnis ilia istiusmodi ordinationis impuritas simul expurgata censeatur? Imo quia sic animum per Dei gratiam mutavit, quo ore, quo pudore, qua conscientia papismum quidem detestabitur, suam autem inordinatissimam ordinationem non ejurabit? aut si, ejuret, quomodo ex illius jure auctoritatem dicendi habebit? Nec tamen nego quin tales, si probe doctrinam veram tenere, si honestis moribus præditi, si ad gregem pascendum apti comperiantur, ex pseudoepiscopis novi pastores, legitimè designentur." Thus he, who was thought then to speak the sense of the churches of Geneva and France, in his book against Saravia about the divers orders of ministers in the church.

His plea for the church-authority of the pope, notwithstanding his being an idolater, a murderer, the man of sin, an adversary of Christ, because a civil magistrate doth not by any moral crime, or those whereof the pope is guilty, lose his jurisdiction and authority, considering the different principles, grounds, ends, laws, rules, privileges, of the authority of the one and the other, and the several tenures whereby the one doth hold and the other pretends to hold his power, is brought in to serve the turn in hand, and may be easily laid aside. And when he shall manifest that there is appointed by Christ one single high priest or prelate in the house of God, the whole church, and that office to be confined to one nation, one blood, one family, propagated by natural generation, without any provision of relief by any other way, person, or family, in case of miscarriage; and when he shall have proved that such an officer as the pope of Rome, in any one particular that constituteth him such an officer, was once instituted by Christ, — I shall farther attend unto his reason for his authority from that of the high priest's among the Jews, which was not lost, as to its continuance in the family of Aaron, notwithstanding the miscarriage of some individual persons vested therewithal. In the close of the chapter he re-assumes his charge of my renouncing my own ordination, which, with great confidence, and without the least scruple, he had asserted in his answer. Of that assertion he now pretends to give the reasons, whereof the first is this: —

1. "*The world looks on him as an Independent of the highest note; therefore, he hath renounced his ordination, and therefore I dare to say so.*" So much for that reason. I understand neither the logic nor morality of this first reason.

2. He *knows from good hands that some of the brethren have renounced their ordination; therefore, he durst say positively that I have renounced mine*, Prov. xii. 18.

3. He hath heard that *I dissuaded others from their ordination*; and therefore he durst say I renounced my own. And yet I suppose he may possibly dissuade some from episcopal ordination; but I know it not, no more than he knows what he affirms of me, which is false.

4. He concludes from the principles in my book of schism, because I said that to insist upon *a succession of ordination from antichrist and the beast of Rome would, if I mistake not, keep up in the this particular what God would have pulled down*, therefore I renounced my ordination, when he knows that I avowed the validity of ordination on another account.

5. If all this will not do, he tells me of something that was said at a *public meeting* (at dinner, it seems) with the canons of Christ Church, — namely, that I *valued not my ordination by the bishop of Oxford any more than a crumb upon my trencher*; which words, whether ever they were spoken or no, or to what purpose, or in reference to what ordination (I mean of the two orders), or in what sense, or with what limitation, or as part of what discourse, or in comparison of what else, or whether solely in reference to the Roman succession, — in which sense I will have nothing to do with it, — I know not at all, nor will concern myself to inquire, being greatly ashamed to find men professing the religion of Jesus Christ so far forgetful of all common rules of civility and principles of of human society as to insist upon such vain, groundless reports as the foundation of accusations against their brethren. Nor do I believe that any one of the reverend persons quoted will own this information, although I shall not concern myself to make inquiry into their memories concerning any such passage or discourse.

Much relief, for future, against these and the like mistakes may be afforded, from an easy obviation of the different senses wherein the term of *ordination* is often used. It is one thing when it is taken largely, for the whole appointment of a man to the ministry, — in which sense I desire our author to consider what is written by Beza among the Reformed, and Gerhard among the Lutheran divines, to omit innumerable others, — another thing when taken for the imposition of hands, whether by bishops or presbyters; concerning which single act, both as to its order and efficacy, I have sufficiently delivered my judgment, if he be pleased to take notice of it. I fear, indeed, that when men speak of an "ordained ministry,' — which, in its true and proper sense, I shall with them contend for, — they often relate only to that solemnity, restraining the authoritative making of ministers singly thereunto, contrary to the intention and meaning of that expression in Scripture, antiquity, and the best reformed divines, both Calvinists and Lutherans; and yet it is not imaginable how some men prevail, by the noise and sound of that word, upon the prejudiced minds of partial, unstudied men. A little time may farther manifest, if it be not sufficiently done already, that another account is given of this matter by Clemens, Tertullian, Cyprian, Origen, Justin Martyr, and generally all the first writers of the Christians, besides the councils of old and late, with innumerable protestant authors of the best note, to the same purpose.

This, I say, is the ground of this mistake: Whereas sundry things concur to *the calling of ministers*, as it belongs to the church of God, the pillar and ground of truth, the spouse of Christ Ps. xlv. 9, and mother of the family, or her that tarrieth at home, Ps. lxviii. 12, unto whom all ministers are stewards, 1 Cor. iv. 1, even in the house of God, 1 Tim. iii. 15; and sundry qualifications are indispensably previously required in the persons to be called; overlooking the necessity of the qualifications required and omitting the duty an authority of the church, Acts i. 15–26, vi. 2–6, xiii. 2, 3, xiv. 23, the act of them who are not the whole church, Eph. iv. 11, 12, but only a part of it, 1 Cor. iii. 5, 2 Cor. i. 24, 1 Pet. v. 3, as to ministry, consisting in the approbation and solemn confirmation of what is supposed to go before, hath in some men's language gotten the name of "ordination," and an interpretation of that name, to such an extent as to inwrap in it all that is indispensably necessary to the constitution or making of ministers: so that where that is obtained, in what order soever, or by whomsoever administered, who have first obtained it themselves, there is a lawful and sufficient calling to the ministry! Indeed, I know no error about the institutions of Christ attended with more pernicious consequences to the church of God than this, should it be practised according to the force of the principle itself. Suppose six, eight, or ten men, who have themselves been formerly ordained, but now perhaps, not by any ecclesiastical censure, but by an act of the civil magistrate, are put out of their places for notorious ignorance and scandal, should concur and ordain a hundred ignorant and wicked persons like themselves to be ministers, must they not, on this principle, be all accounted ministers of Christ, and to be invested with all ministerial power, and so be enabled to propagate their kind to the end of the world? And, indeed, why should not this be granted, seeing the whole bulk of the papal ordination is contended for as valid? whereas it is notoriously known that sundry bishops among them (who perhaps received their own ordination as the reward of a whore), being persons of vicious lives, and utterly ignorant of the gospel, did sustain their pomp and sloth by selling "holy orders," as they called them, to the scum and refuse of men. But of these things more in their proper place.

Take then, reader, the substance of this chapter in this brief recapitulation:— 1. "He denies our churches to be true churches, and our ministers true ministers;" 2. "He hath renounced his own ordination;" 3. "When some young men came to advise about their ordination, he dissuaded them from it;" 4. "He saith he would maintain against all the ministers of England there was in Scripture no such thing as ordination;" 5. "That when he was chosen a parliament-man, he would not answer whether he was a minister or not;" — all which are notoriously untrue, and some of them, namely, the last two, so remote from any thing to give a pretence or colour unto them, that I question whether Satan have impudence enough to own himself their author. And yet, from hear-says, reports, rumours, from table-talk, "vox populi," and such other grounds of reasoning, this reverend author hath made them his own; and by such a charge he hath, I presume, in the judgment of all unprejudiced men, discharged me from farther attending to what he shall be prompted from the like principles to divulge, for the same ends and purposes which hitherto he hath managed, for the future. For my judgment about their ministry and ordination, about the nature and efficacy of ordination, the state and power of particular churches, my own station in the ministry, which I shall at all times, through the grace and assistance of Our Lord Jesus Christ, freely justify against men and devils, it is so well known that I shall not need here farther to declare it. For the true nature and notion of schism, alone by me inquired after in this chapter, as I said, I find nothing offered thereunto. Only, whereas I restrained the ecclesiastical use of the word "schism" to the sense wherein it is used in the places of Scripture that mention it with relation to church affairs, — which that it ought not to be so, nothing but asseverations to the contrary are produced to evince, — this is interpreted to extend to all that I would allow as to the nature of schism itself, which is most false; though I said, if I would proceed no farther, I might not be compelled so to do, seeing in things of this nature we may crave allowance to think and speak with the Holy Ghost. However, I expressly comprised in my proposition all the places wherein the nature of schism is delivered, under what terms or words soever. When, then, I shall be convinced that such discourses as those of this treatise, made up of diversions into things wholly foreign to the inquiry by me insisted on in the investigation of the true notion and nature of schism, with long talks about Anabaptists, Brownists, Sectaries, Independents, Presbyterians, ordination, with charges and reflections grounded on this presumption, [prove] that this author and his party (for we will no more contend about that expression) are "in solidum" possessed of all true and orderly church-state in England, so that whosoever are not of them are "schismatics," and I know not what besides, he being

— "gallinæ filius albæ,
Nos viles pulli nati infelicibus ovis," Juv., xiii. 141,

I shall farther attend unto them.

I must farther add, that I was not so happy as to foresee that, because I granted the Roman party before the Reformation to have made outwardly a profession of the religion of Christ, — although I expressed them to be really a party combined together for all ends of wickedness, and, in particular, for the extirpation of the true church of Christ in the world, having no state of union but what the Holy Ghost calls "Babylon," in opposition to "Zion," — our reverend author would conclude, as he doth, p. 34, that I allowed them to be a true church of Christ; but it is impossible for wiser men than I to see far into the issue of such discourses, and therefore we must take in good part what doth fall out. And if the reverend author, instead of having his zeal warmed against me, would a little bestir his abilities to make out to the understandings and consciences of uninterested men, that, all ecclesiastical power being vested in the pope and councils, by the consent of that whole combination of men called the Church of Rome, and flowing from the pope in its execution to all others, — who, in the derivation of it from him, owned him as the immediate fountain of it, which they sware to maintain in him, and this in opposition to all church-power in any other persons whatsoever, — it was possible that any power should be derived from that combination but what came expressly from the fountain mentioned; I desire our author would consider the frame of spirit that was in this matter in them who first laboured in the work of reformation, and to that end peruse the stories of Lasitius[17] and Regenuolscius[18] about the churches of Bohemia, Poland, and those parts of the world, especially the latter, from pp. 29, 30, and forward. And as to the distinction used by some between the Papacy and the church of Rome, which our author makes use of to another purpose than those did who first invented it (extending it only to the consideration of the possibility of salvation for individual persons living in that communion before the Reformation), I hope he will not be angry if I profess my disability to understand it. All men cannot be wise alike. If the Papacy comprise the pope, and all papal jurisdiction and power, with the subjection of men thereunto; if it denote all the idolatries, false worship, and heresies of that society of men, — I do know that all those are confirmed by church-acts of that church, and that, in the *church-public sense*

---

17 Joannes Lasitius wrote a large work on the Bohemian Brethren. The eighth book of this work under the title, "Historiæ de Origine et Rebus Gestis Fratrum Bohemorum;" etc., was published by Comenis in 1649. — Ed.

18 Regenuolscius, or rather, according to his true name, Wingerscius, was the author of "Systema Historico-Chronologicum Ecclesiarum Slavonicarum." — Ed.

of that church, no man was a member of it but by virtue of the union that consisted in that Papacy, it being placed always by them in all their definitions of their church; as also, that there was neither church-order, nor church-power, nor church-act, nor church-confession, nor church-worship amongst them, but what consisted in that Papacy.

Now, because nothing doth more frequently occur than the objection of the difficulty of placing the dispensation of baptism on a sure foot of account, in case of the rejection of all authoritative influence from Rome into the ministry of the reformed churches, with the insinuation of a supposition of the non-baptization of all such as derive not a title unto it by that means, they who do so being supposed to stand upon an unquestionable foundation, I shall a little examine the grounds of their security, and then compare them with what they have to plead who refuse to acknowledge the deriving any sap or nourishment from that rotten corrupt stock.

It is, I suppose, taken for granted that an unbaptized person can never effectually baptize, let him receive what other qualifications soever that are to be super-added as necessary thereunto. If this be not supposed, the whole weight of the objection, improved by the worst supposition that can be made, falls to the ground. I shall also desire, in the next place, that as we cannot make the popish baptism better than it is, so, that we would not plead it to be better, or any other than they profess it to be, nor pretend that though it be rotten or null in the foundation, yet by continuance and time it might obtain validity and strength. When the claim is by succession from such a stock or root, if you suppose once a total intercision in the succession from that stock or root, there is an utter end put to that claim. Let us now consider how the case is with them from whom this claim is derived.

1. It is notoriously known that, amongst them, the *validity of* the sacraments depends upon *the intention of the administrator*. It is so with them as to every thing they call a sacrament. Now, to take one step backwards, that baptism will by some of ours be scarce accounted valid which is not administered by a lawful minister. Suppose now that some pope, ordaining a bishop in his stable to satisfy a whore, had not an intention to make him a bishop (which is no remote surmise), he being no bishop rightly ordained, all the priests by him afterward consecrated were

indeed no priests, and so, indeed, had no power to administer any sacraments: and so, consequently, the baptism that may lie, for aught we know, at the root of that which some of us pretend unto, was originally absolutely null and void, and could never by tract of time be made valid or effectual, for, like a muddy fountain, the farther it goes, the more filthy it is. Or, suppose that any priest, baptizing one who afterwards came to be pope, from whom all authority in that church doth flow and is derived, had no intention to baptize him, what will become of all that ensues thereon?

It is endless to pursue the uncertainties and entanglements that ensue on this head of account, and sufficiently easy to manifest that whosoever resolves his interest in gospel privileges into this foundation can have no assurance of faith, nay, nor tolerably probable conjecture that he is baptized, or was ever made partaker of any ordinance of the gospel. Let them that delight in such troubled waters sport themselves in them. For my own part, — considering the state of that church for some years if not ages, wherein the fountains of all authority amongst them were full of filth and blood, their popes, upon their own confession, being made, set up, and pulled down, at the pleasure of vile, impudent, domineering strumpets, and supplying themselves with officers all the world over of the same spirit and stamp with themselves, and that for the most part for hire, being in the meantime all idolaters to a man, — I am not willing to grant that their good and upright intention is necessary to be supposed as a thing requisite unto my interest in any privilege of the gospel of Christ.

2. It is an ecclesiastical determination, of irrefragable authority amongst them, that whosoever he be that administers baptism, so he use *the matter and form*, that baptism is good and valid, and not to be reiterated; yea, Pope Nicholas, in his resolutions and determinations upon the inquiry of the Bulgarians (whose decrees are authentic and recorded in their councils, tom. 2. Crab. p. 144), declares the judgment of that church to the full. They tell him that many in their nation were baptized by an unknown person, a Jew or a Pagan, they knew not whether, and inquire of him whether they were to be rebaptized or no; whereunto he answers: "Si in nomine S. S. Trinitatis, vel tantum in Christi nomine, sicut in Actis apostolorum legimus, baptizati sunt, unum quippe idemque est, ut S. Ambrosius ex-

pressit, constat eos denuo non esse baptizandos." If they were baptized in the name of the Trinity, or of Christ, they are not to be baptized again. Let a blasphemous Jew or Pagan do it, so it be done, the work is wrought, grace conveyed, and baptism valid! The constant practice of women baptizing amongst them is of the same import. And what doth Mr Cawdrey think of this kind of baptism? Is it not worth the contending about, to place it in the derived succession of ours? Who knows but that some of these persons, baptized by a counterfeit impostor, on purpose to abuse and defile the institutions of our blessed Saviour, might come to be baptizers themselves, yea, bishops or popes, from whom all ecclesiastical authority was to be derived? and what evidence or certainty can any man have that his baptism doth not flow from this fountain.

3. Nay, upon the general account, if this be required as necessary to the administration of that ordinance, that he that doth baptize be rightly and effectually *baptized himself*, who can in faith bring an infant to any to be baptized, unless he himself saw that person rightly baptized?

As to the matter of baptism, then, we are no more concerned than as to that of ordination. By what ways or means soever any man comes to be a minister according to the mind of Jesus Christ, by that way and means he comes to have the power for a due administration of that ordinance; concerning which state of things our author may do well to consult Beza in the place mentioned. Many other passages there are in this chapter that might be remarked, and a return easily made according to their desert of untruth and impertinency; but the insisting on such things looks more like children's playing at push-pin than the management of a serious disputation. Take an instance. Page 23, he seems to be much offended with my commending him, and tells me, as Jerome said of Rufinus, "I wrong him with praises;" when yet the utmost I say of him is, that "I had received a better character of him than he had given of himself in his book," p. 10 [214]; and that "his proceeding was unbecoming his worth, gravity, and profession," p. 46 [227], or "so grave and reverend a person as he is reported to be;" p. 121 [234]; wherein, it seems, I have transgressed the rule, Μήποτ' εὖ ἔρδειν γέροντα.

The business of his second chapter is, to make good his former charge of my inconstancy and inconsistency with myself as to my former and present opinions, which he had placed in the frontispiece of his other treatise. The impertinency of this chapter had been intolerable, but that the loose discourses of it are relieved by a scheme of my self-contradictions, in the close. His design, he professeth, in his former discourse, was, not to blast my reputation or to "cause my person to suffer, but to prevent the prevalency of my way by the authority of my person;" that is, it was not his intention, it was only his intention for such a purpose! I bless my God I have good security, through grace, that whether he, or others like-minded with himself, intend any such thing or no, in those proceedings of his and theirs, which seemed to have in their own nature a tendency thereunto, my reputation shall yet be preserved in that state and condition as is necessary to accompany me in the duties and works of my generation, that I shall, through the hand of God, be called out unto. And, therefore, being prepared in some measure to go through good report and bad report, I shall give him assurance that I am very little concerned in such attempts, from whatever intention they do proceed; only, I must needs tell him that he consulted not his own reputation with peaceable, godly men, whatever else he omitted, in the ensuing comparing of me to the seducers in Jude, called "wandering planets," for their inconstancy and inconsistency with themselves, — according to the exposition that was needful for the present turn.

But seeing the scheme at the close must bear the weight of this charge, let us briefly see what it amounts unto, and whether it be a sufficient basis of the superstructure that is raised upon it. Hence it is that my inconsistency with myself must be remarked in the title page of his first treatise; from hence must my authority (which what it is I know not) be impaired, and myself be compared to cursed apostates and seducers, and great triumph be made upon my self-inconsistency.

The contradictions pretended are taken out of two books, the one written in the year 1643, the other in 1657, and are as follow:—

| He spake of Rome as a "collapsed, corrupted church-state," p. 40 [p. 37.] | He says, "Rome we account no church at all," p. 156 [p. 155.] |

"Crimen inauditum, C. Cæsar." "Is it meet that any one should be tolerated that is thus woefully inconsistent with himself? What! speak of Rome as a *collapsed church* in Italy, and within thirteen or fourteen years after to say it is no *church at all*." Well! though I may say there is indeed no contradiction between these assertions, seeing in the latter place I speak of Rome as that church is stated by themselves, when yet I acknowledge there may be corrupted churches both in Rome and Italy, in the same treatise; yet I do not find that in the place directed unto, I have in terms, or in just consequence, at all granted the church of Rome to be a collapsed church; nay, the church of Rome is not once mentioned in the whole page, nor as such is spoken of. And what shall we think of this proceeding? But yet I will not so far offend against my sense of my own weakness, ignorance, and frailty, as to use any defensative against this charge. Let it pass at any rate that any sober man, freed from pride, passion, self-fullness, and prejudice, shall be pleased to put upon it:—

— ὁδὲ ὁρῶν τοὺς νόμουςΛίαν ἀκριβῶς, συκοφάντης φαίνεται.

But the second instance will make amends, and take more of the weight of this charge upon its shoulders. Take it, then, as it lies in its triple column:—

"Gifts in the person and consent of people are warrant enough to make a man a preacher, in an extraordinary case only," pp. 15, 40 [pp. 18, 37].	Denying our ordination to be sufficient, he says "he may have that which indeed constitutes him a minister, — namely, gifts and submission by the people," p. 198 [p. 172].	"I am punctually of the same mind still," p. 40 [p. 226]. Yet had said in his first book, p. 46 [p. 43], "As to formal teaching is required, 1. Gifts; 2. Authority from the church," — if he do not equivocate.

I must confess I am here at a stand to find out the pretended contradiction, especially laying aside the word "only" in the first column, which is his, and not mine. By a "preacher," in the first place, I intend a "minister." Gifts, and consent or submission of the people, I affirm in both places to be sufficient to constitute a man a minister in extraordinary cases, — that is, when imposition of hands by a presbytery may not be obtained in due order, according to the appointment of Jesus Christ. That the consent and submission of the people, which include election, have nothing of authority in them, I never said. The superadded act of the imposition of hands by a presbytery, when it may be regularly obtained, is also necessary. But that there is any contradiction in my words (although, in truth, they are not my words, but an undue collection from them), or in this author's inference from them, or any colour of equivocation, I profess I cannot discern. In this place Mr Cawdrey, οὐκ ἀλλ' ἐδόκησεν ἰδεῖν διὰ νύκτα σιλήνην. Pass we to the third:—

| He made the union of Christ and believers to be mystical, p. 21 [p. 129]. | He makes the union to be personal, pp. 94, 95 [p. 22]. |

I wish our reverend author, for his own sake, had omitted this instance, because I am enforced, in my own necessary defence, to let him know that what he assigns to me in his second column is notoriously false, denied and disproved by me in the very place and treatise wherein I have handled the doctrine of the indwelling of the Spirit; and whether he will hear or forbear, I cannot but tell him that this kind of dealing is unworthy his calling and profession. His following deductions and inferences, whereby he endeavours to give countenance to this false and calumnious charge, arise from ignorance of the doctrine that he seeks to blemish and oppose. Though the same Spirit dwell in Christ and us, yet *he* may have him in *fulness*, *we* in *measure*; — fulness and measure relating to his communication of graces and gifts, which are arbitrary to him; indwelling, to his person. That the Spirit animates the catholic church, and is the author of its spiritual life by a voluntary act of his power, as the soul gives life to the body by a necessary act, by virtue of its union, — for [that] life is "actus vivificantis in vivificatum per unionem utriusque," — is the common doctrine of divines. But yet the soul being united to the body as "pars essentialis suppositi," and the Spirit dwelling in the person as a free inhabitant, the union between Christ and the person is not of the same kind with the union of soul and body. Let our author consult Zanchy on the second of the Ephesians, and he will not repent him of his labour; or, if he please, an author whom I find him often citing, namely, Bishop Hall, about union with Christ. And for my concernment in this charge, I shall subjoin the words from whence it must be taken, p. 133 of my book of Perseverance.[19]

---

19 See vol. xi. of Owen's works, chap. viii.

"1. The first signal issue and effect which is ascribed to this indwelling of the Spirit is union; not a personal union with himself, which is impossible. He doth not assume our nature, and so prevent our personality, which would make us one person with him; but dwells in our persons, keeping his own, and leaving us our personality infinitely distinct. But it is a spiritual union, the great union mentioned so often in the Gospel, that is the sole fountain of our blessedness, our union with the Lord Christ, which we have thereby.

"Many thoughts of heart there have been about this union; what it is, wherein it doth consist, the causes, manner, and effects of it, The Scripture expresses it to be very eminent, near, durable; setting it out for the most part by similitudes and metaphorical illustrations, to lead poor weak creatures into some useful, needful acquaintance with that mystery, whose depths, in this life, they shall never fathom. That many, in the days wherein we live, have miscarried in their conceptions of it is evident. Some, to make out their imaginary union, have destroyed the person of Christ; and, fancying a way of uniting man to God by him, have left him to be neither God nor man. Others have destroyed the person of believers; affirming that, in their union with Christ, they lose their own personality, — that is, cease to be men, or at least those are [or?] these individual men.

"I intend not now to handle it at large, but only, — and that I hope, without offence, — to give in my thoughts concerning it, as far as it receiveth light from, and relateth unto, what hath been before delivered concerning the indwelling of the Spirit, and that without the least contending about other ways of expression." So far there, with much more to the purpose. And in the very place of my book of schism referred to by this author, I affirm, as the head of what I assert, that by the indwelling of the Spirit, *Christ personal* and his church do become one *Christ mystical*, 1 Cor. xii. 12; the very expression insisted on by him in my former treatise. And so you have an issue of this self-contradiction; concerning which, though reports be urged for some other things, Mr Cawdrey might have said what Lucian doth of his true history, Γράφω τοίνυν περὶ ὧν μετ' εἶδον, μετ' ἔπαθον, μήτε παρ' ἄλλων ἐπυθόμην.

Let us, then, consider the fourth, which is thus placed:—

1. "In extraordinary cases, every one that undertakes to preach the gospel must have an immediate call from God," p. 28 [p. 28.]	2. Yet required no more of before but "the gifts and consent of the people, which are ordinary and mediate calls," p. 15 [p. 18], neither is here any need or use of an immediate call, p. 53 [p. 48.]	3. To assure a man that he is extraordinarily called, he gives three ways: "1. Immediate revelation; 2. Concurrence of Scripture rule; 3. Some outward acts of providence;" — the two last whereof are mediate calls, p. 30 [p. 29.]

All that is here remarked and cast into three columns, I know not well why, is taken out of that one treatise of "The Duty of Pastors and People;" and could I give myself the least assurance that any one would so far concern himself in this charge as to consult the places from whence the words are pretended to be taken, to see whether there be any thing in them to answer the cry that is made, I should spare myself the labour of adding any one syllable towards their vindication, and might most safely so do, there being not the least colour of opposition between the things spoken of. In brief, extraordinary cases are not all of one sort and nature; in some an extraordinary call may be required, in some not. Extraordinary calls are not all of one kind and nature neither. Some may be immediate from God, in the ways there by me described; some calls may be said to be extraordinary, because they do in some things come short of or go beyond the ordinary rule that ought to be observed in well-constituted churches. Again concurrence of Scripture rules and acts of outward providence may be such sometimes as are suited to an *ordinary*, sometimes to an *extraordinary call*; all which are at large unfolded in the places directed unto by our author, and all laid in their own order, without the least shadow of contradiction. But it may sometimes be said of good men, as the satirist said of evil women, "Fortem animum præstant rebus quas turpiter audent?" Go we to the next:—

| 1. "The church government from which I desire not to wander is the presbyterial." | 2. He now is engaged in the independent way. | 3. Is settled in that way, which he is "ready to maintain, and knows it will be found his rejoicing in the day of the Lord Jesus". |

"Hinc mihi sola mali labes." This is that inexpiable crime that I labour under. An account of this whole business I have given in my review, so that I shall not here trouble the reader with a repetition of what he is so little concerned in. I shall only add, that whereas I suppose Mr Cawdrey did subscribe unto the three articles at his ordination, were it of any concernment to the church of God or the interest of truth, or were it a comely and a Christian part to engage in such a work, I could manifest contradictions between what he then solemnly subscribed to and what he hath since written and preached, manifold above what he is able to draw out of this alteration of my judgment. Be it here, then, declared, that whereas I some time apprehended the *presbyterial, synodical* government of churches to have been fit to be received and walked in (then when I knew not but that it answered those principles which I had taken up, upon my best inquiry into the word of God), I now profess myself to be satisfied that I was then under a mistake, and that I do now own, and have for many years lived in, the way and practice of that called *congregational*. And for this alteration of judgment, of all men I fear least a charge from them, or any of them, whom within a few years we saw reading the service-book in their surplices, etc.; against which things they do now inveigh and declaim. What influence the perusal of Mr Cotton's book of the Keys had on my thoughts in this business I have formerly declared. The answer to it (I suppose that written by himself) is now recommended to me by this author, as that which would have perhaps prevented my change; but I must needs tell him, that as I have perused that book, many years ago, without the effect intimated, so they must be things written with another frame of spirit, evidence of truth, and manner of reasoning, than any I can find in that book, that are likely for the future to lay hold upon my reason and understanding. Of my settlement in my present persuasion I have not only given him an account formerly, but, with all Christian courtesy, tendered myself in a readiness personally to meet him, to give him the proofs and reasons of my persuasions; which he is pleased to decline, and return, in way of answer, that "I complimented him after the mode of the times," when no such thing was intended; and thereupon my words of desiring liberty to wait upon him are expressed, but the end and purpose for which it was desired are concealed in an "etc." But he adds another instance:—

| "Men ought not to cut themselves from the communion of the church, to rend the body of Christ, and break the sacred bond of charity," p. 48 [p. 45.] | He says, "separation is no schism, nor schism any breach of charity," pp. 48, 49 [pp. 110, 111.] | "There is not one word in either of these cautions that I do not still own and allow," p. 44 [p. 226] sure not without equivocation. |

I have before owned this caution as consistent with my present judgment, as expressed in my book of schism, and as it is indeed; wherein lies the appearance of contradiction I am not able to discern. Do not I, in my book of schism, declare and prove that men ought not to cut themselves from the communion of the church; that they ought not to rend the body of Christ; that they ought not to break the sacred bonds of charity? Is there any word or tittle in the whole discourse deviating from these principles? How and in what sense separation is not schism, that the nature of schism doth not consist in a breach of charity, the treatise instanced will so far declare, as withal to convince those that shall consider what is spoken, that our author scarce keeps close either to truth or charity in his framing of this contradiction. The close of the scheme lies thus:—

| "I conceive they ought not at all to be allowed the benefit of private meeting who wilfully abstain from the public congregations." | "As for liberty to be allowed to those that meet in private, I confess myself to be otherwise minded." |

I remember that about fifteen years ago, meeting occasionally with a learned friend, we fell into some debate about the liberty that began then to be claimed by men, differing from what had been, and what was then likely to be, established. Having at that time made no farther inquiry into the grounds and reasons of such liberty than what had occurred to me in the writings of the Remonstrants, all whose plea was still pointed towards the advantage of their own interest, I delivered my judgment in opposition to the liberty pleaded for, which was then defended by my learned friend. Not many years after, discoursing the same difference with the same person, we found immediately that we had changed stations, — I pleading for an indulgence of liberty, he for restraint. Whether that learned and worthy person be of the same mind still that then he was or no, directly I know not; but this I know, that if he be not, considering the compass of circumstances that must be taken in to settle a right judgment in this case of liberty, and what alterations influencing the determination of this case we have had of late in this nation, he will not be ashamed to own his change, being a person who despises any reputation but what arises from the embracing and pursuit of truth. My change I here own; my judgment is not the same, in this particular, as it was fourteen years ago: and in my change I have good company, whom I need not to name. I shall only say, my change was at least twelve years before the "Petition and Advice," wherein the parliament of the three nations is come up to my judgment. And if Mr Cawdrey hath any thing to object to my present judgment, let him, at his next leisure, consider the treatise that I wrote in the year about toleration, where he will find the whole of it expressed. I suppose he will be doing, and that I may almost say of him, as Polyeuctus did of Spensippus, Τὸ μὴ δύνασθαι ἡσυχιάν ἄγειν ὑπὸ τῆς τύχης ἐν πεντασυρίγγῳ νόσῳ δεδεμένον. And now, Christian reader, I leave it to thy judgment whether our author had any just cause of all his outcries of my inconstancy and self-contradiction, and whether it had not been advisable for him to have passed by this seeming advantage for the design he professed to manage, rather than to have injured his own conscience and reputation to so little purpose.

Being sufficiently tired with the consideration of things of no relation to the cause at first proposed (but, "This saith he, this the Independents, this the Brownists and Anabaptists," etc.), I shall now only inquire after that which is set up in opposition to any of the principles of my treatise of schism before mentioned, or any of the propositions of the syllogisms wherein they are comprised at the beginning of this discourse; remarking in our way some such particular passages as it will not be to the disadvantage of our reverend author to be reminded of. Of the nature of the thing inquired after, in the third chapter I find no mention at all; only, he tells me by the way that the doctor's assertion that "my book about schism was one great schism," was not nonsense, but usual rhetoric; wherein profligate sinners may be called by the name of sin, and therefore a book about schism may be called a schism. I wish our author had found some other way of excusing his doctor than by making it worse himself.

In the fourth chapter he comes to the business itself; and if, in passing through that, with the rest that follow, I can fix on any thing rising up with any pretence of opposition to what I have laid down, it shall not be omitted. For things by myself asserted, or acknowledged on all hands, or formerly ventilated to the utmost, I shall not again trouble the reader with them. Such are the positions about the general nature of schism in things national and political, antecedently considered to the limitation and restriction of it to its ecclesiastical use; the departure from churches, voluntary or compelled, etc.; — all which were stated in my first treatise, and are not directly opposed by our author. Such, also, is that doughty controversy he is pleased to raise and pursue about the seat and subject of schism, with its restriction to the instituted worship of God, pp. 18, 19; so placed by me to distinguish the schism whereof we speak from that which is national, as also from such differences and breaches as may fall out amongst men, few or more, upon civil and national accounts; — all which I exclude from the enjoyment of any room or place in our consideration of the true nature of schism, in its limited ecclesiastical sense. The like, also, may be affirmed concerning the ensuing strife of words about *separation* and *schism*, as though they were, in my apprehension of them, inconsistent: which is a fancy no better grounded than sundry others which our reverend author is pleased to make use of. His whole passage, also, receives no other security than what is afforded to it by turning my universal proposition into a particular. What I say of all places in the Scripture where the name or thing of schism is used in an ecclesiastical sense, as relating to a gospel church, he would restrain to that one place of the Corinthians, where alone the word is used in that sense. However, if that one place be all, my proposition is universal. Take, then, my proposition in its extent and latitude, and let him try once more, if he please, what he hath to object to it, for as yet I find no instance produced to alleviate its truth. He much, also, insists that there may be a separation *in* a church where there is no separation *from* a church; and saith this was at first by me denied. That it was denied by me he cannot prove; but that the contrary was proved by me is evident to all impartial men that have considered my treatise, although I cannot allow that the separation in the church of Corinth was carried to that height as is by him pretended, — namely, as to separate from the ordinance of the Lord's supper. Their disorder and division about and in its administration are reproved, not their separation from it. Only, on that supposition made, I confess I was somewhat surprised with the delivery of his judgment in reference to many of his own party, whom he condemns of schism for not administering the Lord's supper to all the congregation with whom they pray and preach. I suppose the greatest part of the most godly and able ministers of the presbyterian way in England and Scotland are here cast into the same condition of schismatics with the Independents; and the truth, is, I am not yet without hopes of seeing a fair coalescency in love and church-communion between the reforming Presbyterians and Independents, though for it they shall with some suffer under the unjust imputation of schism.

But it is incredible to think whither men will suffer themselves to be carried "studio partium," and ἀμετρίᾳ ἀνθολκῆς. Hence have we the strange notions of this author about schism: decays in grace are schism, and errors in the faith are schism; and schism and apostasy are things of the same kind, differing only in degree, because the one leads to the other, as one sin of one kind doth often to another, — drunkenness to whoredom, and envy and malice to lying; and differences about civil matters, like that of Paul and Barnabas, are schism; and this, by one blaming me for a departure from the sense of antiquity, unto which these insinuations are so many monsters. Let us, then, proceed.

That Acts xiv. 4, xix. 9, 18, are pertinently used to discover and prove the nature of schism in an evangelically-ecclesiastical sense, or were ever cited by any of the ancients to that purpose, I suppose our author, on second consideration, will not affirm. I understand not the sense of this argument: "'The multitude of the city was divided, and part held with the Jews, and part with the apostles;' therefore, schism in a gospel church-state is not only a division in a church," or that it is a separation into new churches, or that it is something more than the breach of the union appointed by Christ in an instituted church. Much less doth any thing of this nature appear from Paul's separating the disciples whom he had converted to the faith from the unbelieving, hardened Jews; an account whereof is given us, Acts xix. 9. So, then, that in this chapter there is any thing produced "de novo" to prove that the precise Scripture notion of schism, in its ecclesiastical sense, extends itself any farther than differences, divisions, separations in a church, and that a particular church, I find not; and do once more desire our author, that if he be otherwise minded, to spare such another trouble to ourselves and others as that wherein we are now engaged, he would assign me some time and place to attend him for the clearing of the truth between us.

Of schism, Acts xx. 30, Heb. x. 25, Jude 19, there is no mention; nor are those places interpreted of any such thing by any expositors, new or old, that ever I yet saw; nor can any sense be imposed on them inwrapping the nature of schism with the least colour or pretence of reason.

But now, by our author schism and apostasy are made things of one kind, differing only in degrees, p. 107; so confounding schism and heresy, contrary to the constant sense of all antiquity. Acts xx. 30, the apostle speaks of men "speaking perverse things, to draw away disciples," — that is, teaching them false doctrines, contrary to the truths wherein they had been by him instructed, in his revealing unto them "the whole counsel of God," verse 27. This by the ancients is called heresy, and is contradistinguished from schism by them constantly; so Austin a hundred times. To draw men from the church by drawing them into pernicious errors, false doctrine being the cause of their falling off, is not schism, nor so called in Scripture, nor by any of the ancients that ever yet I observed. That the design of the apostle, in the Epistle to the Hebrews, is to preserve and keep them from apostasy unto Judaism, besides that it is attested by a cloud of witnesses, is too evident from the thing itself to be denied. Chap. x. 25, he warns them of a common entrance into that fearful condition which he describes, verse 26. Their neglect of the Christian assemblies was the door of their apostasy to Judaism. What is this to schism? Would we charge a man with that crime whom we saw neglecting our assemblies, and likely to fall into Judaism? Are there not more forcible considerations to deal with him upon? and doth not the apostle make use of them? Jude 19 hath been so far spoken unto already that it may not fairly be insisted on again. "Parvas habet spes Troja, si tales habet."

In the entrance of the fifth chapter he takes advantage from my question, p. 147 [p. 263], "Who told him that raising causeless differences in a church, and then separating from it, is not in my judgment schism?" where the first part of the assertion included in that interrogation expresseth the *formal nature* of schism, which is not destroyed, nor can any man be exonerated of its guilt, by the subsequent crime of separation, whereby it is aggravated. 1 John ii. 19 is again mentioned to this purpose of schism, to as little purpose; so also is Heb. x. 25. Both places treat of apostates, who are charged and blamed under other terms than that of schism. There is in such departures, as in every division whatever of that which was in union, somewhat of the general nature of schism; but that particular crime and guilt of schism, in its restrained, ecclesiastical sense, is not included in them.

In his following discourse he renews his former charges, of denying their ordinances and ministry, of separating from them, and the like. As to the former part of this charge I have spoken in the entrance of this discourse; for the latter, of separating from them, I say we have no more separated from them than they have from us. Our right to the celebration of the ordinances of God's worship, according to the light we have received from him, is, in this nation, as good as theirs; and our plea from the gospel we are ready to maintain against them, according as we shall at any time be called thereunto. If any of our judgment deny them to be churches, I doubt not but he knows who comes not behind in returnal of charges on our churches. Doth the reverend author think or imagine that we have not, in our own judgment, more reason to deny their churches and to charge them with schism, though we do neither, than they have to charge us therewith and to deny our churches? Can any thing be more fondly pretended than that he hath proved that we have separated from them? upon which, p. 105, he requires the performance of my promise to retreat from the state wherein I stand upon the establishment of such proof. Hath he proved the due administration of ordinances amongst them whom he pleads for? Hath he proved any church-union between them as such and us? Hath he proved us to have broken that union? What will not self-fulness and prejudice put men upon!

How came they into the sole possession of all church-state in England, so that whoever is not of them and with them must be charged to have separated from them? Mr Cawdrey says, indeed, that the episcopal men and they agree in substantials, and differ only in circumstantials, but that they and we differ in substantials. But let him know they admit not of his compliances; they say he is a schismatic, and that all his party are so also. Let him answer their charge solidly upon his own principles, and not think to own that which he hath the weakest claim imaginable unto, and was never yet in possession of. We deny that, since the gospel came into England, the *presbyterian* government, as by them stated was ever set up in England, but in the wills of a party of men; so that here, as yet, unless as it lies in particular congregations, where our right is as good as theirs, none have separated from it that I know of, though many cannot consent unto it. The first ages we plead ours, the following were unquestionably *episcopal*.

In the beginning of chapter the sixth he attempts to disprove my assertion, that the union of the church catholic visible, which consists in the "professing of the saving doctrine of the gospel," etc., is broken only by apostasy. To this end he confounds apostasy and schism, affirming them only to differ in degrees; which is a new notion, unknown to antiquity, and contrary to all sound reason. By the instances he produceth to this purpose he endeavours to prove that there are things which break this union, whereby this union is not broken. Whilst a man continues a member of that church, which he is by virtue of the union thereof and his interest therein, by no act doth he, or can he, break that union.

The partial breach of that union, which consists in the profession of the truth, is *error* and heresy, and not *schism*. Our author abounds here in new notions, which might easily be discovered to be as fond as new, were it worth while to consider them; of which in brief before. Only, I wonder why, giving way to such thoughts as these, he should speak of men with contempt under the name of *notionists*, as he doth of Dr Du Moulin; but the truth is, the doctor hath provoked him. And were it not for some considerations that are obvious to me, I should almost wonder why this author should sharpen his leisure and zeal against me, who scarce ever publicly touched the grounds and foundations of that cause which he hath so passionately espoused, and pass by him who, both in Latin and English, hath laid his axe to the very root of it, upon principles sufficiently destructive to it, and so apprehended by the best learned in our author's way that ever these nations brought forth. But, as I said, reasons lie at hand why it was more necessary to give me this opposition; which yet hath not altered my resolution of handling this controversy in another manner, when I meet with another manner of adversary.

Page 110, he fixes on the examination of a particular passage about the disciples of John, mentioned Acts xix. 2, 3, of whom I affirmed that it is probable they were rather ignorant of the miraculous dispensations of the Holy Ghost than of the person of the Holy Ghost; alleging to the contrary, that the words are "more plain and full than to be so eluded, and, for aught appears, John did not baptize into the name of the Holy Ghost." I hope the author doth not so much dwell at home as to suppose this to be a *new notion* of mine. Who almost of late, in their critical notes, have not either (at least) considered it or confirmed it? Neither is the question into whose name they were expressly baptized, but in what doctrine they were instructed. He knows who denies that they were at all actually baptized, before they were baptized by Paul. Nor ought it to be granted, without better proof than any which as yet hath been produced, that any of the saints under the Old Testament were ignorant of *the being of the Holy Ghost*; neither do the words require the sense by him insisted on. Ἀλλ' οὐδὲ εἰ Πνεῦμα ἅγιόν ἐστιν, ἠκούσαμεν, do no more evince the person of the Holy Ghost to be included in them than in those other, John vii. 39, Οὔπω ἦν Πνεῦμα ἅγιον. The latter, in the proper sense, he will not contend for; nor can, therefore, the expression being uniform, reasonably for the former. Speaking of men openly and notoriously wicked, and denying them to be members of any church whatever, he bids me answer his arguments to the contrary from 1 Cor. v. 7, 2 Thess. iii. 14; and I cannot but desire him that he would impose that task on them that have nothing else to do: for my own part, I shall not entangle myself with things to so little purpose. Having promised my reader to attend only to that which looks toward the merit of the case, I must crave his pardon that I have not been able to make good my resolution. Meeting with so little, or nothing at all, which is to that purpose, I find myself entangled in the old diversions that we are now plentifully accustomed unto; but yet I shall endeavour to recompense this loss by putting a speedy period to this whole trouble, despairing of being able to tender him any other satisfaction whilst I dwell on this discourse. In the meantime, to obviate all strife of words, if it be possible, for the future, I shall grant this reverend author that, in the general large notion of schism, which his opposition to that insisted on by me hath put him upon, I will not deny but that *he* and *I* are both *schismatics*, and any thing else shall be so that he would have to be so, rather than to be engaged in this contest any farther. In this sense he affirms that there was a schism between Paul and Barnabas, and so one of them at least was a schismatic; as also, he affirms the same of two lesser men, though great in their generation, Chrysostom and Epiphanius. So error and heresy, if he please, shall be schism from the catholic church; and scandal of life shall be schism. And his argument shall be true, that schism is a breach of union in a church of Christ's institution; therefore, in that which is so only by call, not to any end of joint worship as such; — of any union, that which consists in the profession of the saving truths of the gospel; and so there may be a schism in the catholic church. And so those Presbyterians that reform their congregations, and do not administer the sacraments to all promiscuously, shall be guilty of schism; and, indeed, as to me, what else he pleaseth, for my inquiry concerns only *the precise limited nature of schism*, in its evangelically-ecclesiastical sense.

Neither shall I at present (allotting very few hours to the despatch of this business, which yet I judge more than it deserves) consider the scattered ensuing passages about ordination, church-government, number of elders, and the like; which all men know not at all to belong unto the main controversy which was by me undertaken, and that they were, against all laws of disputation, plucked violently into this contest by our reverend author. One thing I cannot pass by, and it will, upon the matter, put a close to what I shall at present offer to this treatise. Having said that "Christ hath given no direction for the performance of any duty of worship of sovereign institution, but only in them and by them" (meaning particular churches), he answers, that "if he would imply that a minister in or of a particular church may perform those ordinances without those congregations, he contradicts himself, by saying a particular church is the seat of all ordinances." But why so, I pray? May not a particular church be the seat of all ordinances subjectively, and yet others be the object of them, or of some of them? "But," saith he, "if he mean those ordinances of worship are to be performed only by a minister of a particular congregation, what shall become of the people?" I suppose they shall be instructed and built up according to the mind of Christ; and what would people desire more? But whereas he had before said that I "denied a minister to be a minister to more than his own church," and I had asked him "who told him so," adding that explication of my judgment, that for "so much as men are appointed the objects of the dispensation of the word, I grant a minister, in the dispensation of it, to act ministerially towards not only the members of the catholic church, but the visible members of the world also in contradistinction thereunto;" he now tells me a story of passages between the learned Dr Wallis and myself, about his question in the Vespers, 1654, — namely, that as to that question, "An potestas ministri evangelici ad unius tantum ecclesiæ particuiaris membra extendatur?" I said that Dr Wallis had brought me a challenge, and that, if I did dispute on that question, I must dispute "ex animo." Although I grant that a minister, as a minister, may preach the word to more than those of his own congregation, yet knowing the sense wherein the learned Dr Wallis maintained that question, it is not impossible but I might say, if I did dispute I must do it "ex animo." For his bringing me a challenge, I do not know that either he did so or that I put that interpretation on what he did; but I shall crave leave to say, that if the learned Dr Wallis do find any ground or occasion to bring a challenge unto me, to debate any point of difference between us, I shall not waive answering his desire, although he should bring Mr Cawdrey for his second. For the present I shall only say, that as it is no commendation to the moderation or ingenuity of any one whatever thus to publish to the world private hear-says, and what he hath been told of private conferences; so if I would insist on the same course, to make publication of what I have been told hath been the private discourse of some men, it is not unlikely that I should occasion their shame and trouble. Yet in this course of proceeding a progress is made out in the ensuing words, and Mr Stubbes (who is now called my "amanuensis;" who some five years ago transcribed about a sheet of paper for me, and not one line before or since) is said to be employed, or at least encouraged, by me to write against the learned Dr Wallis, his Thesis being published. This is as true as much of that that went before, and as somewhat of that that follows after; and whereas it is added, that I said what he had written on that subject was "a scurrilous, ridiculous piece," it is of the same nature with the rest of the like reports. I knew that Mr Stubbes was writing on that subject, but not until he had proceeded far in it. I neither employed him nor encouraged him in it, any otherwise than the consideration of his papers, after he had written them, may be so interpreted; and the reason why I was not willing he should proceed, next to my desire of continuance of peace in this place, was, his using such expressions of me, and some things of mine, in sundry places of his discourse, as I could not modestly allow to be divulged. The following words to the same purpose with them before mentioned, I remember not, nor did ever think to be engaged in the consideration of such transgressions of the common rules of human society as those now passed through. Reports, hear-says, talks, private discourse between friends, allegations countenanced by none of these, nor any thing else, are the weapons wherewith I am assaulted! "I have heard," "I am told," "if reports be true," "it was 'vox populi' at Oxford," "is it not so?" "I presume he will not deny it," are the ornaments of this discourse! Strange! that men of experience and gravity should be carried, by the power of these temptations, not only to the forgetfulness of the royal law of Christ, and all gospel rules of deportment towards his professed disciples, but also be engaged into ways and practices contrary to the dictates of the law of nature, and such as sundry heathens would have abhorred. For my own part, had not God by his providence placed me in that station wherein others also that fear him are concerned in me, I should not once turn aside to look upon such heaps as that which I have now passed over. My judgment on most heads and articles of Christian religion is long since published to the world, and I continue, through the grace and patience of God, preaching in public answerably to the principles I do profess; and if any man shall oppose what I have delivered, or shall so deliver, in print, or the pulpit, or in divinity lectures, as my judgment, I shall consider his opposition, and do therein as God shall guide. With evil surmises, charges upon hear-says and reports, attended with perpetual excursions from the argument in hand, I shall no more contend.

Some few observations on scattered passages will now speedily issue this discourse. Page 112, to that assertion of mine, that "if Rome be no particular church, it is no church at all, for the catholic church it is not," he replies, that "though it be not such a particular congregation as I intend, yet it may be a particular patriarchal church." But, — 1. Then, it seems, it is a particular church; which grants my inference. 2. It was a particular Church of Christ's institution that I inquired after. Doth our author think that Christ hath appointed any patriarchal churches? A patriarchal church, as such, is such from its relation to a patriarch; and he can scarce be thought to judge patriarchs to be of divine institution who hath cast off and abjured episcopacy.

The Donatists are mentioned again, p. 113; and I am again charged with an attempt to vindicate them from schism. My thoughts of them I have before declared to the full, and have no reason to retract any thing from what was then spoken, or to add any thing thereunto. If it may satisfy our author, I here grant they were schismatics, with what aggravations he pleaseth; and wherein their schism consisted I have also declared. But he says, I undertake to exempt some others from schism (I know whom), that suffer with them, in former and after ages, under the same imputation. I do so, indeed; and I suppose our author may guess at whom I intend, — himself, amongst others! I hope he is not so taken up in his thoughts with charging schism on others as to forget that many, the greatest part and number of the true churches of Christ, do condemn him for a schismatic, a Donatistical schismatic. I suppose he acknowledges the church of Rome to be a true church; the Lutheran I am persuaded he will not deny, nor perhaps the Grecian, to be so; the Episcopal church of England he contends for; — and yet all these, with one voice, cry out upon him for a schismatic. And as to the plea of the last, how he can satisfy his conscience as to the rejection of his lawful superiors, upon his own principles, without pretending any such crime against them as the Donatists did against Cæcilianus, I profess I do not understand. New mention is made of episcopal ordination, p. 120, and they are said to have had their successive ordination from Rome who ordained therein. So, indeed, some say, and some otherwise. Whether they had or no is nothing to me; I lay no weight upon it. They held, I am sure, that place in England, that without their approbation no man could publicly preach the gospel. To say they were presbyters, and ordained as presbyters, I know not what satisfaction can arise unto conscience thereby. Party and argument may be countenanced by it. They profess they ordained as bishops; that for their lives and souls they durst not ordain but as such. So they told those whom they ordained, and affirm they have open injury done them by any one's denial of it. As it was, the best is to be made of it. This shift is not handsome. Nor is it ingenuous, for any one that hath looked into antiquity, to charge me with departing from their sense in the notion of schism, declared about the third and fourth ages, and at the same time to maintain an equality between bishops and presbyters, or to say that bishops ordained as presbyters, not as bishops. Nor do I understand the excellency of that order which we see in some churches, where they have two sorts of elders, the one made so by ordination without election, and the other by election without ordination; those who are ordained casting off all power and authority of them that ordained them, and those who are elected immediately rejecting the greatest part of those that chose them.

Nor did I, as is pretended, plead for their presbyterian way in the year [16]46; all the ministers almost in the county of Essex know the contrary, one especially, being a man of great ability and moderation of spirit, and for his knowledge in those things not behind any man I know in England of his way, with whom in that year, and the next following, I had sundry conferences at public meetings of ministers as to the several ways of reformation then under proposal. But the frivolousness of these imputations hath been spoken of before, as also the falseness of the calumny which our author is pleased to repeat again about my turning from ways in religion.

My description of a particular church he once more blames as applicable to the catholic church invisible, and to the visible catholic church (I suppose he means as such), when a participation in the same ordinances numerically is assigned as its difference. He asks whether it becomes my ingenuity to interpret the capability of a church's reduction to its primitive constitution by its own fitness and capacity to be so reduced, rather than by its external hinderances or furtherances; but with what ingenuity or modesty that question is asked, I profess I understand not. And, p. 134, he hath this passage (only I take notice of his introduction to his answer, with thanks for the civility of the inquiry in the manner of its expression):— "My words were these: 'Whether our reverend author do not in his conscience think there was no true church in England till;' etc.; which puts me into suspicion that the reverend doctor was offended that I did not always (for oft I do) give him that title of the 'reverend author,' or the 'doctor,' which made him cry out he was never so dealt withal by any party as by me; though, upon review, I do not find that I gave him any uncivil language, unbeseeming me to give or him to receive; and I hear that somebody hath dealt more uncivilly with him in that respect, which he took very ill."

Let this reverend author make what use of it he please, I cannot but again tell him that these things become neither him nor any man professing the religion of Jesus Christ, or that hath any respect to truth or sobriety. Can any man think that in his conscience he gives any credit to the insinuation which here he makes, that I should thank him for calling me "reverend author" or "reverend doctor," or be troubled for his not using these expressions? Can the mind of an honest man be thought to be conversant with such mean and low thoughts? For the title of "reverend,' I do give him notice that I have very little valued it ever since I have considered the saying of Luther, "Nunquam periclitatur religio nisi inter reverendissimos;" so that he may, as to me, forbear it for the future, and call me as the Quakers do, and it shall suffice. And for that of "doctor," it was conferred on me by the university in my absence, and against my consent, as they have expressed it under their public seal, nor doth any thing but gratitude and respect unto them make me once own it; and freed from that obligation, I should never use it more, nor did I use it until some were offended with me, and blamed me for my neglect of them. And for that other whom he mentions, who before this gave so far place to indignation as to insinuate some such thing, I doubt not but by this time he hath been convinced of his mistake therein, being a person of another manner of ability and worth than some others with whom I have to do; and the truth is, my manner of dealing with him in my last reply, which I have since myself not so well approved of, requires the passing by such returns. But you will say, then, why do I preface this discourse with that expression, "With thanks for the civility of the inquiry in the manner of its expression?" I say, this will discover the iniquity of this author's procedure in this particular. His inquiry was, "Whether I did not in my conscience think that there were no true churches in England until the Brownists our fathers, the Anabaptists our elder brothers, and ourselves, arose and gathered new churches?" Without once taking notice or mentioning his titles that he says he gave me, I used the words in a sense obvious to every man's first consideration, as a reproof of the expressions mentioned,. That which was the true cause of my words our author hides in an "etc.;" that which was not by me once taken notice of is by him expressed to serve an end of drawing forth an evil surmise and suspicion, that hath not the least colour to give it countenance. Passing by all indifferent readers, I refer the honesty of this dealing with me to the judgment of his own conscience. Setting down what I neither expressed nor took notice of, nor had any singular occasion in that place so to do, the words being often used by him, hiding and concealing what I did take notice of and express, and which to every man's view was the occasion of that passage, that conclusion or unworthy insinuation is made, which a good man ought to have abhorred.

Sundry other particulars there are, partly false and calumniating, partly impertinent, partly consisting in mistakes, that I ought at the first view to have made mention of; but, on several accounts, I am rather willing here to put an end to the reader's trouble and my own.

A BRIEF VINDICATION OF THE NONCONFORMISTS FROM THE CHARGE OF SCHISM.

as it was managed against them in a sermon preached before the Lord Mayor by Dr Stillingfleet, Dean of St Paul's.

> "Coitio Christianorum merito sane illicita, si illicitis par; merito damnanda, si quis de ea queritur eo titulo quo de factionibus querela est. In cujus perniciem aliquando convenimus? Hoc sumus congregati quod et dispersi; hoc universi quod et singuli; neminem lædentes, neminem contristantes; quum probi, cum boni coeunt, cum pii, cum casti congregantur, non est factio dicenda, sed curia." — *Tertul.*

Prefatory Note.

In 1680, when the nation was under strong fears lest, with the help and favour of the Court, Popery should resume its old domination in Britain, the celebrated Stillingfleet, at that time Dean of St Paul's, preached a sermon on the 2d of May before the Lord Mayor of London. It was published under the title, "On the Mischief of Separation." His object was to prove the Nonconformists guilty of schism, on the ground that they admitted the Church of England to be a true church of Christ, and yet lived in a state of dissent and separation from it. His text was Phil. iii. 16.

Perhaps no sermon has ever given rise to a controversy in which a greater number of writers has appeared on both sides; and among these were names signally eminent for worth and learning. Besides the following pamphlet by Owen, Baxter published his "Answer to Dr Stillingfleet's Charge of Separation," in terms of vehement invective against the injustice with which he had treated Dissent. John Howe addressed to the offending Dean "A Letter written from the Country to a Person of Quality in the City," protesting with all his characteristic mildness and candour, but most firmly, against the insinuations of Stillingfleet. Vincent Alsop also took the field, in a work brimful of wit and humour to the very title-page, "The Mischief of *Impositions*." Mr Barret of Nottingham, in allusion to the "Irenicum," written by Stillingfleet when rector of Sutton, to reconcile conflicting sects by proving that no form of church-government could plead divine authority in its favour, published, "The Rector of Sutton Committed with the Dean of St Paul's," etc. Besides these authors, to whom Stillingfleet replies in his "Unreasonableness of Separation," Mr John Troughton of Bicester published "An Apology for the Nonconformists; showing their reasons both for their not conforming and for their preaching publicly, though forbidden by law: with an Answer to Dr Stillingfleet's Sermon and his Defense of it, 1681." An account of the work in which Stillingfleet replied to the first five of these antagonists will be found in a prefatory note to Owen's answer to it, vol. xv. p. 183, of Owen's works. But Stillingfleet had to encounter fresh attacks:— "More Work for the Dean," by Mr Thomas Wall; Mr Barret's second "Attempt to Vindicate the Principles of the Nonconformists, not only by Scripture, but by Dr Stillingfleet's Rational Account;" the "Modest and Peaceable Inquiry," by Mr Lob; Baxter's "Second True Defence of the mere Nonconformists;" Humphrey's "Answer to Dr Stillingfleet's Book, as far as it concerned the Peaceable Design;" and "The Rational Defense of Nonconformity," in 1689, by Mr Gilbert Rule.

To the rescue of the Dean from this host of opponents, there advanced, with his vizor down and name withheld, Dr Sherlock, in his "Discourse about Church Unity, being a Defence of Dr Stillingfleet's 'Unreasonableness of Separation,' in answer to several late pamphlets, but principally to Dr Owen and Mr Baxter, 1681." This work was followed up by "A Continuation and Vindication of the Defense of Dr Stillingfleet, in answer to Mr Baxter, Mr Lob, and others." Mr Long of Exeter, wandering from the points in debate into most offensive personalities against Baxter, published "The Unreasonableness of Separation, the Second Part; or, a farther impartial account of the history, nature, and pleas, of the present separation from the

Church of England, with special remarks on the life and actions of Richard Baxter, 1682." Richard Hook, D.D., vicar of Halifax, was the author of the "Nonconformist Champion, his Challenge Accepted; or, an answer to Mr Baxter's Petition for Peace, with remarks on his Holy Commonwealth, his Sermon to the House of Commons, his Nonconformist's Plea, and his Answer to Dr Stillingfleet, 1682." The famous Sir Roger L'Estrange could not refrain from taking part in this curious mêlée with all his coarse but clever wit, of which the title of his work is a specimen, "The Casuist Uncased, in a Dialogue betwixt Richard and Baxter, with a moderator between them for quietness' sake."

The sermon which embroiled so many able men in disputes that lasted for ten years may well excite curiosity; and yet it would be difficult to say why it should have roused such a storm of controversy, resounding over the breadth of a kingdom. It is calm and measured in its tone, and contains no reckless invective, no impeachment of motives, no envenomed intensity of language. Its strength lay in its calmness, and in the extreme plausibility with which the case of the Church of England is stated against Dissenters. That the latter should admit it to be a church of Christ, and yet hold themselves justified in their nonconformity; and that the common grounds of objection to the Established Church should refer to the terms on which men were admitted to *office* in it, and did not, as the Dean alleged, affect their admission to *membership*, were points which such a controversialist could handle most effectively for his own cause. That Nonconformists, who had suffered so much in resisting popish encroachment, should be exhibited as practically the friends of Popery in opposing the Church of England, reputed to be the chief defence against it; while they, on the other hand, had been warning the nation for years against the vantage-ground which Popery had in the constitution and rites of the English Church; and that all this should have been done, not in the vulgar abuse which refutes itself, but in downright and deliberate logic, was sufficiently galling, and fitted to bring upon them no small odium from the temper of the nation, roused at the time by the fear of popish aggression and ascendency. It was, in truth, an attempt not merely to spike the best guns of Dissent, but to turn them against itself.

This "Vindication" by Owen in reply is all that could be wished, in strength of reasoning, civility of language, and crushing effect. There is a passage of eloquent pathos at the close, in allusion to the long sufferings of the Nonconformists. — ED.

A Brief Vindication of the Nonconformists from the Charge of Schism.

It was no small surprise unto many, first to hear of, and then to see in print, the late sermon of the Rev. Dean of St Paul's, preached at Guildhall, May 2, 1680, being the first Sunday in Easter term, before the Lord Mayor, etc.

Whatever there might be of truth in it, yet they judged the time both of the one and the other, the preaching and printing of it, to be somewhat unseasonable; for they say that this is a time wherein the agreement of all Protestants, so far as they have attained, is made more than ordinarily necessary. And whereas the Nonconformists do agree in religion with all the sober protestant people of the nation, which is the church of England, they do suppose that ordinary prudence would advise unto a forbearance of them in those few things wherein they dissent, not indeed from the body of the protestant people, but from some that would impose them on their consciences and practices. Who knows not that the present danger of this nation is from Popery, and the endeavours that are used both to introduce it and enthrone it, or give it power and authority among us? And it is no part of the popish design to take away and destroy those things wherein the Nonconformists do dissent from the present ecclesiastical establishment, but rather to confirm them. Their contrivance is, to ruin and destroy the religion of the body of the Protestants in this kingdom, wherein the Nonconformists are one with them, and equally concerned with any of them. Wherefore it cannot but be grievous unto them, as well as useless unto the common interest of the protestant religion, that at such a time and season they should be reflected on, charged, and severely treated, on the account of those lesser differences which in no way disenable them from being useful and serviceable unto the government and nation, in the defence and preservation of the protestant religion. And that it is their resolution so to be, they have given sufficient evidence, equal at least with that given by any sort of people in the nation. Yea, of their diligence in opposition unto Popery, and their readiness to observe the direction of the magistrates therein, whilst the plot hath been in agitation, they suppose the honourable person unto whom this sermon is dedicated can and will bear them witness.

In these circumstances, to be required severely to change their judgments and practices, as it were "momento turbinis," immediately and in an instant, or else to be looked on and treated as adversaries, many do think as unseasonable as to command a good part of an army, when it is actually engaged against an enemy, to change all their order, postures, discipline, and advantages, or immediately to depart out of the field. And they do withal suppose that such a sudden change is least of all to be expected to be wrought by such severe charges and reflections as are made on all Nonconformists in this discourse. Such like things as these do men talk concerning the season of the preaching and publishing of this sermon; but in such things every man is to be left unto his own prudence, whereof he may not esteem himself obliged to give an account.

For my part, I judge it not so unseasonable as some others do; for it is meet that honest men should understand the state of those things wherein they are greatly and deeply concerned. Nonconformists might possibly suppose that the common danger of all Protestants had reconciled the minds of the conforming ministry unto them, so as that they were more than formerly inclined unto their forbearance; and I was really of the same judgment myself. If it be not so, it is well they are fairly warned what they have to expect, that they may prepare themselves to undergo it with patience. But we shall pass by these things, and attend a little unto the consideration of the sermon itself.

The design of this discourse seems to consider in these three things, or to aim at them:—

1. To prove all the Nonconformists to be guilty of schism and a sinful separation from the church of England.

2. To aggravate their supposed guilt and crime, both in its nature and all the pernicious consequences of it that can be imagined.

3. To charge them, especially their ministers, with want of sincerity and honesty in the management of their dissent from

the church of England, with reference unto the people that hear them.

What there is of truth in these things, or what there may be of mistake in them, it is the duty of Nonconformists to try and examine. But some few things must have a previous consideration before we come to the merits of the cause itself:—

1. The reverend author of this discourse affirms, that in the preaching of this sermon he was "far from intending to stir up the magistrates and judges unto a persecution of dissenters, as some ill men have reported," Epist. Ded. Without this information, I confess I could not but judge it would have been as liable unto a supposition of such a design as the actings of the Nonconformists, in the management of their cause, are unto that of insincerity in the judgment of this reverend author; for, —

(1.) It was not preached unto Nonconformists, perhaps not one of them being present; so that the intention of preaching it could not be their conviction. They were not likely either to hear the charge or the reasons of it.

(2.) It was preached unto them who were no way guilty of the pretended crime reproved, but peculiarly to such as were intrusted with the execution of the penal laws against them that were supposed guilty, magistrates and judges; which in another would have but an ill aspect. If a man should go unto a justice of the peace, and complain that his neighbour is a thief, or a swearer, or a murderer, though he should give the justice never so many arguments to prove that his neighbour did very ill in being so and doing so, yet his business would seem to be the execution of the law upon him. But let the will of God be done; Nonconformists are not much concerned in these things.

We are likewise informed, in the same epistle, that there are "no sharp and provoking expressions" on the persons of any. It is, indeed, beneath the gravity and dignity of this reverend author to bring reviling or railing accusations against any; neither will he, I am sure, give countenance to such a practice in others, which is seldom used but by men of very mean consideration: but I am not satisfied that he hath not used even great severity in reflections on a whole party of men, and that unprovoked; nor do I know how persons, on a religious account, can be more severely reflected on, — and that not only as unto their opinions and practices, but also as unto the sincerity of their hearts and honesty of their designs, — than the Nonconformists are in this sermon.

I have seen a collection made of such reflections, by the hand of a person of honour, a member of the church of England, with his judgment upon them; wherein they appear to me not to be a true resemblance or representation of Christian love and charity.

2. A great part of this discourse being such as became a popular auditory, consisting in generals on all hands acknowledged, as, the good of union, the evil of schism and causeless separation, etc., — which will indifferently serve any party, until it be determined where the original fault and mistake doth lie, — I shall not at all take notice of it, though it be so dressed as to be laid at the door of Nonconformists, in a readiness for an application unto their disadvantage but nothing that, by way of argument, testimony, or instance, is produced to prove the charge mentioned, and the consequents of it, shall be omitted.

3. Some few things may be taken notice of in the passage of the author unto his text. Of that nature is his complaint, p. 2: "There is just cause for many sad reflections, when neither the miseries we have felt nor the calamities we fear, neither the terrible judgments of God upon us, nor the unexpected deliverance vouchsafed unto us, nor the common danger we are yet in, have abated men's hearts, or allayed their passions, or made them more willing to unite with our established church and religion; but, instead of that, some stand at a greater distance, if not [in] defiance." It is acknowledged willingly by us that the warnings and calls of God unto this nation have been great and marvellous, and yet continue so to be; but it is worthy our inquiry, whether this be to be looked on as the only end and design of them, that the Nonconformists do immediately in all things comply with the established church and religion, and are evidences of God's displeasure because they do not so, when He who searcheth their hearts doth know that they would do it were it not for fear of His displeasure? What if it should be the design of God in them to call the nation, and so the church of England, unto repentance and reformation? which, when all is done, is the only way of reconciling all protestant dissenters. What if God should in them testify against all the atheism, profaneness, sensuality, that abound in this nation, unto the public scandal of it, with the dread and terror of those by whom they

are duly considered, the persons guilty of them being no way proceeded against by any discipline of the church, nor any reformation of the church itself from such horrible pollutions once attempted? Every man who knows any thing of Christ, of his law, gospel, rule, and discipline, — of the nature, end, and use of them, with the worship of God to be performed in them and by them; and doth withal consider the terror of the Lord, unto whom an account is to be given of these things; must acknowledge that, both in persons and things, there is a necessity of reformation among us, on the utmost peril of the displeasure of Christ Jesus: yet no such reformation is so much as endeavoured in a due manner. It is no encouragement unto conscientious men to unite themselves absolutely and in all things unto such a church as doth not, as will not, or as cannot, reform itself, in such a degenerate state as that which many churches in the world are at this day openly and visibly fallen into. And, to deal plainly with our brethren (if they will allow us to call them so), — that they may know what to expect, and, if it be the will of God, be directed unto the only true way of uniting all Protestants in the only bands of evangelical union, order, and communion, — unless those who are concerned will endeavour, and until they are enabled in some measure to effect, a reformation in the ministry and people, as unto their relation to the church, as also in some things in the worship of God itself, it is vain to expect that the Nonconformists should unite with the church, however established. And may we not think that those many warnings and calls of God may have some respect unto those abominations that are found in the nation, yea, such as, without a due reformation of them, will issue in our desolation? I do know that with the Nonconformists also there are "sins against the LORD their God;" and it will be a great addition unto their sins, as also an aggravation of their guilt, if they comply not with the "warnings of God," as they are here expressed by this reverend author, so as to reform whatever is amiss in them, and return wholly unto God from all their wanderings. But as unto those things which are usually charged on them, they are such as interest, hatred, and the desire of their ruin, suggest unto the minds of their adversaries, or are used by some against their science and conscience to further that end, without the least pretence to be raised from any thing in them, — their opinions, practices, or conversation in the world. Doth atheism abound among us? — it is from the differences in religion made by Nonconformists! Is there danger of Popery? — it is because of the Nonconformists! Are the judgments of God coming on the nation? — it is for Nonconformity! So was it of old with the Christians: "Si Tybris ascendit in mænia, si Nilus non ascendit in arva, si cœlum stetit, si terra movit, si fames, si lues, statim, 'Christianos ad leonem!'"

4. The immediate introduction unto the opening of his text is an account of the differences and divisions that were in the primitive churches, occasioned by the Judaizing Christians, who contended for the observation of the ceremonies of the law. But some things may be added unto his account, which are necessary unto the right stating of that case, as it may have any respect unto our present differences. And we may observe, —

(1.) That those with and concerning whom the apostle dealeth in his epistle were principally those of the Jewish church and nation who had owned the gospel, professed faith in Christ Jesus, had received (many of them) spiritual gifts, or "tasted of the powers of the world to come," and did join in the worship of God in the assemblies of the Christians. I only mention this, because some places quoted usually in this matter do relate directly unto the unbelieving Jews, which went up and down to oppose the preaching of Christ and the gospel, in rage and fury, stirring up persecution everywhere against them that were employed in it.

(2.) This sort of persons were freely allowed by the apostle to continue in the use of those rites and ceremonies which they esteemed themselves obliged unto by virtue of Moses' law, granting them in all other things the privilege of believers, and such as whom they would not in any thing offend. So do James and the elders of the church declare themselves, Acts xxi. 20, etc. Yea, —

(3.) Out of tenderness unto them, and to prevent all offence to be taken by them at the liberty of the Gentiles, they did order that the believers of the Gentiles should forbear for a season the use of their natural liberty in some few things, whereby the other were, in their common meetings, as in eating and drinking together, usually scandalized; giving them, also, unto the same end, direction concerning one thing evil in itself, whose long usage and practice among the Gentiles had obliterated a sense of its guilt, wherewith they could not but be much offended.

(4.) With this determination or state of things, thus settled by the apostles, no doubt but that a multitude of the Jewish believers did rest content and satisfied; but certain it is that with many of them it was otherwise: they were no way pleased that they were left unto the freedom of their own judgment and practice in the use and observance of the legal ceremonies, but they would impose the observation of them on all the churches of the Gentiles wherever they came. Nothing would serve their turn but that all other churches must observe their ceremonies, or they would not admit them unto communion with them. And, in the pursuit of this design, they prevailed for a season on whole churches to forego the liberty wherewith Christ hath made them free, and to take on them the yoke of bondage which they imposed on them; as it was with the churches of the Galatians.

I have mentioned these things only to show how remote we are from any access unto those opinions and practices which caused the first divisions in Christian churches, and among all sorts of believers. We agree with our brethren in the faith of the gospel, as the Gentiles did with the believing Jews; we have nothing to impose in religion on the consciences or practices of any other churches or persons; we are not offended that others, be they many or few, should use their own choice, liberty, and judgment, in the government, discipline, worship, and ceremonies, of pretended order, nor do envy them the advantages which they have thereby; We desire nothing but what the churches of the Gentiles desired of old, as the only means to prevent division in them, — namely, that they might not be imposed on to observe those things which they were not satisfied that it was the mind of Christ they should observe, for he had taken all the churches under his own power, requiring that they should be taught to do and observe all that he commanded them, and nothing else, that we know of. We desire no more of our governors, rulers, brethren (if they think so) in the ministry, but that we be not, with outward force and destructive penalties, compelled to comply with and practice in the worship of God such things as, for our lives, and to save ourselves from the greatest ruin, we cannot conceive that it is the mind of Christ that we should do and observe; — that, whilst we are peaceable and useful in our places, firmly united unto the body of the Protestants in this nation (which, as this author tells us, is the church of England), in confession of the same faith and common interest, for the maintenance and preservation of that one religion which we profess, we be not deprived of that liberty which God and nature, Christ and the gospel, the example of the primitive churches, and the present protestant interest of this nation, do testify to be our due.

These things being premised, because I have no design to except against any thing in the discourse of the reverend author of this sermon wherein the merit of the cause is not immediately concerned, nor to seek for advantages from expressions, nor to draw a saw of contention about things not necessary unto that defence of our innocency which alone I have undertaken (as is the way of the most in the management of controversies), I shall pass on unto the charge itself, or the consideration of the arguments and reasons whereon all Nonconformists are charged with schism, etc.

But yet because there are some things insisted on by the author, in the progress of his discourse, according as he judged the method to be most convenient for the managing of his charge, which I judge not so convenient unto the present defence, I shall speak briefly unto them, or some of them, before I proceed unto what is more expressly argumentative; as, —

1. He chargeth the Nonconformist ministers for concealing their opinions and judgments from the people about the lawfulness of their communion with the church, and that for ends easily to be discerned (that is, their own advantage); that is, they do indeed judge that it is lawful for the people to hold communion with the church of England, but will not let them know so much, lest they should forsake their ministry:—

Pages 19, 20, "I do not intend to speak of the terms upon which persons are to be admitted among us to the exercise of the function of the ministry, but of the terms of lay-communion; that is, those which are necessary for all persons to join in our prayers and sacraments, and other offices of divine worship. I will not say there hath been a great deal of art to confound these two (and it is easy to discern to what purpose it is), but I dare say the people's not understanding the difference of these two cases hath been a great occasion of the present separation; for, in the judgment of some of the most impartial men of the dissenters at this day, although they think the case of the ministers very hard, on account of subscriptions and declarations required of them, yet they confess very little is to be said on the behalf of the people, from whom none of those things are required. So that the people are condemned in their separation by their own teachers; but how they can preach lawfully to a people who commit a fault in hearing them I do not understand."

And the same thing is yet managed with more severity, pp. 37, 38, in words that I shall at large transcribe:—

"I dare say if most of the preachers at this day, in the separate meetings, were soberly asked their judgment, whether it were lawful for the people to join with us in the public assemblies, they would not deny it: and yet the people that frequent them generally judge otherwise; for it is not to be supposed that faction among them should so commonly prevail beyond interest, and, therefore, if they thought it were lawful for them to comply with the laws, they would do it. But why, then, is this kept up as such a mighty secret in the breasts of their teachers? why do they not preach to them in their congregations? Is it for fear they should have none left to preach to? — that is not to be imagined of mortified and conscientious men. Is it lest they should seem to condemn themselves, whilst they preach against separation in a separate congregation?

"This, I confess, looks oddly, and the tenderness of a man's mind in such a case may, out of mere shamefacedness, keep him from declaring a truth which flies in his face while he speaks it.

"Is it that they fear the reproaches of the people, which some few of the most eminent persons among them have found they must undergo if they touch upon this subject? (for, I know not how it comes to pass, that the most godly people among them can the least endure to be told of their faults;) but is it not as plainly written by St Paul, 'If I yet pleased men, I should not be the servant of Christ,'[20] as, 'Woe be unto me if I preach not the gospel?' If they, therefore, would acquit themselves like honest and conscientious men, let them tell the people plainly that they look on our churches as true churches, and that they may lawfully communicate with us in prayers and sacraments; and I do not question but in time, if they find it lawful, they will judge it to be their duty: for it is the apostle's command here, 'Whereto we have already attained, let us walk by the same rule, let us mind the same thing.'"

---

20 Gal. i. 10.

A crime this is which, if true, is not easily to be expiated; nor can men give greater evidence of their own hypocrisy, insincerity, and government by corrupt ends and designs, than by such abominable arts and contrivances. So, if it should prove not to be true, it cannot but be looked on as animated by such an evil surmise as is of no small provocation in the sight of God and men.

This reverend author makes a distinction about communion with the church, p. 20, between what is required of ministers and that which is called "lay-communion," which is the foundation of this charge:—

"I do not confound bare suspending communion in some particular rites, which persons do modestly scruple, and using it in what they judge to be lawful, with either total or at least ordinary forbearance of communion in what they judge to be lawful, and proceeding to the forming of separate congregations, — that is, under other teachers and by other rules than what the established religion allows. And this is the present case of separation which I intend to consider, and to make the sinfulness and mischief of it appear."

But he knows that by the communion and uniting ourselves unto the church, which is pressed either on ministers or people, a total submission unto the rule, as established in the Book of Canons and Rubric of the Liturgy, is required of them all. When this is once engaged in, there is no suspending of communion in particular rites to be allowed; they who give up themselves hereunto must observe the whole rule to a tittle. Nor is it in the power of this reverend author, who is of great dignity in the church, and as like as any man I know to be inclined thereunto, to give indulgence unto them in their abstinence from the least ceremony enjoined. Wherefore, the question about lay-communion is concerning that which is absolute and total, according unto all that is enjoined by the laws of the land, or by the canons, constitutions, and orders of the church. Hereby are they obliged to bring their children to be baptized with the use of the aerial sign of the cross; to kneel at the communion; to the religious observation of holidays; to the constant use of the liturgy in all the public offices of the church, unto the exclusion of the exercise of those gifts which Christ continues to communicate for its edification; to forego all means of public edification besides that in their parish churches, where, to speak with modesty, it is ofttimes scanty and wanting; to renounce all other assemblies wherein they have had great experience of spiritual advantage unto their souls; to desert the observation of many useful gospel duties, in their mutual watch that believers of the same church ought to have one over another; to divest themselves of all interest of a voluntary consent in the discipline of the church and choice of their own pastors; and to submit unto an ecclesiastical rule and discipline which not one in a thousand of them can apprehend to have any thing in it of the authority of Christ or rule of the gospel: and other things of the like nature may be added.

This being the true state of lay-communion, which will admit of no indulgence if the rule be observed, I must say that I do not believe that there are six nonconformist ministers in England that do believe this communion to be lawful for the people to embrace; and, on the other hand, they cease not to instruct them wherein their true communion with the church of England doth consist, — namely, in faith and love, and all the fruits of them, unto the glory of God.

I heartily wish these things had been omitted, that they had not been spoken; — not to cover any guilt in the Nonconformists, whose consciences are unto them a thousand witnesses against such imputations; but whereas the ground of them is only surmises and suspicions, and the evil charged of the highest nature that any men can involve themselves in the guilt of, it argues such a frame of spirit, such a habit of mind, as evidenceth men to be very remote from that Christian love and charity which, on all hands, we sometimes pretend unto. Of the same nature is another charge of the like want of sincerity, p. 46: "Those," saith he, "who speak now most against the magistrate's power in matters of religion had ten substantial reasons for it when they thought the magistrates on their own side;" for which is quoted an "Answer unto Two Questions," 1659;[21] — that is, they change their opinions according to their interest. I know not directly whom he intends. Those who are commonly called Independents expressed their apprehension of the magistrate's power in and about religion in their Confes-

---

21 Stillingfleet alludes to one of Owen's tracts under this title. See this vol., p. 507. — Ed.

sion, made 1659.[22] That any of them have, on what hath ensued, changed their opinion therein I know not. And, for my part, I have on this occasion perused the answer unto the two questions directed unto, and do profess myself at this day to be of the same judgment with the author of them, as it is expressed in that paper. There are things, not easily to be numbered, wherein we acknowledge the magistrate's power and duty in matters of religion, as much as ever was in the godly kings of Judah of old, or was at first claimed by the first Christian emperors. Yet there are some who, although they are fed and warmed, promoted and dignified, by the effects of the magistrate's power in and about religion, will not allow that any thing is ascribed unto him, unless we grant that it is in his rightful power, and his duty, to coerce and punish with all sorts of mulcts, spoiling of goods, imprisonments, banishments, and in some cases death itself, such persons as hold the Head and all the fundamental principles of Christian religion entire, whose worship is free from idolatry, whose conversations are peaceable and useful, unless in all things they comply with themselves, when possibly some of them may be as useful in and unto the church of God as those that would have them so dealt withal. And it may be, common prudence would advise a forbearance of too much severity in charges on others for changing their opinions, lest a provocation unto a recrimination on them that make them should arise of changing their opinions also, not without an appearing aspect to their own interests; but we have some among the Nonconformists who are so accustomed, not only unto such undue charges as that here insisted on, but unto such unjust accusations, false reports, malicious untruths, concerning them, their words, doctrines, and practices, — which, being invented by a few ill men, are trumpeted abroad with triumph by many,

---

22 The first edition of the Savoy Confession, — so called from an old building in the Strand founded by an Earl of Savoy, — was printed in 1659. In doctrine it agrees with the Westminster Confession. A chapter on "the institution of churches" was substituted in the Savoy Declaration for those chapters on the power of synods, church censures, marriage, divorce, and the magistrate's power in regard to religion, which are to be found in the Westminster Confession. The chapter substituted details the principles of Congregationalism. — Ed.

— as that they are come to a resolution never to concern themselves in them any more.

2. As unto the state of the question, we are told that "he speaks not of the separation or distinct communion of whole churches from each other; which, according to the Scripture, antiquity, and reason, have a just right and power to govern and reform themselves. By whole churches, I mean the churches of such nations, which, upon the decay of the Roman empire, resumed their just right of government to themselves, and, upon their owning Christianity, incorporated into one Christian society, under the same common ties and rules of order and government," p. 16.

I do suppose that particular churches or congregations are hereby exempted from all guilt of schism in not complying with rules of communion imposed on them by other churches. I am sure, according unto the principles of Nonconformists, they are so; for they judge that particular or congregational churches, stated with their officers according to the order of the gospel, are entire churches, that have a just right and power to govern and reform themselves. Until this be disproved, — until it be proved either that they are not churches because they are congregational, or that, although they are churches, yet they have not power to govern and reform themselves, — they are free from the guilt of schism in their so doing.

But the reverend author seems, in the ensuing discourse, to appropriate this right and power unto national churches, whose rise he assigns unto the dissolution of the Roman empire, and the alteration of the church government unto that of distinct kingdoms and provinces. But this is a thing that fell out so long after the institution of churches and propagation of Christian religion, that we are not at all concerned in it; especially considering that the occasion and means of the constitution of such churches was wholly foreign unto religion and the concerns of it.

The right and power of governing and reforming themselves here spoken of is that which is given by Christ himself unto his churches; nor do I know where else they should have it. Wherefore, those national provincial churches, which arose upon the dissolution of the Roman empire, must first be proved to be of his institution before they can be allowed to have their power given them by Jesus Christ. In what kings, potentates, and other supreme magistrates, might do to accommodate the outward profession of religion unto their rule and the interest thereof, we are not at all concerned, nor will give interruption unto any of them, whilst they impose not the religious observation of their constitutions unto that end upon our consciences and practice. Our sole inquiry is, what our Lord Jesus Christ hath ordained; and which, if we are compliant withal, we shall fear neither this nor any other charge of the like nature.

But to give strength hereunto it is added: "Just as several families united make one kingdom, which at first had a distinct and independent power; but it would make strange confusion in the world to reduce kingdoms back again to families, because at first they were made up of them," p. 17; which is again, insisted on, p. 31. But the case is not the same; for if, indeed, God had appointed no other civil government in the world but that of families, I should not much oppose them who would endeavour peaceably to reduce all government thereunto. But whereas we are certain that God, by the light of the law of nature, by the ends and uses of the creation of man, and by express revelation in his word, hath, by his own authority, appointed and approved other sorts of civil government in kingdoms and common-weals, we esteem it not only a madness to endeavour a reduction of all government into families, as unto the possibility of the thing, but a direct opposition unto the authority, command, and institution of God. So, if these national churches were of the immediate institution of Christ himself, we should no more plead the exemption of particular churches from any power given them by Christ as such, than we do to exempt private families from the lawful government of public magistrates. And we must also add, that whatever be their original and constitution, if all their governors were as the apostles, yet have they no power but what is for edification, and not for destruction. If they do or shall appoint and impose on men what tends unto the destruction of their souls, and not unto their edification, as it is fallen out in the church of Rome, not only particular churches, but every individual believer is warranted to withdraw from their communion: and hereon we ground the lawfulness of our separation from the church of Rome, without any need of a retreat unto the late device of the power of provincial churches to reform themselves. Let none mistake themselves herein; believers are not made for churches, but churches are appointed for believers. Their edification, their guidance and direction in the profession of the faith and performance of divine worship in assemblies, according to the mind of God, is their use and end; without which they are of no signification. The end of Christ in the constitution of his churches was, not the moulding of his disciples into such ecclesiastical shapes as might be subservient unto the power, interest, advantage, and dignity, of them that may in any season come to be over them, but to constitute a way and order of giving such officers unto them as might be in all things useful and subservient unto their edification; as is expressly affirmed, Eph. iv. 11–16.

As it should seem, an opinion opposite unto this notion of national churches is examined and confuted, p. 17: "And it is a great mistake, to make the notion of a church barely to relate to acts of worship, and, consequently, that the adequate notion of a church is an assembly for divine worship, — by which means they appropriate the name of churches to particular congregations, — whereas, if this hold true, the church must be dissolved as soon as the congregation is broken up; but if they retain the nature of a church when they do not meet together for worship, then there is some other bond that unites them, and whatever that is, it constitutes the church." I am far from pretending to have read the writings of all men upon this subject, nay, I can say I have read very few of them, though I never avoided the reading of any thing written against the way and order which I approve of; wherefore there may be some, as far as I know, who have maintained this notion of a church, or that it is only an assembly for divine worship; but for my part, I never read nor heard of any who was of this judgment. Assemblies for divine worship we account indispensably necessary for the edification of the churches; but that this is that which gives them their constitution and formeth that which is the bond of their union, none of the Nonconformists, as I know of, do judge; for it will not only hence follow, as the reverend author observes, "that the church is dissolved when the congregation is broken up" (on which account churches at this time would be dissolved almost every week, whether they would or no), but that any sort of persons, who have no church relation unto one another, meeting occasionally for divine worship, do constitute a church, which it may be within an hour they cease to be. It is not, therefore, on this account that we appropriate the name of churches unto particular congregations; there is quite another way and means, another bond of union, whereby particular churches are constituted, which hath been sufficiently declared. But if the meaning of the "appropriating the name of churches unto particular congregations" be, that those societies which have not, or which cannot have, assemblies for divine worship, are not churches properly so called, it is a thing of another consideration, that need not here be insisted on. But when such societies as whose bounds and limits are not of divine institution, as were those of the national church of the Jews; no, nor yet of the prudence and wisdom of men, as were the distribution of the ancient church into patriarchates and dioceses; but a mere natural and necessary consequent of that prevailing sword which, on the dissolution of the Roman empire, erected distinct kingdoms and dominions, as men were able, — such societies as are not capable of any religious assemblies for divine worship, and the ministration of Christian discipline in them, — such as are forced to invent and maintain a union by ways and means, and officers and orders, which the Scripture knows nothing of, — are proved to be churches of Christ's institution, I shall embrace them as such. In the meantime, let them pass at their own proper rate and value, which the stamp of civil authority hath put upon them. What is farther discoursed by the author on this subject, proceeding no farther but why may it not be so and so, we are not concerned in.

3. Pages 23, 24, there is a distribution of all dissenters into two parties:— (1.) Such as say, "That although they are in a state of separation from our church, yet this separation is no sin." (2.) Such as say, "That a state of separation would be sin, but, notwithstanding their meeting in different places, yet they are not in a state of separation." The difference of these two parties seems to me to be only in the different ways of expressing themselves, — the one granting the use of the word "separation" in this case, which others will not admit; for their practice, so far as I can observe, is one and the same, and therefore their principles must be so also, though they choose several ways of expressing them. Both sorts intended do plead that in sundry things they have communion with the church of England; and in some things they have not, nor can have it so. Some knowing the word "separation" to be of an indifferent signification, and to be determined as unto its sense by what it is applied unto,

do not contend but that, if any will have it so, the state wherein they are should be denominated from their dissent unto those things wherein they cannot hold communion with the church of England, and so are not offended if you call it a state of separation; howbeit this hinders not but that they continue their communion with the church of England, as was before mentioned. Others seem to take "separation" in the same sense with "schism," which is always evil, or at least they pretend it is their right to have the denomination of their state taken from what they agree in with the church of England, and not from their dissent in other things from it; and therefore they continue in a practice suitable unto that dissent. Wherefore, I judge that there is no need of this distinction, but both parties intended are equally concerned in the charge that is laid against them for their dissent in some things from the church.

These things being premised, that we may not be diverted from the substance of the cause in hand, as they would otherwise occur unto us in our progress, I shall proceed unto the consideration of the charge itself laid against the Nonconformists, and the arguings whereby it is endeavoured to be confirmed.

The charge is, "That all the Nonconformists, of one sort or another, — that is, Presbyterians and Independents — are guilty of sin, of a sinful separation from the church of England;" and therefore, as they live in a known sin, so they are the cause thereby of great evils, confusion, disturbances among ourselves, and of danger unto the whole protestant religion: whence it is meet that they should, etc.

The matter of fact being thus far mutually acknowledged, that there is such a stated difference between the church of England and the Nonconformists, the next inquiry naturally should be on these two heads:—

1. Who or what is the cause of this difference or distance? without which we cannot judge aright on whom the blame of it is to be charged; for that all men are not presently to be condemned for the withdrawing from the communion of any church, because they do so, without a due examination of the causes for which they do it, will be acknowledged by all Protestants. In plain terms, our inquiry is, Whether the cause hereof be, on the one hand, the imposition of terms of communion, without any obligation in conscience to make that imposition so much as pleaded or pretended from the nature of the things

imposed; or the refusal of compliance with those impositions, under a profession that such a compliance would be against the light of conscience and the best understanding in them who so refuse which they can attain of the mind and will of God in the Scripture?

2. Whereas the parties at difference do agree in all substantial parts of religion, and in a common interest as unto the preservation and defence of the protestant religion, living alike peaceably under the same supreme authority and civil government, Whether the evils and inconveniences mentioned are necessary and inseparable effects of such a difference; or whether they do not wholly owe themselves unto passions, corrupt affections, and carnal interests of men, which ought on all hands to be mortified and subdued? For as, it may be, few wise men, — who know the nature of conscience, how delicate and tender it is, what care is required in all men to keep it as a precious jewel, whose preservation from defilements and affronts God hath committed unto us, under the pain of his eternal displeasure; how unable honest men are to contravene the light of their own minds, in things of the smallest importance, for any outward advantages whatever; how great care, diligence, and accuracy ought to be used in all things relating unto the worship of God, about which he so frequently declares his jealousy, and displeasure against those who in any thing corrupt or debase it, with sundry other things of the like nature, — will admire that these differences are not ended among us by an absolute acquiescency of the one party in the judgments, dictates, and impositions of the other: so, upon the supposition before mentioned, — of an agreement in all the foundations of religion, in all things, from themselves and God's appointment, necessary unto salvation; of that union of affections which our joint interest in the unity of the faith doth require; and of that union of interest which both parties have in the preservation of the protestant religion, and that of obedience and subjection unto the same civil government; and on the satisfaction which the dissenting parties have in that the others do enjoy all those great advantages which the public profession of religion in this kingdom is accompanied withal, not in the least pretending to or contending for any share therein, — many wise men do and cannot but admire that the inconveniences and evils pretended should ensue on this difference as it is stated among us, and that

the dissenters should be pursued with so much vehemency as they have been, even unto their ruin. But we must proceed in the way and method here proposed unto us.

First, the foundation whereon the reverend author manageth his charge of schism, with all its consequents, against the Nonconformists, is taken from the words of his text, and declared, pp. 10–14 of his book. I shall not transcribe his words, principally because I would not oblige myself to take notice of any thing that is ἔξω τοῦ πράγματος, which, in such discourses, do commonly administer occasion of unnecessary strife. The force of the argument, unto the best of my understanding, consists in the things that follow:— 1. That all churches and the members of them, by virtue of the apostolical precept contained in the text, ought to walk according unto rule. 2. That the rule here intended is not the rule of charity and mutual forbearance in the things wherein they who agree in the foundation are differently minded or otherwise than one another. But, 3. This was a standing rule for agreement and uniformity in practice in church order and worship, which the apostles had given and delivered unto them. 4. That this rule they did not give only as *apostles*, but as governors of the church, as appears from Acts xv.. 5. Wherefore, what the apostles so did, that any church hath power to do, and ought to do, namely, to establish a rule of all practice in their communion. 6. That not to comply with this rule in all things is schism, the schism whereof Nonconformists are guilty. This, to the best of my understanding, is the entire force of the argument insisted on, and that proposed unto the best advantage for the apprehension of its force and strength, etc.

Let us, therefore, hereon a little inquire whether this will bear the weight of so great a charge as that which is built upon it and resolved into it, with all the dismal consequents pretended to ensue thereon; and we shall not pass by, in so doing, any thing that is offered to give an especial enforcement unto the charge itself. But in our entrance into the consideration of these things, I must needs say it is somewhat surprising unto me to see a charge wherein the consciences, reputation, liberty, etc., of so many are concerned, founded on the exposition of a text which no sober expositor that I know of did ever find out, propose, or embrace. But if it be true and according unto the mind of the Holy Ghost, this ought to be no disparagement unto it, though it be applied unto such an end. This is that which we are to examine. I say, therefore, —

1. We no way doubt but that the apostles did give rules of faith, obedience, and worship, not only unto private Christians, but to whole churches also; which we find recorded in the Scripture. Unto all these rules we do declare our assent and consent with an entire conformity; and do hope that with indifferent, unbiassed persons this is enough to free us from the charge of schism. 2. For the rule here intended, some take it to be the rule of *faith* in general, or divine revelation; some, to be the rule of *charity* and brotherly condescension; some, to be the particular rule here laid down, of *walking together in the different measures* of faith, light, and knowledge, which we do attain unto. The apostle, in the foregoing verses, having given an account of the glorious excellencies of the mysteries of the gospel, and of his own endeavour after the full attainment of them, yet affirms that he had not attained unto that perfection in the comprehension of them which he designed and aimed at. Herein, in the instance of himself, he declares the condition of the best believers in this life; which is not a full measure and perfection in the comprehension of the truths of the gospel, or enjoyment of the things themselves contained in them: but withal he declares their duty, in pressing continually, by all means, after that measure of attainment which is proposed unto their acquisition. Hereupon he supposes what will certainly ensue on the common pursuit of this design: which is, that men will come unto different attainments, have different measures of light and knowledge, yea, and different conceptions or opinions about these things; some will be "otherwise minded" than other some will be, in some things only. 3. Hereupon he, gives direction how they should walk and behave themselves in this state and condition; and unto those who have attained that measure whence, in comparison of others, they may be styled "perfect," that they press on unanimously towards the end proposed; and as for those who in any things differed from others, he encourageth them to wait on the teachings of God, in that use of the means of instruction which they enjoyed. And having prescribed to each supposed party their especial duties as such, he lays down the duty of them both in common; which is, that in and with respect unto what they had attained, they should "walk by the same rule," namely, which he had now laid down, and "mind the same

thing," as he had before enjoined them. Wherefore, these words of the apostle are so far from being a foundation to charge them with schism who, agreeing in the substance of the doctrine of the gospel, do yet dissent from others (probably the greater part of the church are intended) in some things, that they enjoin a mutual forbearance among those who are so differently minded. 4. But our author affirms that it cannot be a rule of charity and mutual forbearance that is intended, because the apostle had spoken of that just before. But it is apparent that he speaks these words with reference unto what he had said just before; and if this be that which those who are "otherwise minded" are not obliged unto, then are they not obliged at all to "walk by the rule" intended; which is not the mind of the apostle. So himself declares out of Cajetan, that "the apostle subjoins the last words to the former, lest the persons he there speaks unto should think themselves excused from going as far as they can in the same rule," p. 37.

But "a rule," he says, "it is limiting and determining the practice, requiring uniformity in observing the same standing rule." The Nonconformists hereon do say, that if the apostles, or any one apostle, did appoint such a rule as this intended, let it be produced with any probability of proof to be theirs, and they are all ready to subscribe and conform unto it. On supposition that any rule of this nature was appointed by the apostles and declared unto the churches, as the reverend author I suppose doth intimate that it was (though I dare not affix a determinate sense unto his words in this place), all that can be required of us is, that we do conform and walk according unto that rule so appointed and declared by them. This we are always ready to do. Sundry general rules we find in the Scripture given unto us, relating unto the constitution and edification of churches, to their order, and worship, and government; sundry particular rules for ministers and others, how they should behave themselves in church societies and assemblies, are also laid down therein; — all which we embrace, and submit unto the authority of Christ in them. And if any other government or particular rule can be produced given by them, which is not recorded in the Scripture, so it can be proved to be theirs, we will engage to conform unto it.

5. If the rule pretended to be given by the apostles be of any use in this case, or can give any force unto the argument in

hand, it must be such a one as appointed and required things to be observed in the worship of God that were never divinely appointed, imposing the observation of them on the consciences and practice of all the members of the church, under penalties spiritual and temporal; a rule constituting national churches, with a government and discipline suited unto that constitution, with modes and ceremonies of worship nowhere intimated in the Scripture, nor any way necessary in the light of reason. Such a rule, I say, it must be, since, although I should grant (which yet I do not) that the consequent is good, that because the apostles made rules for the practice of the church, that believers were bound in conscience to submit unto, therefore ordinary governors of the church may do so also, yet it will by no means follow that because the apostles appointed a rule of one sort, present church governors may appoint those of another. We know full well, and it is on all hands agreed, what is the rule that our conformity is required unto. If this be done from any rule given by the apostles, it must be a rule of the same nature or to the same purpose; otherwise, by a pretence of their pattern or example, rules may be made directly contrary unto and destructive of all the rules they ever really gave; as it is actually fallen out in the church of Rome. But, —

6. We deny that the apostles made or gave any such rules to the churches present in their days, or for the use of the churches in future ages, as should appoint and determine outward modes of worship, with ceremonies in their observation, stated feasts and fasts, beyond what is of divine institution, liturgies or forms of prayer, or discipline to be exercised in law courts, subservient unto a national ecclesiastical government. What use, then, they are or may be of what benefit or advantage may come to the church by them, what is the authority of the superior magistrate about them, we do not now inquire or determine. Only we say, that no rule unto these ends was ever prescribed by the apostles; for, —

(1.) There is not the least intimation of any such rule to be given by them in the Scripture. There are in it, as was before observed, many express rules, both general and particular, about churches, their faith, worship, and men's walking in them, thoroughly sufficient to direct the duty and practice of all believers in all cases and occurrences relating to them: but of any such rule as that here pretended there is no mention; which certainly, if it had been given, and of the importance which now it is pleaded to be of, — such as that without it neither peace, nor unity, nor order, can be preserved in churches, — some intimation at least would have been made of it therein. Especially, we may judge it would have been so, seeing sundry things (every thing, so far as we can understand) wherein the edification of the church is any way concerned are recorded in it, though of little or no use in comparison of what so great and general a rule would be of. Besides, there is that doctrine delivered, and those directions given by them, in the Scripture, concerning the liberty of believers and forbearance of dissenters, as is inconsistent with such a rule and the imposition of it.

(2.) The first churches after their times knew nothing of any such rule given by them; and, therefore, after they began to depart from the simplicity of the gospel in any things, as unto worship, order, and rule, or discipline, they fell into a great variety of outward observances, orders, and ceremonies, every church almost differing in some thing or other from others, in some such observations, yet all "keeping the unity of the faith in the bond of peace." This they would not have done if the apostles had prescribed any one certain rule of such things that all must conform unto, especially considering how scrupulously they did adhere unto every thing that was reported to be done or spoken by any of the apostles, were the report true or false.

(3.) In particular, when a difference fell out amongst them in a business of this nature, namely, in a thing of outward order, nowhere appointed by the authority of Christ, — namely, about the observation of Easter, — the parties at variance appealed on the one side to the practice of Peter, on the other to the practice of John (both vainly enough): yet was it never pretended by any of them on either side that the apostles had constituted any rule in the case; and therefore it is not probable that they esteemed them to have done so in things of an alike nature, seeing they laid more weight on this than on any other instance of the like kind.

(4.) It is expressly denied, by good and sufficient testimony among them, that the apostles made any law or rule about outward rites, ceremonies, times, and the like. See Socrat., lib. v. cap. 21.

However, then, the apostles might, by their epistles and presence with the churches, reform abuses that were creeping or had crept in among them, and set things in order among them, with renewed directions for their walking; and though all Christians were obliged unto the observation of those rules, as all those still are unto whom they are applicable in their circumstances; yet all this proves nothing of their appointing such a general rule as is pretended: and such a rule alone would be pleadable in this case; and yet not this neither, until either it were produced in a scheme of canons, or it were proved that because they had power to make such a rule, so others may do the like, adding unto what they prescribed, leaving place unto others to add to their rule by the same right, and so endlessly.

The truth is, if God would be pleased to help us, on all hands, to lay aside prejudices, passions, secular interests, fears, and every other distempered affection, which obstruct our minds in passing a right judgment on things of the nature treated on, we [should] find in the text and context spoken unto a sacred truth divinely directive of such a practice as would give peace and rest unto us all; for it is supposed that men, in a sincere endeavour after acquaintance with the truths and mysteries of the gospel, with an enjoyment of the good things represented and exhibited in them, may fall, in some things, into different apprehensions about what belongs unto faith and practice in religion. But whilst they are such as do not destroy or overthrow the foundation, nor hinder men from "pressing towards the mark for the prize of the high calling of God in Christ Jesus," that which the apostle directs unto them who are supposed to be ignorant of or to mistake in the things wherein they do differ from others, is only that they wait for divine instruction in the use of the means appointed for that end, practising in the meantime according to what they have received. And as unto both parties, the advice he gives them is, that "whereunto they have attained," wherein they do agree, — which were all those principles of faith and obedience which were necessary unto their acceptance with God, — they should "walk by the same rule, and mind the same thing;" that is, "forbearing one another" in the things wherein they differ: which is the substance of what is pleaded for by the Nonconformists.

And that this is the meaning and intention of the apostle in this place is evident from the prescription of the same rule in an alike case, Rom. xiv.. This the reverend author saw, — namely, that the rule there laid down is such as expressly requires mutual forbearance in such cases, where men are unsatisfied in conscience about any practice in religion; which seems, in the same case, to be quite another rule than that which he supposeth to be intended in this place to the Philippians. But hereunto he answers, that "the apostle did act like a prudent governor, and in such a manner as he thought did most tend to the propagation of the gospel and the good of particular churches. In some churches that consisted mostly of Jews, as the church of Rome at this time did, and where they did not impose the necessity of keeping the law on the Gentile Christians (as we do not find they did at Rome), the apostle was willing to have the law buried as decently and with as little noise as might be; and, therefore, in this case he persuades both parties to forbearance and charity in avoiding the judging and censuring of one another, since they had an equal regard unto the honour of God in what they did. But in those churches where the false apostles made use of this pretence of the Levitical law being still in force, to divide the churches and to separate the communion of Christians, the apostle bids them beware of them and their practices, as being of a dangerous and pernicious consequence," pp. 14, 15. First, No man ever doubted of the prudence of the apostle as a governor, though in this place he acts only as a teacher divinely inspired, instructing the churches in the mind of God as unto the differences that were among them. Secondly, The difference then among the Romans was about the observation of the Mosaical ceremonies and worship; that is, so far as they might be observed in the countries of the Gentiles, out of the limits of the church, the land of Canaan. It could not be, therefore, concerning such things as whose discharge and practice was confined unto the temple or that land, which yet the Jews of Jerusalem adhered unto, Acts xxi. 20–24. Their controversy, therefore, was principally about meats and drinks, days of feasting or fasting, and the like, all founded on a supposed necessity of circumcision. Thirdly, It is well observed by our author, that the Judaizing Christians (which, in all probability, at this time were the greatest number at Rome, the Gentile church not making any great increase before the coming of the apostle thither) did not impose the necessity of keeping the law on the Gentile Christians; at least not in that manner as was done by the false teachers who troubled the churches of the Galatians and others, so as to eject them who complied not with them out of church-communion, and from all hopes of salvation: but yet both parties continued in their different practices; which, through want of instruction what was their duty in such cases, produced many inconveniences among them, as judging or despising one another, contrary to the rule of Christian love and charity. In this state the apostle prescribes unto them the rule of their duty; which is, plainly, to bear with one another, to love one another, and, according to the nature of charity, to believe all things, — to believe that each party was accepted with God, whilst they served him according unto the light which they had received. And as it is to be thought that, upon the giving of this rule and direction, they utterly laid aside all the animosities in judging and despising one another which they had been guilty of; so it is certain that they continued in their different practice a long time after without any rebuke or reproof; yea, some learned men do judge, and that not on grounds to be despised, that the parties who differed were gathered into distinct churches, and so continued to walk, even to the days of Adrian the emperor, when the last and final destruction of the whole nation of the Jews did befall them; after which those who were not hardened to the utmost gave off all expectation of any respect to be had with God of their old institution. I do not know how the present case between the church of England and the Nonconformists could have possibly been more plainly and distinctly stated and exemplified, in any thing that the churches were capable of or liable unto in those days, than it is in this case here stated and determined by the apostle; in whose direction, rule, and determination we do fully acquiesce. But, Fourthly, It is true also which this reverend author observes, that when the false apostles, or any other Judaizing teachers pretending to authority, did impose the observation of the rites and ceremonies of the Levitical law on any churches, unto their disturbance and division, the apostle looks hereon as that which so far altered the case that he gives other rules and directions about it. And if such impositions might be yet forborne in the like case, especially as accompanied with the severe supplement and addition of all sorts of outward penalties, to be inflicted on them who cannot comply with them, an open door would appear into all that agreement, peace, and quietness among us which are desired.

I have treated thus far of these things, not to manage a controversy with this author or any other, but only to show that there is no ground to be taken from this text or its context to give countenance unto the severe censure of schism and all the evil consequents of it, as maintained by ill arts and practices, upon the Nonconformists.

The procedure of our author in the management of his charge, is in a way of proving, from the assertions and concessions of the several parties whereinto he hath distinguished Nonconformists, that they have no just cause to withhold full communion from the church of England, especially in its parochial assemblies. And as unto the first party, whom he affirms to grant that they are in a state of separation, he quotes some sayings out of a discourse of a nameless author, concerning Evangelical Love, Church-Peace, and Unity;[23] and together with some concessions of his, he adds his judgment, that communion in ordinances must be only in such churches as Christ himself instituted by unalterable rules, which were only particular and congregational churches. As I remember, that author hath at large declared in his discourse what communion believers ought to have with the church, or all churches, — the church in every sense wherein that name is used in the Scripture. But I shall not trouble myself to inquire into his assertions or concessions; nor at present can I do so, not having that book with me where I now am. My business is only to examine, on this occasion, what this reverend author excepteth against or opposeth unto his assertion about congregational churches, and the answering his charge of schism, notwithstanding this plea of the institution of particular churches for the celebration of divine ordinances. This he doth p. 25: "Granting this to be true, how doth it hence appear not to be a sin to separate from our parochial churches, which, according to their own concessions, have all the essentials of true churches? And what ground can they have to separate and divide those churches, which, for all that we can see, are of the same nature with the churches planted by the apostles at Corinth, Philippi, or Thessalonica?"

Ans. 1. We will allow at present that the parochial churches, at least some of them, in this nation are true churches; that is, that they are not guilty of any such heinous errors in doctrine or idolatrous practice in worship as should utterly deprive them of the being and nature of churches. Yet we suppose it will not

---

23   See a work by our author under this title, published in 1672, vol. xv. p. 57. — Ed.

be made a rule, that communion may not be withheld or withdrawn from any church in any thing, so long as it continues, as unto the essence of it, to be so. This author knows that testimonies may be produced out of very learned protestant writers to the contrary.

2. We do not say, it is not pleaded, that because "communion in ordinances must be only in such churches as Christ himself hath instituted," etc., that therefore it is lawful and necessary to separate from parochial churches; but it may be pleaded thence, that if it be on other grounds necessary to so separate or withhold communion from them, it is the duty of them who do so to join themselves in or unto some other particular congregations.

The reasons why the Nonconformists cannot join in that communion with those parochial churches which were before described are quite of another nature, which are not here to be pleaded; however, some of them may be mentioned, to deliver us from this mistake, that the ground of separation from them is the institution of particular congregational churches. And they are such as these:—

(1.) There are many things in all parochial churches that openly stand in need of reformation. What these are, both with respect unto persons and things, hath been before intimated, and shall be farther declared if occasion require. But these parochial churches neither do, nor indeed can, nor have power in themselves to reform the things that ought, by the rule of the Scripture, to be reformed; for none among us will plead that they are intrusted with power for their own government and reformation. In this case we judge it lawful for any man peaceably to withdraw communion from such churches, [and] to provide for his own edification in others.

(2.) That there are many things, in the constant and total communion of parochial churches, imposed on the consciences and practices of men, which are not according to the mind of Christ. The things of this nature I shall not here mention in particular.

(3.) There is no evangelical church discipline administered in such parochial churches, which yet is a necessary means unto the edification of the churches, appointed by Christ himself, and sacredly attended unto by the primitive churches; and we dare not renounce our interest in so blessed an ordinance of Christ in the gospel.

(4.) The rule and government which such parochial churches are absolutely under, in the room of that rule and discipline which ought to be in and among themselves, — namely, that by the courts of bishops, chancellors, commissaries, etc., — is unknown to the Scriptures, and in its administration is very remote from giving a true representation of the authority, wisdom, love, and care of Christ to his church; which is the sole end of all church rules and discipline. The yoke hereof many account themselves not obliged to submit unto.

(5.) There is in such churches a total deprivation of the liberty of the people, secured unto them by the rules and practices of several ages from the beginning, of choosing their own pastors; whereby they are also deprived of all use of their light and knowledge of the gospel in providing for their own edification.

(6.) It cannot be denied but that there is want of due means of edification in many of those parochial churches, and yet provision is made by the government that those churches are under that none shall, by any way, provide themselves of better means for that great end of all church-society.

It is on these and the like reasons that the Nonconformists cannot join in total communion, such as the rule pleaded for requireth, with parochial churches. In this state, as was said, the Lord Christ having instituted particular congregations, requiring all believers to walk in them, it is the duty of those who are necessitated to decline the communion of parochial churches, as they are stated at present, to join themselves in and unto such congregations as wherein their edification and liberty may be better provided for according unto rule.

But hereon the reverend author proceeds to oppose such particular congregations or churches, I think, as unto their original and necessity; for so he speaks, pp. 25, 26: "But I must needs say farther, I have never yet seen any tolerable proof that the churches planted by the apostles were limited to congregations." Howbeit, this seems to be so clear and evident in matter of fact, and so necessary from the nature of the thing itself, that many wise men, wholly unconcerned in our controversies, do take it for a thing to be granted by all without dispute. So speaks Chief-Justice Hobart,[24] p. 149, in the case of Colt and Glover *cont.*

---

24 Sir Henry Hobart, Lord Chief-Justice of the Court of Common Pleas, published, in 1650, a work under the title of "Reports in the Reign of King James I., with some few Cases in the Reign of

Bishop Coventry and Litchfield: "And we know well that the primitive church, in its greatest purity, was but voluntary congregations of believers, submitting themselves to the apostles, and after to other pastors; to whom they did minister of their temporals as God did move them." Of the same judgment are those who esteem the first government of the church to be democratical. So speaks Paulus Sarpius: "In the beginning, the government of the holy church had altogether a democratical form, all the faithful intervening in the chiefest deliberations. Thus we see that all did intervene at the election of Matthias unto the apostleship, and in the election of the six deacons; and when St Peter received Cornelius, a heathen centurion, unto the faith, he gave an account of it to all the church; likewise in the council celebrated in Jerusalem, the apostles, the priests, and the other faithful brethren did intervene, and the letters were written in the name of all these three orders. In success of time, when the church increased in number, the faithful retiring themselves to the affairs of their families, and having left those of the congregation, the government retained only in the ministers, and became aristocratical, saving the election, which was popular." And others also of the same judgment may be added.

But let us hear the reasoning of this learned author against this apprehension; this he enters upon, p. 26: "It is possible at first there might be no more Christians in one city than could meet in one assembly for worship; but where doth it appear that when they multiplied into more congregations, they did make new and distinct churches, under new officers, with a separate power of government? Of this, I am well assured, there are no marks or footsteps in the New Testament nor the whole history of the primitive church. I do not think it will appear credible to any considerate man that the five thousand Christians in the church of Jerusalem made one stated and fixed congregation for divine worship, not if we make all the allowances for strangers which can be desired; but if this were granted, where are the unalterable rules that as soon as the company became too great for one particular assembly, they must become a new church, under peculiar officers and an independent authority? It is very strange that those who contend so much for the Scripture being

---

Queen Elizabeth." The fifth edition was revised and corrected by Lord Ch. Nottingham, 1724. — Ed.

a perfect rule of all things pertaining to worship and discipline should be able to produce nothing in so necessary a point."

I answer, — 1. It is possible that an impartial account may, ere long, be given of the state and ways of the first churches after the decease of the apostles; wherein it will be made to appear how they did insensibly deviate in many things from the rule of their first institution, so as that, though their mistakes were of small moment, and not prejudicial unto their faith and order, yet occasion was administered to succeeding ages to increase those deviations, until they issued in a fatal apostasy. An eminent instance hereof is given us in the discourse of Paulus Sarpius about matters beneficiary, lately made public in our own language.[25]

2. The matter of fact herein seems to me evidently to be exemplified in the Scripture; for although, it may be, there is not express mention made that these or those particular churches did divide themselves into more congregations with new officers, yet are there instances of the erection of new particular congregations in the same province, as distinct churches, with a separate power of government. So the first church in the province of Judea was in Jerusalem; but when that church was complete, as to the number of them who might communicate therein unto their edification, the apostles did not add the believers of the adjacent towns and places unto that church, but erected other particular congregations all the country over. So there were different churches in Judea, Galilee, and Samaria, — that is, many in each of them, Acts ix. 31. So the apostle mentions the churches of God that were in Judea, 1 Thess. ii. 14, and nowhere speaks of them as one church, for worship, order, and government. So he speaks again, that is constantly, Gal. i. 22, "I was unknown by face unto the churches of Judea." And that these churches were neither national nor diocesan, but particular congregations, is, as I suppose, sufficiently evident. So was it in the province of Galatia. There is no mention of any church therein that should be comprehensive of all the believers in that province; but many particular churches there were, as it is testified chap. i. 2. So was it also in Macedonia. The first church planted in that province was at Philippi, as it is declared Acts xvi.; and

---

25 Appended to the edition of Paul Sarpi's "History of the Council of Trent," published in 1676, will be found also his "Treatise of Beneficiary Matters." — Ed.

it was quickly brought into complete order, so as that when the apostle wrote unto it, there were in it the "saints" whereof it was constituted, with "bishops and deacons," Phil. i. 1. But that church being so complete, the apostle appointed other particular congregational churches in the same province, which had officers of their own, with a power of government; these he mentions and calls "The churches of Macedonia," 2 Cor. viii. 1, 23. Wherefore we need no more directions in this matter than what are given us by the apostle's authority, in the name and authority of Jesus Christ, nor are concerned in the practice of those who afterward took another course, of adding believers from other places unto the church first planted, unless it were in case of a disability to enjoy church-communion among themselves elsewhere. Whatever, therefore, is pretended unto the contrary, we have plain Scripture evidence and practice for the erecting particular distinct congregations, with power for their own rule and edification, in the same province, be it as small as those that were of Samaria or Galilee. It cannot, surely, be said that these churches were national, whereof there were many in one small province of a small nation, nor yet metropolitical or diocesan; nor, I suppose, will it be denied but that they were intrusted with power to rule and govern themselves in all ordinary cases, especially when in every one of them elders were ordained; which the apostles were careful to see done, Acts xiv. 23. This is the substance of what we plead as unto particular congregations.

3. It is not probable that any of the first churches did, for a long time, increase in any city unto such a number as might exceed the bounds of a particular church or congregation; for such they might continue to be, notwithstanding a multiplication of bishops or elders in them, and occasional distinct assemblies for some acts of divine worship. And it seems if they did begin to exceed in number beyond a just proportion for their edification, they did immediately erect other churches among them or near them. So, whereas there was a mighty increase of believers at Corinth, Acts xviii. 10, there was quickly planted a distinct church at Cenchrea, which was the port of the city, Rom. xvi. 1. And notwithstanding the great number of five thousand that were converted at Jerusalem upon the first preaching of the gospel, yet were they so disposed of or so dispersed, that some years after this there was such a church only there as did meet

together in one place as occasion did require, even the whole multitude of the brethren, who are called the "church" in distinction from the "apostles and elders," who were their governors, Acts xv. 4, 12, xxi. 22. Nor was that church of any greater number when they all departed afterward and went out into Pella, a village beyond Jordan, before the destruction of the people, city, and temple. And though many alterations were before that time introduced into the order and rule of the churches, yet it appears that when Cyprian was bishop of the church at Carthage, the whole community of the members of that church did meet together to determine of things that were for their common interests, according unto what was judged to be their right and liberty in those days; which they could not have done had they not all of them belonged unto the same particular church and congregation. But these things may be pleaded elsewhere if occasion be given thereunto. But yet, —

4. I must say that I cannot discern the least necessity of any positive rule or direction in this matter, nor is any such thing required by us on the like occasion; for this distribution of believers into particular congregations is that which the nature of the thing itself, and the duty of men with respect unto the end of such churches, do indispensably require. For what is the end of all churches, for which they are instituted? is it not the edification of them that do believe? They will find themselves mistaken who suppose that they were designed to be subservient unto the secular interest of any sort of men. What are the means appointed of Christ in such churches for that end? Are they not "doctrine and fellowship, breaking of bread, and prayers," — that is, the joint celebration of the ordinances of Christ in the gospel, in preaching the word, administering the sacraments, mutual watchfulness over one another, and the exercise of that discipline which he hath appointed unto his disciples? I desire to know whether there be any need of a new revelation to direct men who are obliged to preserve churches in their use unto their proper end, to take care of such things as would obstruct and hinder them in the use of means unto the end of their edification? Whereas, therefore, it is manifest that, ordinarily, these means cannot be used in a due manner but in such churches as wherein all may be acquainted with what all are concerned in, the very institution itself is a plain command to plant, erect, and keep all churches in such a state as wherein this end may be at-

tained. And, therefore, if believers in any place are so few, or so destitute of spiritual gifts, as not to be able of themselves jointly to observe these means for their edification, it is their duty not to join by themselves in a church-state, but to add themselves as members unto other churches; and so when they are so many as that they cannot orderly communicate together in all these ordinances, in the way of their administration appointed in the Scripture, unto the edification of them, it is their duty, by virtue of the divine institution of churches, to dispose of their church-state and relation into that way which will answer the ends of it, — that is, into more particular churches or congregations.

I speak not these things in opposition unto any other church-state which men may erect or establish out of an opinion of its usefulness and conveniency, much less against that communion which ought to be among those particular churches, or their associations for their common rule and government in and by their officers; but only to manifest that those Nonconformists who are supposed to adhere unto the institution of particular churches in a peculiar way, do not thereby deserve the imputation of so great and intolerable a guilt as they are here charged withal. And whereas I have hereby discharged all that I designed with respect unto the first sort of Noncomformists, as they are here distinguished, I might here give over the pursuit of this argument; but because I seek after truth and satisfaction also in these things, I shall a little farther consider what is offered by this reverend author unto the same purpose with what we have passed through. So, therefore, he proceeds, pp. 26, 27, "If that of which we read the clearest instance in Scripture must be the standard of all future ages, much more might be said for limiting churches to private families than to particular congregations; for do we not read of the church that was in the house of Priscilla and Aquila at Rome, of the church that was in the house of Nymphas at Colosse, and in the house of Philemon at Laodicea? Why, then, should not churches be reduced to particular families, when by that means they may fully enjoy the liberty of their consciences and avoid the scandal of breaking the laws? But if, notwithstanding such plain examples, men will extend churches to congregations of many families, why may not others extend churches to those societies which consist of many congregations?"

I answer, — 1. Possibly a church may be in a family, or consist only of the persons that belong to a family: but a family, as a family, neither is nor can be a church; for as such it is constituted by natural and civil relations. But a church hath its form and being from the voluntary spiritual consent of those whereof it consists unto church-order: "They gave," saith the apostle, "their own selves to the Lord, and unto us by the will of God," 2 Cor. viii. 5. Neither is there any mention at all in the Scripture of the constitution of churches in private families, so as that they should be limited thereunto.

2. What is spoken of the church in the houses of Aquila, Nymphas, and Philemon, doth not at all prove that there was a particular church in each of their houses, consisting only of their own families as such; but only that there was a church which usually assembled in their respective houses. Wherefore, —

3. There is no such example given of churches in private families in the whole Scripture as should restrain the extent of churches from congregations of many families. And the inquiry hereon, that "if men will extend churches to congregations of many families, why may not others extend churches unto societies which consist of many congregations," hath not any force in it; for they who extended churches unto congregations of many families were the apostles themselves, acting in the name and authority of Jesus Christ, It cannot be proved that ever they stated, erected, or planted any one church, but it was composed of many persons out of many families; nor that ever they confined a church unto a family, or taught that families, though all of them believers and baptized, were churches on the account of their being families. "So others may extend churches unto those societies which consist of many congregations;" — yet not so as those who cannot comply or join with them should thereon be esteemed schismatics, seeing such societies were not appointed by Christ and his apostles. If such societies be so constituted as that there is but a probable plea that they are ordained by Christ, there may be danger in a dissent from them merely on this account, that they consist of many congregations; but this is not our case, as hath been before declared.

The remainder of this section consists in an account of the practice of the churches in some things in following ages. This though of importance in itself, and deserving a full inquiry into, yet belongeth not unto our present case, and will, it may be, in due time be more fully spoken unto.

Those supposed of the first way and judgment, who grant a separation from the established form of the church of England, are dismissed with one charge more on and plea against their practice, not without a mixture of some severity in expression p. 30: "But suppose the first churches were barely congregated, by reason of the small number of believers at that time, yet what obligation lies upon us to disturb the peace of the church we live in to reduce churches to their infant state?" which is pressed with sundry considerations in the two following pages. But we say, — 1. That the first churches were not "congregated by reason of the small number of believers," but because the Lord Christ had limited and determined that such a state of his churches should be under the New Testament, as best suited unto all the ends of their institution. 2. That which is called the "infant state of churches" was, in truth, their sole perfect estate; — what they grew up unto afterward, most of them, we know well enough; for leaving, as it is called, their "infant state" by degrees, they brought forth at last "The man of sin." 3. No obligation lies upon us from hence to "disturb the peace" of any church; nor do we do so, let what will be pretended to the contrary. If any such disturbance do ensue upon the differences that are between them and us, as far as I know, the blame will be found lying upon them who [are] not [only] satisfied that they may leave the first state of the churches, under a pretence of its infancy, and bring them into a greater perfection than was given them by Christ and his disciples, but compel others also to forego their primitive constitution, and comply with them in their alteration thereof.

The remainder of the discourse of this section, so far as I can understand, proceeds on this principle, that the sole reason and cause of our nonconformity is this persuasion of the divine institution of particular churches; but all men know that this is otherwise. This of all things is least pleaded, and commonly in the last place, and but by some, among the causes and reasons of our withholding communion, so far as we do so, from the church of England, as unto the way and manner wherein it is required of us. Those reasons have been pleaded already, and may yet be so farther in due time. For the rest of the discourse, we do not, we cannot, believe that the due and peaceable observation of the institutions of Christ doth of itself give any disturbance unto any churches or persons whatever, nor that a peaceable endeavour to practice ourselves according unto those institutions, without imposing that practice on them, can be justly blamable. We do not, we cannot, believe that our refusal of a total compliance with a rule for order, discipline, worship, and ceremonies in the church, not given by Christ and his apostles, but requiring of us sundry things either in themselves or as required of us directly contrary unto, or inconsistent with, the rules and directions given us by them unto those ends (as, in our judgment and light of our consciences, is done in and by this rule), is either schism or blamable separation. We do judge ourselves obliged to preserve peace and unity among Christians by all the means that Christ hath appointed for that end, — by the exercise of all graces, the performance of all duties, the observation of all rules and directions given us for that end; but we do not, we cannot, believe that to neglect the means of our own edification, appointed unto us by Christ himself, to cast away the liberty wherewith he hath made us free, and to destroy our own souls for ever by acting against his authority in his word, and our own consciences guided thereby, in a total complying with the rule proposed unto us, is a way or means for the attaining of that end. And we do believe that, in the present state of the differences among us, an issue whereof is not suddenly to be expected in an absolute agreement in opinion and judgment about them, the rule of the Scripture, the example of the first churches, the nature of Christian religion, and the present interest of the protestant religion among us, do call for mutual forbearance, with mutual love, and peaceable walking therein. And we begin to hope, that whereas it is confessed that the foundations of Christian religion are preserved entire among us all, and it is evident that those who dissent from the present ecclesiastical establishments, or any of them, are as ready to do and suffer what they shall be lawfully called unto in the defence and for the preservation of the protestant religion, wise men will begin to think that it is better for them to take up quietly in what the law hath provided for them, and not turmoil themselves and others in seeking to put an end unto these differences by force and compulsion; which by these ways they will never whilst they live attain unto. And we do suppose that many of them who do cordially own and seek the preservation of the protestant religion in this nation, — men, I mean, of authority, power, and interest, — will be no more instrumental to help one part [to] ruin and destroy another, unduly weakening the whole interest of Protestantism thereby; but, considering how little the concern of themselves or their posterity can be in these lesser differences, in comparison of what it is in the whole protestant cause, will endeavour their utmost to procure an equal liberty (though not equal outward advantages) for all that are firm and stable in their profession of that protestant religion which is established by law in this kingdom. I know that learned and eloquent men, such as this author is, are able to declaim against mutual forbearance in these things, with probable pleas and pretences of evil consequents which will ensue thereon; and I do know that others, though not with equal learning or eloquence, do declare and set forth the inequality, unrighteousness, and destructive events of a contrary course, or the use of force and compulsion in this cause; — but it must be granted that the evil consequences pretended on a mutual forbearance do follow from the corrupt affections and passions of men, and not from the thing itself; but all the evils which will follow on force and compulsion do naturally arise from the thing itself.

I shall close this part of my discourse with an observation on that wherewith it is closed by this author, in his management of it. Saith he, "To withdraw from each other into separate congregations tempts some to spiritual pride, and scorn and contempt of others, as of a more carnal and worldly church than themselves; and provokes others to lay open the follies, and indiscretions, and immoralities of those who pretend to so much purity and spirituality above their brethren," pp. 32, 33. If there be any unto whom this is such a temptation as is mentioned in the first place, and being so, doth prevail upon them, it is their sin, arising from their own lusts, by which every man is tempted, and is not at all occasioned by the thing itself. And for the other part, let those who delight in that work proceed as they shall see cause; for if they charge upon us things that are really foolish, indiscreet, and immoral, as in many things we sin all, we hope we shall learn what to amend, and to be diligent therein, as for other reasons, so because of our observers. But if they do what some have done, and others yet continue to do, — fill their discourses with false, malicious defamations, with scorn, contempt, railing, and revilings, scandalous unto Christian religion, like a sermon lately preached before my Lord Mayor, and since put in print (I intend not that under consideration), — We are no way concerned in what they do or say, nor do, as we know of, suffer any disadvantage thereby; yea, such persons are beneath the offence and contempt of all men pretending unto the least wisdom and sobriety.

For what remains of this discourse, I esteem not myself concerned to insist on the examination of it; for I would not so express my judgment in these things as some are here represented to declare themselves, and I know that those who are principally reflected on are able to defend both their principles and practices. And besides, I hear (in the retirement wherein I live, and wherein I die daily) that some of those most immediately concerned have returned an answer unto this part of the discourse under consideration. I shall, therefore, only observe some few things that may abate the edge of this charge; for although we judge the defence of the truth which we profess to be necessary when we are called thereunto, yet at present, for the reasons intimated at the entrance of this discourse, we should choose that it might not be brought under debate. But the defence of our innocency, when the charge against us is such as in itself tends to our distress and ruin, is that alone which is our present design, and which wise men, no way concerned in our nonconformity, for the sake of the protestant religion and public peace of the nation, have judged necessary.

The principal strength of this part of the reverend author's discourse consists in his application of the reasons of the [Westminster] Assembly against those who desired forbearance, in distinct communion from the rule sought then to be established, unto those who now desire the same forbearance from the church of England. I will not immerse myself in that controversy, nor have any contention with the dead. This only I say, that the case then between the Presbyterians and those who dissented from them is so vastly different from that now between the church of England and the Nonconformists, and that in so many material instances and circumstances, that no light can be communicated unto the right determination of the latter from what was pleaded in the former. In brief, those who pleaded then for a kind of uniformity or agreement in total communion did propose no one of those things, as the condition of it, which are now pleaded as the only reasons of withholding the same kind of conformity from the church of England, and the non-imposition of any such things they wade the foundation of their plea for the compliance of others with them; and those on the other side, who pleaded for liberty and forbearance in such a case as wherein there were no such impositions, did it mostly on the common liberty which, as they judged, they had with their other brethren to abide by the way which they had declared and practised long before any rule was established unto its prejudice. And these things are sufficient to give us, as unto the present case under debate, an absolute unconcernment in what was then pleaded on the one side or the other, and so it shall be here dismissed.

The especial charge here managed against the Nonconformists is, that they allow that to "live [in] a state of separation from such churches as many at least of ours are is a sin;" yet that themselves so do, which is manifest in their practice. But it may be said, — 1. That this concession respects only parochial churches, and that some of them only; but the conformity in general required of us respects the constitution, government, discipline, worship, and communion of the national church and diocesan churches therein. 2. Persons who thus express themselves are to be allowed the interpretation of their own minds, words, and expressions; for if they do judge that such things do belong unto a state of separation from any churches, as, namely, a causeless renouncing of all communion with them, a condemnation of them as no church, and on that ground setting up churches against them, which they know themselves not to be guilty of, they may both honestly and wisely deny themselves to be in a state of separation, nor will their present practice prove them so to be. And, on the other hand, those who do acknowledge a separation as unto distinct local presential communion with the church of England, yet do all of them deny those things which, in the judgment of those now intended, are necessary to constitute a state of separation. But on this account, I cannot see the least contradiction between the principles and practice of these brethren, nor wherein they are blameworthy in their concessions, unless to be in too much earnestness to keep up all possible communion with the church of England. "Forgive them that wrong." Yet I say not this as though those who are here supposed to own a state of separation were not as zealous also for communion in faith, love, and doctrine of truth with the body of Protestants in this nation as they are. 3. That which animates this part of the discourse, and which is the edge of this charge, is, that "the ministers do conceal from the people what their judgment is about the lawfulness of communion with the church of England." How this can be known to be so, I cannot understand; for that it is their judgment that they may do so is proved only, so far as I know, from what they have written and published in print unto that purpose. And certainly what men so publish of their own accord, they can have no design to conceal from any, especially not from them who usually attend on their ministry, who are most likely to read their books with diligence. But this hath been spoken unto before.

In these things we seek for no shelter nor countenance from what is pleaded by any concerning the obliging power of an "erroneous conscience," which the reverend author insists on, pp. 42–44; for we acknowledge no rule of conscience in those things which concern churches, their state, power, order, and worship, but divine revelation only, — that is, the Scripture, the written word of God, — and sure enough we are not deceived in the choice of our rule, so as that we desire no greater assurance in any concerns of religion. And by the Scripture as our rule, we understand both the express words of it, and whatever may, by just and lawful consequence, be educed from them. This rule we attend unto, and inquire into the mind of God in it, with all the diligence we are able, and in the use of all the means that are usually and truly pleaded as necessary unto the attainment of a right understanding thereof; and if any one can inform us of any thing required of us thereby which yet we have not received, we shall with all readiness comply therewithal. We have no prejudices, no outward temptations, that should bias our minds and inclinations unto those principles, and practices on them, which we judge ourselves guided and directed unto by this rule; but all such considerations as might be taken from the most moderate desires, even of food and raiment, do lie against us. We are hereon fully satisfied that we have attained that knowledge in the mind of God about these things as will preserve us from evil or sin against him, from being hurtful or useless unto the rest of mankind, if we submit unto the light and conduct of it. Wherefore, we seek no relief in, we plead no excuse from, the obligation of an erroneous conscience, but do abide by it that our consciences are rightly informed in these things; and then it is confessed on all hands what is their power, and what their force to oblige us, with respect unto all human commands.

I know not of any farther concern that the Nonconformists have in the discourse of this reverend author, unless it be in the considerations which he proposeth unto them, and the advice which he gives them in the close of it. I shall only say, concerning the one and the other, that having weighed them impartially, unto the best of my understanding, I find not any thing in them that should make it the duty of any man to invent and constitute such a rule of church communion as that which is proposed unto the Nonconformists for their absolute compliance withal, nor any thing that should move the Nonconformists unto such compliance, against the light of their consciences and understanding in the mind of Christ; which alone are the things in debate between us. But if the design of the author, in the proposal of these considerations and the particulars of his advice, be, that we should take heed to ourselves, that during these differences among us we give no offence unto others, so far as it is possible, nor entertain severe thoughts in ourselves of them from whom we differ, we shall be glad that both he and we should be found in the due observance of such advice. One head of his advice I confess might be, if I am not mistaken, more acceptable with some of the Nonconformists, if it had not come in the close of such a discourse as this is; and it is, that "they should not be always complaining of their hardships and persecution," p. 54: for they say, after so many of them have died in common jails; so many have endured long imprisonments, not a few being at this day in the same durance; so many have been driven from their habitations into a wandering condition, to preserve for a while the liberty of their persons; so many have been reduced unto want and penury by the taking away of their goods, and from some the very instruments of their livelihood; after the prosecutions which have been against them in all courts of justice in this nation, on informations, indictments, and suits, to the great charge of all of them who are so persecuted, and ruin of some; after so many ministers and their families have been brought into the utmost outward straits which nature can subsist under; after all their perpetual fears and dangers wherewith they have been exercised and disquieted, — they think it hard they should be complained of for complaining by them who are at ease. It may be remembered what one speaks very gravely in the Comedian, —

> "Sed, Demea, hoc tu facito cure animo cogites,Quàm vos facillime agitis, quàm estis maxumePotentes, dites, fortunati, nobiles;Tam maxume vos æquo animo æqua noscereOportet, si vos voltis perhiberi probos." —
> [Ter. Ad. iii., iv., 54.]

Indeed, men who are encompassed with an affluence of all earthly enjoyments, and in the secure possession of the good things of this life, do not well understand what they say when they speak of other men's sufferings. This I dare undertake for all the Nonconformists: let others leave beating them, and they shall all leave complaining. She is thought but a curst[26] mother who beats her child for crying, and will not cease beating until the child leave crying; which it cannot do whilst it is continually beaten. Neither do I know that the Nonconformists are "always complaining of their sufferings," nor what are their complaints that they make, nor to whom; yea, I do suppose that all impartial men will judge that they have borne their sufferings with as much patience and silence as any who have gone before them in the like state and condition. And they do hope that men will not be angry with them if they cry unto God for deliverance from those troubles which they judge they undergo for his sake. Thankful, also, they are unto God and men for any release they have received from their sufferings; wherein their chief respect amongst men hitherto is unto the king himself. But that they should be very thankful to those who esteem all their past and present sufferings to be light, and do really endeavour to have them continued and increased (among whom I do not reckon this reverend author, for I do not know that I can truly do so), is not to be expected.

I shall add no more, but that whereas the Nonconformists intended in this defence are one, or do completely agree, with the body of the people in this nation that are Protestants, Or the church of England, in the entire doctrine of faith and obedience, in all the instances whereby it hath been publicly declared or established by law, — which agreement in the unity of faith is the

---

26 Not our English "cursed," but an adjective, said to be derived from the Dutch "korst," signifying crusty, ill-tempered. — Ed.

principal foundation of all other union and agreement among Christians, and without which every other way or means of any such union or agreement is of no worth or value, and which if it be not impeached is in itself a sufficient bond of union, whatever other differences may arise among men, and ought to be so esteemed among all Christians; — and whereas they are one with the same body of the people, that is, in its magistracy and those who are under rule, in one common interest, for the maintenance and preservation of protestant religion, whereunto they are secured by a sense of their duty and safety, and without whose orderly and regular concurrence in all lawful ways and actings unto that end it will not be so easily attained as some imagine; — and whereas also they are one with them in all due legal subjection unto the same supreme power amongst us, and are equally ready with any sort of persons of their respective qualities or condition in the nation to contribute their assistance unto the preservation of its peace and liberty; — and whereas in their several capacities they are useful unto the public faith and trust of the nation, the maintenance and increase of the wealth and prosperity of it; — considering what evidences there are of the will of God in the constitution of our natures, under the conduct of conscience, in immediate subordination unto himself; the different measures of light, knowledge, and understanding which he communicates unto men; as also of the spirit, rule, and will of Jesus Christ, with the example of the apostles and the primitive churches for mutual forbearance, in such different apprehensions of and practices about religion, as no way intrencheth on the unity of faith, or any good of public society; — I cannot but judge (in which persuasion I now live, and shall shortly die) that all writings tending to exasperate and provoke the dissenting parties one against another are at this day highly unseasonable; and all endeavours, of what sort soever, to disquiet, discourage, trouble, punish, or distress such as dissent from the public rule, in the way before described, are contrary to the will of God, obstructive of the welfare of the nation, and dangerous unto the protestant religion.

www.ingramcontent.com/pod-product-compliance
Lightning Source LLC
Chambersburg PA
CBHW011315080526
44587CB00024B/3998